A HISTORY OF THETFORD

A HISTORY OF THETFORD

Alan Crosby

Phillimore

1986

' Published by
PHILLIMORE & CO. LTD.
Shopwyke Hall, Chichester, Sussex

ISBN 0 85033 604 X

Typeset in the United Kingdom by:
Fidelity Processes - Selsey - Sussex

Printed in Great Britain at the
University Press, Oxford

*In memory of Edwin W. Burgin
with respect and affection*

CONTENTS

LIST OF PLATES
(between pages 48 and 49)

Acknowledgements for plates:

Thetford Ancient House Museum (Norfolk Museums Service), 1, 2, 3, 7, 9, 10, 11, 13, 14, 15, 20, 25, 26 and 29. David Osborne provided all the other illustrations. My grateful thanks are due to David for his great help and for allowing me to use some of his extensive collection of pictures and photographs of Thetford. I am grateful to Chad Goodwin, Curator of the Museum, for permission to reproduce the map of Thetford by Thomas Martin, and other material in his custody, and for his interest and assistance. Plates 2, 3, and 9 are taken from *The Architectural Remains of Thetford*, drawn by the Rev. Joseph Wilkinson (vicar of Thetford St Mary), etched by H. Davy, and published in 1822.

LIST OF MAPS

INTRODUCTION AND ACKNOWLEDGEMENTS

THE HISTORY of Thetford began long before there was thought of the town or of its name, thousands of years before an urban community grew on the banks of the Thet and the Little Ouse — names, incidentally, which have no antiquity. The trackway which ran along the eastern edge of the Fens through Suffolk and Norfolk crossed these rivers by a series of fords in the area of the present town. Around these fords settlement developed and very much later the town of Thetford evolved, or perhaps was deliberately laid out, with its focus on the central ford, now marked by the Town Bridge. Almost in the middle of the modern town is the hillfort which was built by the Icenian inhabitants of the district in about 500 B.C., to guard the river crossings and the trackways which converged on the area. The hillfort, later the basis of the Norman castle, provides a tangible reminder that this has been a place of importance for 2,500 years, and remains a key element in the plan and appearance of Thetford.

At the very end of the Iron Age a remarkable complex of buildings was erected on Gallows Hill at the northern edge of the modern town, apparently as a ceremonial or prestige centre for the Icenian royal family, the most celebrated member of which was the now almost legendary Boudicca. The Gallows Hill complex was deliberately razed to the ground after the Boudiccan uprising of A.D. 60. A largely agricultural community occupied the site of modern Thetford throughout the Roman and early Saxon period, but during the second half of the ninth century this expanded rapidly and emerged as a large and flourishing town, spreading across 200 acres on either side of the river. By the time of the Norman Conquest Thetford was the sixth town of England, a major trading, commercial and industrial centre with numerous churches, a mint, religious houses and political importance. This was despite the setbacks posed by its sacking by the Danes in 1004 and 1010.

After the Conquest the town was, for a brief period, the seat of the bishops of East Anglia, until the removal of the see to Norwich, while a large motte and bailey castle was built within the hillfort. By this time, however, Thetford was in the early stages of decline, a contraction in both size and prosperity which lasted, with interruptions, throughout the Middle Ages and into the early modern period. The population in 1066 was about 4,500: in the late 16th century it was less than 1,500. The decline was accompanied by a radical reorientation of the town, which had hitherto been mainly on the south bank. The greater part of the south bank town was abandoned and the new focus became the north bank community. In the 13th century the shape of this district was altered greatly by the creation of a new market place and planned suburb on the southern edge of the castle defences.

In the Middle Ages Thetford was a Borough under the control of its manorial lords in several crucial aspects of its administration and economy. Not until 1574 was it granted a charter of incorporation, thereby achieving virtual self-government. Between that date and 1835 the Corporation was a self-perpetuating and increasingly corrupt body, which did useful work to improve the town in its early years but latterly became interested only in the opportunities for political and financial gain which were offered. This was particularly so in respect of parliamentary elections, for Thetford was one of the most notorious of all pocket boroughs. The needs of the town were completely ignored in the interests of private gain.

During the late 18th century change affected Thetford, as some new industries were developed – paper-making, agricultural engineering, malting and the production of fertilisers – and as the population increased for the first time in centuries. These trends continued for much of the 19th century, and the town became seriously overcrowded and unhealthy. There was very little provision for sanitation or other essentials of public health, severe epidemics were frequent, and on a number of occasions conditions were sufficiently bad to warrant the intervention of central government. Local government, although reformed in 1835 to provide a democratically elected council, consistently failed to take adequate steps to deal with the problems of the town.

Shortly after the First World War the town's biggest employer, Burrell's, the largest traction engine manufacturers in the world, failed. There was very great social and economic distress, with high unemployment and a decline in the population, and during the 1930s Thetford was a seriously depressed town. No new industries could be enticed to the area, and the Second World War provided only a temporary respite in the economic decay of Thetford. After the war the Borough Council took the lead in promoting the revival of fortunes, by agreeing to accept overspill from London and the new industry which accompanied the influx of population. Between 1951 and 1981 Thetford more than quadrupled in population, and in the 1970s was the fastest growing town in Britain, a remarkable reversal of previous trends. This has of course drastically altered the character and shape of the town, and produced a variety of social difficulties of its own. The architect of the change, Thetford Borough Council, was swept away by another form of 'progress': the reorganisation of local government which, in 1974, forced the amalgamation of Thetford with several other authorities to form the new and unwieldy Breckland district.

Thetford was well served by its early historians, but badly served by its Corporation. In 1739 Francis Blomefield, who was educated in the town, wrote a substantial history of Thetford as part of his *History of Norfolk*, and this formed the basis of Thomas Martin's *History of the Town of Thetford*, published posthumously in 1779. Martin probably intended to include substantially more narrative and descriptive material than was eventually published, but nonetheless the book is a work of considerable merit and value, the fruit of extensive and careful research by Blomefield and Martin himself. Martin was allowed to take possession of the records of Thetford Corporation, including those of its medieval predecessors. On his death his literary executors used some of the material to complete the book, and then disposed of the records instead of returning them to the possession of the Corporation. Many of them were given away or destroyed as waste paper, and the vast majority of the medieval material was thus lost for ever. In the late 18th and early 19th centuries George Bird Burrell, a member of the Corporation and a competent amateur historian, collected as many of the surviving records as could be located, and pasted them into scrapbooks or made full transcripts in a series of notebooks. He thereby saved some of the material, but we shall never know just how much was lost. The result is that, apart from the miscellany of deeds, leases and fragmentary account rolls retrieved by Burrell, there are no records of the Borough prior to the Assembly Book which was begun in 1574.

Since Martin wrote his *History* there have been other attempts to update the published record, notably that of Alfred Leigh Hunt, who in 1884 wrote *The Ancient Capital of East Anglia*, much of which is taken directly from Martin. Many of the historical myths of this period — especially that which states that Thetford was *Sitomagus*, a major Roman town — have been repeated faithfully until recent years. So much has changed since Hunt published his book just over a century ago, and there has been such a great deal of historical reappraisal as a result of archaeological and documentary research, that a new history of the town is long overdue. This book attempts to provide such a history. It grew out of a course entitled *The Story of Thetford* which I gave on behalf of the Cambridge Extra-Mural Board.

I would like to thank all those who attended that course for their encouragement, interest and enthusiasm, which inspired me to continue and to put it all down on paper, and which made Saturdays in the autumn of 1984 so enjoyable for me. A very great debt of gratitude is due to my mother, who typed the manuscript, and to my sister and my wife Jacquie, who sacrificed many hours to check the text. I would add that any errors of grammar, style or punctuation are, however, to be attributed to me! I have greatly appreciated the assistance given to me by my friends in the Norfolk Record Office. Above all, I wish to thank Thetford Town Council, which gave me free access to all the material in its custody and which allowed me to spend days working in the imposing setting of the Council Chamber, under the no doubt amused gaze of Leonard Shelford Bidwell and his many successors, the Mayors of the Borough of Thetford, whose portraits line the wall. To the Town Clerk and his Secretary, Mrs. Peel, I am most grateful for their patience and, not least, for the many cups of coffee which sustained me in my labours.

Chapter One

BEGINNINGS

A JOURNEY across East Anglia from east to west reveals to the traveller no dramatic changes of scenery, and no remarkable topographical features. The height above sea level rarely exceeds 300 feet and only exceptionally is the relief sufficiently pronounced to excite comment. Nevertheless, variations in the landscape do exist, and three major divisions can be distinguished between Ely and Diss. These correspond to differences in the underlying geology of the region, and hence the soils.[1] It is these differences, and the impact they have had upon such aspects as the agriculture and communications patterns of East Anglia, which go some way towards providing a background explanation of the location and growth of the town of Thetford, and — thousands of years before it became a town — of the settlement of the earliest human inhabitants of the region (map 1).

Towards the west there are the Fens, a highly distinctive region which in its present form is entirely a product of man's efforts over many centuries to drain, reclaim and improve the land. Until comparatively recently it was difficult of access and awkward to cross, and it is still an area avoided by most main roads. In the prehistoric period the coastline was quite different: a great estuary stretched inland to Wisbech and Denver, with its outlet in the vicinity of the present mouth of the Nene. The northward course of the Great Ouse from Denver via Wiggenhall to Lynn did not then exist: the Wissey flowed westwards towards Wisbech, as did the Little Ouse, and only the Nar flowed out to the Wash at Lynn.

The sea level fell, naturally and not through man's activities, from about A.D. 50, and so the Fenland area began to dry out. The estuary gradually shrank, and it was possible for man to colonise both the silt and mud flats at the northern end of the district, between Holbeach and Wiggenhall, and also the peat tracts farther south, between Wisbech and Ely. Here the Romans began the process of draining, canalising and embanking which has continued to the present day, to produce the geometric landscape of dykes and banks and great rectangular fields which we now see. At the same time they began to alter the whole pattern of Fenland waterways. The sluggish, winding and lengthy courses were inefficient as a means of carrying away flood waters as well as being inconvenient for navigation, and the Romans made the first artificial channels in an attempt to overcome these problems, while in later centuries the Great Ouse and Little Ouse were diverted by a new channel cut directly from Littleport to Brandon Creek, and then by means of widened channels to carry their waters to the sea at Lynn. In prehistoric times, therefore, the Fens were largely undrained and uninhabited: marshy peat moor and wet fen crossed by innumerable channels and by major river-courses, with shallow lakes and treacherous marshes, and with few safe or convenient land routes, while the Wisbech estuary meant that the sea extended 20 miles farther south than it does today.[2]

To the east of Thetford was another difficult area of country, the central — or, as it has rather misleadingly been termed, the 'high' — plateau of East Anglia, stretching southwards from the Fakenham and Aylsham district, through Norfolk and Suffolk and into Essex. This area, which forms the rather dull interior of the region, is a land of gentle topography, with scarcely perceptible ridges and broad shallow valleys. During the last glaciation, which ended about 12,000 years ago, the ice-sheets scraped it flat, and then deposited thick layers of boulder clay, so that the soils are heavy, fertile and difficult to work. The district was eventually thickly wooded, which together with its heavy soils meant that it was not an easy area for agricultural exploitation in the prehistoric period. The main exception was along the river valleys where sheets of gravels and alluvium were much easier to cultivate, and provided excellent sites for

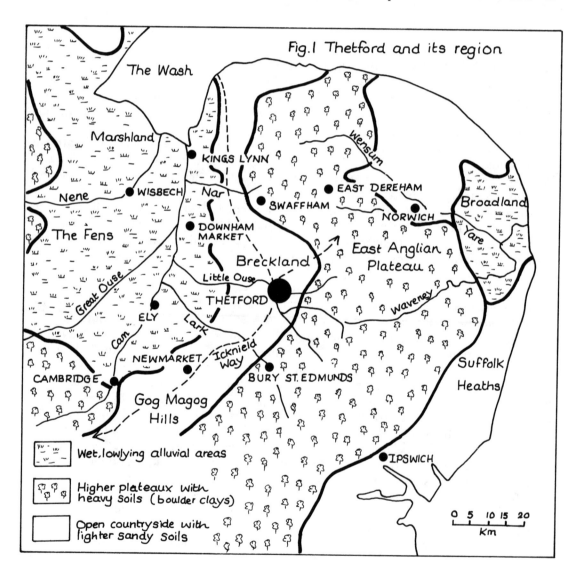

Fig.1 Thetford and its region

settlement. There was undoubtedly some prehistoric penetration of the plateau region, but in contrast to later centuries it was not the most densely occupied or intensively exploited.

Between the wet Fenland and the thickly forested clay plateau was a belt of more open country, running southwards from the ridge behind Snettisham and Dersingham, through Breckland and the Suffolk warrens and then towards Newmarket. This was an area of sandstones and chalks, better drained and therefore drier than the country to the east and west, and with much lighter, more easily-worked soils, less intrinsically fertile but more accessible to prehistoric technology. In the Breckland proper the soils are particularly light, because the underlying chalk is farther below the surface and the basin thus formed is, except along the margin and in the few river valleys which cross the area, filled largely with sands. The combination of porous sands and permeable chalk beneath means that over large areas there is almost no surface drainage, and only where larger rivers have cut down to more impermeable layers of rock does reliable permanent water exist. In the prehistoric period the sandy region — which was not called Breckland until 1894, although this is now a most convenient and widely-used name — was also wooded, although probably less densely than the clay region to the east.[3] Its relative openness made it attractive to the earliest settlers, and it is most fortunate that there is good evidence of how the agricultural systems of these settlers developed and in turn influenced the landscape of the district.

The evidence comes from the mud deposited in the beds of now-vanished lakes and ponds: pollen is trapped in the layers of muds and silts, and the structure of pollen means that it has been preserved extremely well. When core-samples are taken from the lake beds it is possible to analyse the types and quantities of different plant pollens from each period, and so to produce a detailed picture of how the vegetation of the area changed over thousands of years. Breckland provided the first location in Britain for this type of palaeo-botanical analysis, when in 1939 at Hockham Mere investigations produced the earliest reliable evidence for the vegetation of Britain after the ice age, from about 10,000 B.C. The sequence which was recognised began with tundra-type vegetation — birch, pine and willow — in the immediate post-glacial period, followed by the development of grassland in the extensive open spaces, and the gradual appearance of forest trees such as hazel, oak, elm and lime as the climate warmed and deciduous woodland could survive. The amount of grass and fern pollen diminished as the density of woodland increased. About 3000 B.C., however, during the Neolithic period, the quantity of elm began to decline rapidly, and plants such as plantain, dandelion and groundsel, which flourish on cleared sites and cultivated land, showed a very sharp increase, together with cereals and other herbaceous plants.[4]

This means that, about 5,000 years ago, arable agriculture involving extensive clearance of the forest cover began in the Breckland area on a considerable scale. Had this been part of a shifting cultivation system, in which land was used for a few years and then abandoned, it would have been expected that the tree pollen — indicating the forest cover — would have returned, but the evidence from Breckland shows that this was not the case, implying therefore that the scale of agriculture was such as to change the landscape permanently. The land was cleared and then remained as pasture, arable and heathland, because cultivation and cropping by animals prevented the regeneration of the forest cover. Thus the characteristic heaths, commons and 'brecks' of Breckland which were the typical landscape of the district until the early years of this century were man-made phenomena but of extreme antiquity — the result of remarkably intensive and advanced agricultural activity beginning about 3,000 years ago.

In the same area is an even more remarkable example of prehistoric enterprise: the great flint-mining complex, Grime's Graves. The mines have been dated to a period between 2500 and 2200 B.C. It is estimated that the site contains at least 800 shafts, up to 12 metres in depth, over an area of about 35 acres. They cut through a thick overlay of chalk and seams of inferior flint to reach the 'floorstone', flint of excellent quality and ideal for the manufacture of axes, knives and other implements. The volume of material excavated was enormous; when it was dug out by archaeologists Pit No. 1 was found to contain over 10,000 cubic metres of material. The miners were almost certainly skilled rather than casual workers, although the operations may have been seasonal: the assumption is therefore that agricultural workers and hunters must have exchanged foodstuffs for flint products. Flint-mining and working was a traditional industry in Brandon and adjacent villages almost to the present day, the main uses latterly being in flintlock guns and for decorative and building work.[5]

The neolithic production was used for flint axes and knives, although because flint is not easy to assign to a specific location it is not always possible to trace the distribution of axes from this, as opposed to any other, source: this contrasts with the highly distinctive igneous rocks used in axe factories in such places as the Lake District and Cornwall, which can be easily identified as being from a particular site. It is evident, though, that most of the Grime's Graves flint axes were used locally, and the correlation between the period of greatest output here and that of the extensive forest clearing which was undertaken in Breckland is immediately apparent. There can be little doubt that as the clearances developed the demand for axes and other implements increased rapidly, and it became worthwhile to undertake flint-mining locally on a very large scale.

This area, of relatively dense population and advanced agricultural and industrial techniques, had cultural, economic and social contacts with similar areas of southern England, and notably with Salisbury Plain and the Wessex Downs, the heartland of Neolithic culture. At a very early date communications between Wiltshire and Norfolk and the intervening areas of chalk upland were facilitated by the development of a trackway which linked them. This is now called the Icknield Way, the name being derived from the Iceni, occupants of Norfolk and Suffolk during the Iron Age and early Roman period. They lived 2,000 years ago but the trackway which bears their name is probably twice as old, of great antiquity even when Boudicca (Boadicea) made the Iceni a name of national renown.

The Icknield Way ran along the crest of the Chilterns and the Bedfordshire Hills, and skirted the edge of the Fens by following the upland behind Newmarket. It crossed modern Suffolk about three miles east of the present A11, and entered Norfolk at Thetford. Here it seems to have divided, one branch continuing along the spur of higher land across the centre of Breckland towards the sea near Hunstanton, where a ferry across the mouth of the Wash probably connected with a comparable trackway along the summit of the Lincolnshire Wolds, and thence with the Humber and East Yorkshire. The other branch headed north-eastwards across Norfolk, towards Norwich and the surrounding area which was another early centre of Neolithic and Iron Age occupation. Throughout its East Anglian course the Icknield Way carefully followed the belt of drier, more open country between the Fens and the clay plateau, neither of which offered easy conditions for the traveller. It avoided, wherever possible, difficult areas of wet ground, and therefore tended to run just to the east of the heads of the rivers and streams which flowed west to the Fens, a feature particularly apparent north of the present King's Lynn to Norwich road. Inevitably, though, there were places where rivers had to be crossed. In most cases they were no more than small streams, not far from their sources, and only five significant watercourses were encountered between the Thames and the North Sea. Of these the largest, and thus the most serious obstacle, was the Little Ouse, which was joined at Thetford by the Thet. Their combined waters were greater than any of the other five and it was this which, indirectly,

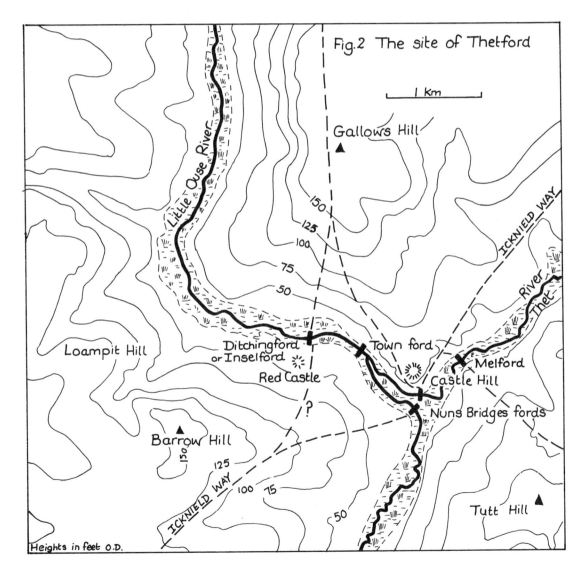

Fig.2 The site of Thetford

seems to have been responsible for the location of Thetford and the growth, thousands of years after the trackway was first evolved, of a town on the site (map 2).

The Icknield Way came northwards across Lackford Warren and Barnham Common and crossed the Little Ouse and the Thet by a long, discontinuous ford. Today this spot is marked by the several arches of Nuns Bridges, and it lies a few hundred yards above the confluence of the two rivers, where they run parallel but separated by a narrow strip of meadowland. Five thousand years ago the channels would undoubtedly have been different — not least because the construction of several mills in the vicinity during the Saxon period affected the waterway network — and it is likely that this was an area with several branching and rejoining channels, separated by low-lying islands and shoals, and so producing shallow and easily-forded waters. Additionally, a spur of slightly higher land, the low hill on which the centre of modern Thetford is built, came close to the river and so afforded a convenient approach route from the north.

There is no doubt that the Nuns Bridges fords were the first in importance, but there were others. The present Town Bridge was certainly preceded by a ford, and on the draft town map drawn by George Burrell in about 1805 this is still clear: the road approached the river from the south and then widened towards the edge of the water, while the Bridge itself was narrow and constricted. The widening was entirely characteristic of a ford, and presumably survived into the early 19th century because it allowed access to the water for livestock and on the occasions when the bridge was too decrepit to be used with safety, a regrettably frequent problem.[6] A third ford was downstream, not far from the site at Red Castle which during the early Saxon period was the location of the main settlement. In all these places the river was probably shallower and wider than it is today.

The Icknield Way was not a single trackway, but had numerous side-tracks and branches to avoid obstacles such as areas flooded in winter, or to provide short cuts and subsidiary routes. Although the Nuns Bridges ford carried the major traffic, each of the other fords will have been crossed by side tracks or branches. The main route seems to have bifurcated just north of Nuns Bridges, with the eastern branch heading for Norwich and roughly following the line of Castle Lane, and the western branch heading north-westwards, probably along the line today represented by Guildhall Street and Earls Street.

In the angle between the two branches is the greatest monument of prehistoric west Norfolk still visible, with the exception of Grime's Graves. Commanding the ford was a hillfort (although this is rather a misnomer as the land was only slightly elevated), sited between the eastern and western routes and thus carefully placed to maximise its strategic function. This hillfort was one of only a few which have been found in East Anglia, although they are frequently found in Southern England. It comprises a double ditch system, oval in shape, with an inner rampart, and was built in the early Iron Age, probably about 500 B.C.[7] The site is excellent: it occupies the tip of the low ridge or spur which extends southwards from Gallows Hill, and not only commands the routeways heading south, north-east and north-west from the Nuns Bridges fords, but also has fine views along the valleys in each direction. The building of a fort at this spot emphasises the great importance of the site of Thetford as a strategic point, and it is no accident that the ramparts of the fort were later used for the Norman castle and are still at the heart of modern Thetford. For over 2,500 years this place has been a focal point of communications.

The builders of the hillfort were not the earliest inhabitants of what was to become Thetford. As might be expected the Neolithic peoples of the district, so active in clearing the forests of Breckland and exploiting the flint resources of Brandon, were also living at Thetford: Neolithic beakers, flints and potsherds dating from about 1700 B.C. were found on the site of the hillfort and elsewhere in the town, including the Red Castle area which was to be the focus of early Saxon Thetford. Bronze Age occupation is represented by isolated finds in the area of the town itself, but more prominently by the existence of tumuli on Gallows Hill and at Snarehill. Undoubtedly there was much other earlier occupation but the evidence for this has either not been recognised, or has been obliterated by later development and redevelopment.

The construction of the hillfort early in the Iron Age was probably associated with the establishment of Icenian control over the district, and from this period it was likely that Thetford lay close to the centre of Icenian power. The distribution of place-names which contain elements deriving from the word 'Iceni' shows a concentration in south-west Norfolk and north-west Suffolk: Ickworth, Icklingham, Ixworth, and Ickburgh being examples. Thetford is geographically central to this area, added to which its strategic position would imply that it had an important position in Icenian society. The hillfort was substantially remodelled in about A.D. 5 by the Iceni, in response to a threat posed by the Belgae, who had occupied most of south-east England and the Home Counties during the previous 50 years. The ditches were either filled in and replaced, or were re-cut, so that in the early years of the first century there were two huge ditches, 30 feet wide and 16 feet deep, with almost vertical sides and flat bottoms, and probably further reinforced by rows of sharpened stakes. These imposing and powerful defences indicate that the Thetford fort was being reinforced as part of the protection of the Icenian heartland. The Belgic threat was countered, and the Iceni survived as a separate kingdom until after the Roman conquest, but it is possible that the southern edge of their territory was pushed back during the conflict to the Waveney–Little Ouse line. This has remained as the boundary between Norfolk and Suffolk until the present day.[8]

Icenian silver and bronze coinage has been found in the area, but remarkable archaeological discoveries made in the early 1980s have produced dramatic evidence of the power of the Icenian state immediately before its destruction.[9] It has always been known that under King Prasutagus and his wife, Boudicca, the Icenians became an allied or client kingdom of the Romans immediately after the Claudian conquest in A.D. 43. In 1980 a unique complex of buildings was discovered by aerial observation on the summit of Gallows Hill, on the northern edge of modern Thetford. It is in a place which commanded views in all directions (or, it could be argued, was easily visible from all sides), and was also beside the western route of the Icknield Way at the point where it begins to descend from the hillspur towards the Little Ouse fords.

The excavation of the site, in advance of development works, revealed a huge rectangular enclosure, covering 11 acres, with a single entrance and an extraordinary triple ditch and bank system. Between the outer and middle ditches was a remarkable fence consisting of several parallel rows of posts, each four inches in diameter and set four inches apart: it has been calculated that the site had no less than 70 miles of fences in total. Within the enclosure, centrally placed opposite the entrance, were three large circular wooden buildings, the purpose of which was unclear. Beyond them was a D-shaped building, the discovery in which of a single bronze oak leaf has led to suggestions that it was a rich and elaborate shrine.

It seems almost certain that this complex of buildings, which is quite unlike anything ever discovered in this country, just predates the Roman conquest. Finds included hand-made pre-Conquest pottery; dies and moulds for coins; clay weights for looms; querns; and silver Icenian brooches and a coin; while post-Conquest Romanised material included wheel-made pottery and bronze brooches: it is thus evident that its existence spanned the Conquest. The items found during excavation allow its construction date to be determined at about A.D. 40 and show that it was deliberately and carefully demolished, and the site levelled, about 20 years later.

There had already been suggestions that an Icenian royal palace, not dissimilar to that of the Regnensian king Cogidubnus at Fishbourne, should have been located in the Lakenheath–Mildenhall area, so the Gallows Hill discovery was immediately interpreted by some observers as such a building. Since the king and queen of the Iceni throughout the period 40–60 were Prasutagus and Boudicca, the name 'Boadicea's Palace' was used in newspaper reports and headlines. The high quality of the design, its scale, its uniqueness and its very prominent location do indeed point to this being the residence or 'headquarters' of the Icenian royal family. It is not obviously a religious complex, although possibly it had a large shrine, and neither is it a military fortress, since although it had heavy and elaborate defences the enclosed area was only two acres, far too small to contain a significant military force. The limited evidence of buildings indicates that a purely domestic function is also unlikely, since they are formal and on a large scale. This implies, therefore, that the Gallows Hill complex was a prestige building designed to assert the status and authority of the occupants or users, and to impress with its magnitude and proportions. The presence of coin-moulds suggests that there was some minting of coins on the spot: this would also indicate that it was a seat of authority. On balance, therefore, the building could well have been a seat of government of the Icenian kingdom, and hence of Prasutagus and Boudicca, although not necessarily their actual residence.[10]

If this is the case, and there is no reason to question that Icenian leaders, royal or not, were living at Thetford in the first half of the first century, then there must also have been some form of civilian settlement in the vicinity. This has not yet been discovered, but could have lain lower down the hill in the area of the railway station and the northern part of the present town.

The destruction of the complex can be dated to approximately A.D. 60, and there can be little doubt that this act was closely connected with, and probably a direct result of, the Boudiccan rebellion which took place in that year. It is tempting to imagine that the rebellion began at Thetford, and that the Gallows Hill buildings were the scene of the celebrated incident which began the uprising: Prasutagus died, leaving his two daughters as heirs to the kingdom, the Romans — as was inevitable — took the opportunity to annex the territory to the province of Britain, but in the process soldiers brutally treated Boudicca, the widow, and raped her daughters, while behaving arrogantly towards the Icenian nation in confiscating its treasury and revenues. The Icenians rebelled, were joined by their neighbours the Trinovantes, and the Boudiccan uprising had begun, to end in defeat near St Albans after the devastation of the Roman towns of Colchester, London and St Albans, and the near-loss of Roman control in

Britain. The careful and deliberate razing of the Gallows Hill site and the removal of all evidence of its existence — to the extent of levelling the ditches and banks — was not the result of a violent siege or the direct consequence of warfare. Rather, it took place after the final defeat of the Iceni, during the process of dismantling and erasing all trace of their separate statehood. A bronze mount from the belt of a Roman soldier, which may have been lost during the work of levelling the site, was found during excavation.

The administrative centre for the former Icenian territory was fixed at *Venta Icenorum*, Caistor St Edmund (just south of Norwich), so that Thetford and its neighbourhood no longer had any political importance. Nevertheless, the Icknield Way continued in use as a major north–south routeway, even though the Peddars Way was developed as a parallel route a few miles to the east. It has been argued that the Peddars Way was primarily a Roman military and commercial road, while the ancient trackway continued to serve the native population. Roman civil settlements were established on the Peddars Way at Brettenham and Ixworth, but no comparable site has yet been found on the East Anglian section of the Icknield Way. It is doubtful whether there was any substantial township at Thetford, and there is no foundation at all for the belief of the 18th-century historians that this was *Sitomagus*, a major Roman town.[11]

Undoubtedly there was occupation of the area of the modern town during the Roman period, but this is likely to have been mainly by peasant farmers, and to have produced no clearly-defined nucleated settlement. Extensive Romano–British occupation was indicated by finds in the Red Castle excavations, and it is very significant that the same area, at the western extremity of the present town, was apparently also the location of the earliest Saxon settlement. This suggests a continuity of use between the two periods.

In the past decade new archaeological discoveries on Gallows Hill have provided further evidence for possible Roman activity in the vicinity of Thetford. While it remains true that a substantial town did not exist, and that most settlement was agricultural, the presence of a greatly more sophisticated and wealthy population has been implied by the discovery of the Thetford Treasure. In 1981, quite independently of the enormous publicity which surrounded the work on 'Boadicea's Palace', Thetford attracted great attention when a Treasure Trove Inquest was held on a discovery made on Gallows Hill two years before. The Thetford Treasure is one of the most significant archaeological discoveries made in Britain this century and, in the words of Catherine Johns of the British Museum, 'it is important not just for the history of Thetford or of Norfolk, but for that of the whole of Britain and Europe, since it gives us new information about the times in which it was made and used, and contains some of the finest pieces of their kind found anywhere in the . . . Roman Empire'.

The Treasure consists of gold jewellery and silver spoons. The jewellery is remarkable for its quality and sophistication, with excellent workmanship and gold of great purity. The softness of the gold and the unusually ornate designs — which would have made the pieces inconvenient and uncomfortable to wear — suggest that the jewellery was largely for ceremonial use. It does not appear to have been worn, and as some of the pieces were not even finished it is reasonable to suppose that the hoard was buried by a jeweller who was probably, although not definitely, working in Norfolk. There are 22 gold rings, many with precious and semi-precious stones held in elaborate settings, as well as bracelets, necklaces, pendants, and a fine gold belt-buckle.

There are 36 silver spoons: 16 have short curled handles terminating in a bird's head, and are about the size of a tablespoon; 17 are small spoons with long pointed handles; and three are perforated for use as strainers. Two of the spoons are partly gilded and engraved, and almost all of them have inscriptions which refer to their dedication to the nature-god, Faunus. His cult was popular in the rural areas of late-Roman Britain, and although there is no evidence as yet to suggest that there was a temple in the Thetford area this is clearly a strong possibility. The Treasure may have been brought from somewhere else to be buried here for safety, but if so the choice of a site close to the Icknield Way seems rather odd. It is very much to be hoped that one day it will be possible to answer the question with confidence.[12]

Close to the site of the Treasure find, and on Gallows Hill also, another hoard had already been uncovered. This was a collection of 47 silver coins (*siliquae*), dating from the period 355-388.[13] The dates of the coins confirm that they were buried during the last decade of the 4th century, and it can be no coincidence that this is also the date which is ascribed to the burial of the Thetford Treasure. The period from 390 onwards was marked by the gradual disintegration of Imperial authority in the province of Britain, when civil unrest and lawlessness were accompanied and exacerbated by raids by Pictish and Saxon pirates. There is no doubt that both hoards were buried for safety during the 390s, only to be lost for almost sixteen centuries.

The evidence for the Roman period in Thetford is scanty, but more may yet come to light and help in the interpretation of the context of the Thetford Treasure. Equally scarce are the indications of how the transition between the 'Roman' and 'Saxon' periods affected the area. The previous assumption of a marked break in 410 is now known to be wrong. Well before that date Saxon mercenaries had been brought in to help against Pictish, Irish and even Saxon incursions, and permanent settlement by the Saxons had started well before the formal withdrawal of Roman authority. Archaeological evidence, particularly from cemeteries, shows that the mercenaries and settlers were most numerous near the Wash and Icknield Way, and so Thetford must have come under Saxon control at very early date, probably near the beginning of the 5th century. We know nothing of the detailed process by which the change was effected, but it is almost certain that the Romano–British farming community will have continued, with little disruption, into the Pagan Saxon period, for such continuity of settlement at this level of society is now widely recognised.[14]

Chapter Two

THE RISE AND FALL OF SAXON THETFORD

THE THREE CENTURIES from 850 were perhaps the most remarkable in the history of Thetford. During that period it grew, with impressive speed, from a small agricultural settlement to a town which was the fifth or sixth largest in England and was effectively, in a phrase much loved by the Victorian historians and the writers of modern tourist publicity, the capital of East Anglia. In the second half of the 11th century Thetford became the seat of the bishops of East Anglia. But thereafter the history of the town shows a startling change. There was a rapid and dramatic shrinking in its size and population, a major re-orientation of its geography, and then centuries of stagnation. Only with the industrial development of the early 19th century was Thetford revived and rejuvenated. The precise reasons for these phenomena, the sudden flourishing and the equally precipitate decline, remain the subject of supposition because, almost inevitably, it is impossible to find definitive evidence. Nevertheless it is possible to offer convincing suggestions for the patterns of growth and decline which have been deduced from archaeological and historical sources. These patterns are important not only for the history of this town, but also in the regional history of East Anglia and even of England, for had Thetford retained its size, significance and influence the urban structure of our country would have been substantially different.

In some senses, despite post-war investigation of its archaeological and historical background, Saxon Thetford remains a mysterious and enigmatic place, but this need not have been the case. Thetford presented perhaps unequalled scope for a thorough, careful and illuminating programme of archaeological research, an opportunity to produce a clear and complete explanation of the beginnings and evolution of urban life. Until 1945 most of the main area of the Saxon town lay beneath fields and open land, untouched since its abandonment in the two centuries following the Norman Conquest. Here was evidence for the street and house plans, the crafts and industries, the trades, the life-styles and the people of the Saxon and Norman town. The opportunity to examine this evidence was, with honourable exceptions, thrown away. The expansion scheme implemented by the Borough Council and the L.C.C. in the 1950s and 1960s was undertaken with scant regard for the history of the town, and in the process most of the vast archaeological potential was destroyed by bulldozers and excavators. As late as the early 1970s the redevelopment of the town centre, an area continuously occupied for 12 centuries, went ahead without any preliminary archaeological investigation, and now it is too late to compensate for the deplorable losses.

The archaeological work which *was* undertaken was of necessity randomly located — although carefully executed — and the total area investigated amounts to no more than five per cent. of the Saxon town. The information derived from this work,

11

although of crucial importance, can in most cases only hint at what might have been. Our knowledge of Saxon and early medieval Thetford is thus derived from the very limited documentary sources, the observations of earlier historians, and the valiant efforts of archaeologists who managed in a few small parts of the town to excavate in advance of the developers.[1] The history of Saxon Thetford comprises a small amount of specific and proven detail, a good deal of generalisation or logical supposition, and a measure of pure hypothesis!

Origins

Thetford evolved as a town in the second half of the ninth century, and until then comprised one or more small agricultural communities on the south bank of the Little Ouse. The three fords which were, as already seen, key factors in explaining the distribution of the earliest human occupation of the area, seem to have been equally important in determining the location of these early Saxon settlements. Indeed, it is likely that there was some degree of physical continuity between the sub-Roman and Pagan Saxon communities: it is illogical to suppose that the district was depopulated in the intervening period, or that the inhabitants moved wholesale to a new location, while the convenient dates for the end of the Roman occupation and the start of the Saxon had no relevance to the daily existence of peasant farming populations. Dating the archaeological evidence for the settlement of the sixth to eighth centuries is far from simple because the only substantial categories of finds are human burials and potteries: both of these remained unchanged in character and appearance for hundreds of years, and so precise dating is impossible. The terms 'Pagan', 'Middle' and 'Later' Saxon, formerly in general use and still employed for the sake of convenience, are also unreliable: in some places the characteristics of one such period could last much longer than in others, and so the selection of a single date for the start or end of these divisions is not acceptable.

With these reservations it is clear that the earliest significant Saxon settlement was at Red Castle, a long-mysterious circular earthwork close to the western end of the later Saxon town and of modern Thetford. When excavated in the 1950s it revealed traces of Roman occupation, and a substantial number of Pagan and Middle Saxon burials, as well as pottery.[2] The earthwork was proved to be of a later date, thrown up in the 11th century *across* the line of the Saxon defensive works, and so not associated with the seventh- and eighth-century settlement. The site lies close to the lowest of the three fords, just above the damp riverside which would probably have been marshland in the early Saxon period, and is beside one of the several routes of the Icknield Way road system. The ford was known to Martin, in the 18th century, as Ditchingford, a name which he interpreted as 'ditch-end ford', i.e. the ford at the end of the defensive ditch of the Saxon town.[3] However, there is no earlier documentary evidence for this name, and in the medieval period it was called Inselford (or one of several close variants), a name which survived into the early 19th century in the place-name Dissilford Common, which suggests that Ditchingford may in fact have been a corruption of the old name, perhaps with a degree of wishful thinking on Martin's part. It has also been suggested that the old name was Redford, or 'reed-ford', associated with the name Red Castle for the adjacent earthwork. Other settlement of the seventh and eighth centuries has been located in the southern part of the town, close to St Margaret's Cemetery and beside Brandon Road, but investigations elsewhere have not produced any concentration of finds.

In particular, the settlement which was anticipated at Weevers Close, just south of the Nuns Bridges, has not yet come to light, although it has long been supposed that it ought to exist. The 18th-century writers noted an earthwork here, allegedly of Saxon date, and the site would in important respects replicate that at Red Castle.[4] But archaeological investigation has been limited to a small series of trial holes, and although it now appears unlikely that any considerable settlement will be found, the possibility of a minor one cannot be ruled out. The apparent importance of this ford, on the eastern branch of the Icknield Way and close to the Iron Age hillfort, would imply that some occupation was likely.

The Red Castle settlement had a church, which according to older historians was dedicated to St Martin: recent research by Alan Davison has revealed that the true dedication was that of St Lawrence, formerly attributed to a supposed church at the top end of King Street. The location of St Martin's church is thus unclear. The Red Castle church was found to date from the Middle Saxon period, that is from the earliest phase of Christianity in the area, and was then a small and simple wooden building, likely to have resembled the still-extant example at Greensted in Essex. In about 1030 the church was reconstructed in stone. The existence of this church at an early date points to the Red Castle site having at least some of the characteristics of a village, although we know nothing of its appearance; whether or not it was a nucleated settlement, for example. Even if the evidence for other early occupation, at Weevers Close or perhaps at the middle ford adjacent to the present Town Bridge, should eventually be found, it seems improbable that these would be as large as the Red Castle settlement.

Development of a town

The sudden growth of the agricultural community or communities into a flourishing, extensive and important town can be explained by several related reasons, a complex of circumstances rather than a clear and easily-distinguished cause: the origins of the Second World War and the Industrial Revolution are, and always will be, the subject of fierce debate, so how much harder it is to procure a watertight explanation of an undocumented and barely-visible development which took place over a thousand years ago. The urban growth of Thetford seems to have been a response to the interaction of factors such as the general expansion of trade and the network of trade routes, the place of Thetford as a focus of such routes, technological advances in the pottery industry, and military and political events in ninth-century England.

The location of Thetford, at a point where the Little Ouse first became navigable and at a major ford on a key north–south route, was clearly conducive to settlement growth once the expansion of trade — regional, national and even international — made these routes economically significant. It should, however, be emphasised that the mere existence of a ford and a navigable river did not make urban growth a foregone conclusion, but rather provided suitable conditions for such development. As the centre of East Anglia became more thickly populated and was increasingly exploited for agriculture in the eighth and ninth centuries the riverhead port at Thetford assumed significance for east to west trade routes, connecting with the Fenland waterways and thence to the sea, as well as with the ancient north to south routeway. Thetford thus became a trading centre for the export of local agricultural produce — grain, wool and timber — and the import of goods from the rest of England and overseas.[5]

The strategic importance of the site cannot be ignored. Its controlling point in the regional communications pattern and its rôle as a 'gateway' to the interior of East Anglia or, for invaders marching westwards, to the English Midlands, gave it military significance for hundreds of years. The two Iron Age strongholds, at the Castle and Gallows Hill, indicate an early appreciation of this, and the growth of the Saxon town, which had substantial defences, was undoubtedly related to that function. Three of the small number of written references to later Saxon Thetford relate to its place as the objective of military campaigns, and in the immediate post-Conquest period the refortification of the town was probably associated with its use as a base for campaigns against rebels in and around the Fenland area. Deriving from the military rôle was a political and administrative importance.

Coinciding with the urbanisation of Thetford was the development of a flourishing and long-lasting pottery industry.[6] Conversely, the decline and failure of the industry during the 12th century accompanied the later stages of the decline in the wealth and population of the town. While it would be a mistake to suppose that the pattern of industrial change alone provides a sufficient explanation for the rise and fall of the town, because so many other factors were involved, there can be no doubt that the growth and eventual demise of a key industry had a profound impact. The manufacture of pottery made Thetford into a significant industrial centre, while its function as a trading town was greatly reinforced by the distribution and export of this commodity.

Other possible reasons for the growth of the town exist, the most tantalising and the least easy to confirm being that there was some degree of deliberate decision involved. A limited amount of evidence from the archaeological investigation of the southern part of the town hinting at elements of regularity in the road pattern and land divisions, as well as the existence of a defensive system, indicate that some type of overall authority operated in Thetford even during the early phases of its life as a town. The rapidity with which the town grew and the fact that it did not grow around the Red Castle nucleus but instead occupied virgin land to the east, together with the possibility of a degree of planning in its layout, suggest that Thetford could have been established and provided with an outline plan as a deliberate act, for economic or more probably strategic and defensive purposes. There are numerous well-documented examples of such actions from later Saxon England, and it is now appreciated that the conscious planning of towns was well known at this time.

Against that, some have argued that the political and military circumstances of East Anglia in the later ninth century were not conducive to urban planning. In 870 the kingdom of East Anglia fell to the Danes, and remained outside the full control of the Saxons until Edward the Elder secured Danish submission in 917. It was during this period that the planned *burhs* of Wessex and Mercia were founded — Oxford and Wallingford are examples — but during these years Thetford lay outside that political system. It is also suggested that the swiftness of the Danish actions in

870, and of their submission in 917, did not allow enough time for the establishment of an extensive network of fortified *burhs*, and that no other examples have been found in East Anglia.[7]

There is some sense in this argument, but it remains evident that Thetford did grow with unusual speed, did have at least a suggestion of a civic authority of some type, and did have a large defensive system which was apparently constructed during the period in question. Excavations in the area south-east of London Road, near the present Dane Close, indicate that even in the later ninth century this was still agricultural land, while investigation of the town defences in several locations seems to imply that they were first constructed around the year 900, when a substantial part of the land so enclosed was undeveloped (map 3). The original defences consisted of a ditch about 20 feet wide, with a bank made of the excavated material: the precise course is not entirely certain, except for a long straight stretch running south-east from Red Castle, across London Road, as far as the cemetery. It is presumed that it continued on that alignment as far as Queensway, turned eastward to Nuns Bridges Road, and then followed the approximate course of that road to Weevers Close and the ford. At the northern end it may have turned sharply to the right, along the edge of the marshes, to Ditchingford, or followed a shorter route direct to the Little Ouse opposite Red Castle. The ditch and bank were still clearly visible in the 18th century, and the Red Castle to London Road section survives today, but the rest has been destroyed by later agricultural and urban expansion.[8]

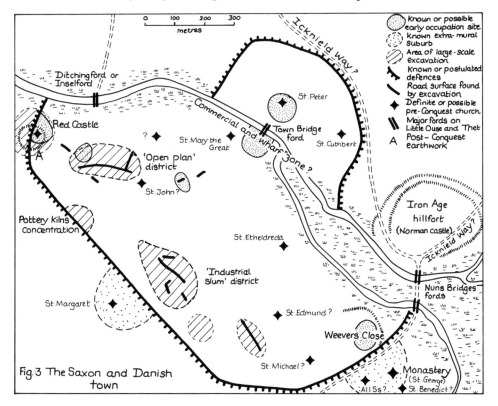

Fig. 3 The Saxon and Danish town

The Saxon town

The greater part of the Saxon town lay south of the Little Ouse, spreading across the gently-sloping land which forms the end of the Barrow Hill ridge. It had a very long river frontage, stretching for a mile between Red Castle and Nuns Bridges, and most of that length is likely to have been a belt of marshy low-lying land, unsuitable for development but used for grazing cattle. There will, however, have been some permanent wharfage for river traders, most probably in the vicinity of the present Town Bridge where the banks are higher and drier than elsewhere. No scientific excavation has ever taken place in that part of the town, and much of the evidence will have been destroyed or damaged by intensive development over the centuries, as well as by river erosion; it may therefore never be possible to establish the details of the riverside features of the town.

The south bank town covered a roughly semi-circular area of about 60 hectares (150 acres) with its centre at the ford on the site of the Town Bridge. That it focused upon what is still the centre of the present town strongly points to the early pre-eminence of that river crossing once urban development had started and to the lesser importance of those upstream at Nuns Bridges and downstream at Ditchingford which had been significant during the agricultural period. Indeed, this might have been the *theodford* (people's ford or chief ford) which is thought to have given its name to the town. It is likely that the late ninth-century town, built around this ford, took traffic away from the other two so that they became secondary crossings.

In 1963 it was suggested on the basis of map evidence and analogy with other Saxon towns, that there was a smaller semi-circular defended area on the north bank of the river, covering approximately 15 hectares (37 acres). Its defences were perhaps a ditch and bank system less substantial than the southern rampart, and were thought to have followed the line of Water Lane, Painter Street and Earls Street to the market place. One suggestion is that they then continued along Guildhall Street towards the site of the old market place and the ramparts of the Iron Age hillfort. However, it will be shown in Chapter 3 that a more likely course was south of this, roughly along the line of Cage Lane and down to the river close to the later Pit Mill. The curve of the supposed rampart from Water Lane to the vicinity of the Guildhall is strikingly clear even on modern maps, although the construction of the A11 relief road has totally destroyed the Water Lane section of its route. Archaeological evidence for the northern defences is as yet lacking, but it is known that there was contemporary occupation of the area, and the case for the north bank town and its defensive line is convincing.[9]

The absence of archaeological evidence is not a real problem: there is, for example, no dispute that the north bank town was intensively occupied throughout the medieval period, but almost no medieval material has been found there. A combination of the destruction of evidence by development over the centuries, and the paucity of scientific investigation, is responsible for the apparent anomaly. The north bank town had its focus at the crossroads just north of the bridge, where White Hart Street, King Street, Bridge Street and Minstergate meet today. The church of St Peter is situated immediately beside this junction, and is known to be a pre-Conquest foundation. It thus seems probable that this was a village-type nucleus even before the rapid urbanisation of Thetford.

A south-bank town with a smaller north bank bridgehead settlement produces an urban form which in its general characteristics is similar to that of some other Saxon towns: Cambridge, Norwich and London, for example. But within the town the street pattern and the distribution of land uses is scarcely understood. There is no map of Thetford earlier than 1807, apart from a rough sketch plan made about 50 years before by Thomas Martin.[10] Medieval documentary evidence, which might at least have helped to locate other streets, is either unhelpful or of limited scope, and therefore the evidence for street patterns is small. It is reasonable to suppose that most of the streets shown on the 1807 map existed in the medieval period and we can presume that at least some were features of pre-Conquest Thetford, but it is perfectly possible that others were not, and that, even if the general line of a street has survived, its detailed alignment and location may have shifted over the centuries. Archaeological sections across existing streets are absent, and until these are available to reconstruct the history of the road and its surfaces all must be based on supposition.

In view of the undoubted importance of the Town Bridge river crossing the approximate alignments of London Road – Bridge Street – White Hart Street, and perhaps of Castle Street – King Street – Minstergate are likely to be ancient. On the south bank Brandon Road, London Road, Star Lane and Bury Road more or less focus upon the bridge and are presumably Saxon in origin. A further clue is the use of the term 'gate' to mean 'street', a word of Danish origin and widespread in Eastern England. It is probable, though by no means certain, that the streets with 'gate' in their names pre-date the Conquest. Minstergate is the chief example today, but formerly there were several more. Bridge Street was previously Bridgegate, Raymond Street was Reymundsgate, and Magdalen Street may have been Wrethamgate. One recent theory, reviving a suggestion made by W. G. Clarke in the early years of this century, is that Brandon Road was known as Westgate, a name recorded in a few medieval deeds.[11]

The road pattern of the south bank town is even less clear than that of the north, because most of its streets disappeared, to be ploughed up for agriculture or buried beneath soil and vegetation, with the abandonment of that area in the late 11th and 12th centuries. There must have been an extensive network of intervening roads and main streets in addition to the radial routes, but there is practically no evidence and certainly no surface trace of this. In the excavations of the 1950s and 1960s short lengths of road were found, but not even a tentative plan can be drawn on the basis of these. A west to east road lay between Red Castle and the present London Road–Brandon Road junction, 12 feet wide and made of flints rammed down onto a slag and sand base. It had been rebuilt and repaired on the same alignment on several occasions, proving that it was a permanent highway. Leading off it were the beginnings of minor roads or lanes, with some indication of one heading approximately at a right angle towards the bank of the river. Other short stretches of paved road were found elsewhere, while there were traces of less formal pathways and alleyways in what seemed to be an industrial area.

The blocks between the road varied in character, some parts of the town apparently being quite open in plan, with a low density of building, while others were intensively developed. The 'open plan' district seemed to have been divided up by deep, narrow ditches (which could have been for drainage or for the delineation of boundaries, or both) into large and approximately regular blocks. Some of these were later amalgamated or subdivided, indicating patterns of land use or tenure which changed over time. The spoil from the ditches was not used to form banks, and had not been spread across adjacent land, suggesting that it had been removed to another location: this has been used as evidence for the existence of some form of civic authority or organising body. Within these blocks there were no major concentrations of buildings along street frontages, but instead they were set back randomly from the roadway within their own yards or smallholdings. Elsewhere there was convincing evidence for a different type of urban form, in which buildings and industrial premises were crowded in a closely-packed, congested belt along the edge of the street. Properties were frequently demolished or abandoned, and new buildings erected on their sites. Industry and housing were inextricably mixed, and associated with these features were networks of ditches, narrow back lanes, and clusters of pits. The excavator, Group Captain Knocker, described this part of the town as an 'industrial slum', and it has also been termed the 'artisans quarter'.[12]

It is entirely to be expected that a town of the size and economic importance of 10th- and 11th-century Thetford would have had zonings of urban land use, with different areas devoted wholly or in part to specific trades, or occupied by different social or ethnic groups. Therefore the existence of these two very dissimilar forms of town plan is unremarkable. The 'open plan' form resembles examples from northern Europe, including well-studied Danish examples at Birka and Hedeby in Jutland, while the densely-developed form is perhaps more characteristic of what is known of Saxon towns in central and southern England. Thetford must have had Danish and English inhabitants, but it is not possible to determine whether the observed differences within the town can be related to the existence of these two groups.[13]

At some stage the success of the town seems to have led to the growth of extra-mural suburbs, as the built-up area expanded to cover the land within the defences. Such suburbs probably dated from the late 10th and early 11th centuries, the period of great prosperity and largest population. It is even possible that for a time in the later Saxon period, between the two phases of Anglo-Danish warfare, the defences themselves were abandoned or neglected, permitting easier movement and development beyond their line. Excavation in the vicinity of the former St Barnabas' Hospital and near the London Road cemetery has shown at least two extra-mural churches — St Margaret and St George — and two others, St Benet and All Saints, are also thought to have been beyond the ditch. The monastery which preceded the medieval nunnery of St George, and which was a daughter house of Bury St Edmunds Abbey, was extra-mural and, since perhaps three of these churches were associated with it, may be presumed to have been a stimulus to the growth of the adjacent suburb.

The churches of Saxon Thetford were numerous (map 4) and in this it closely resembled the other major towns of the time which have — unlike Thetford — retained their importance: Lincoln, York, Norwich and Oxford, for example. Many of the sites of the early churches were still visible in the 18th century, and Blomefield and Martin were able to describe their remains, but the identity of several could even then only be presumed from tradition, and from the inadequate documentary record. Fourteen pre-Conquest churches can be identified with greater or lesser confidence. Some are

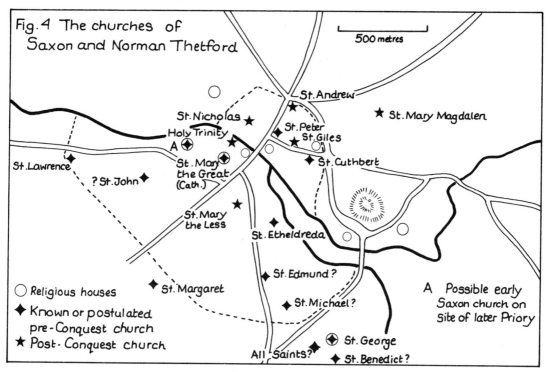

Fig. 4 The churches of Saxon and Norman Thetford

mentioned by name in the Domesday Survey (1086): St Mary the Great (which served as the cathedral), St Peter, St John, St Martin, St Margaret, and St Helen, the last-named being in a remote rural area three miles away on the edge of the borough. Five others have dedications which are characteristic of a Saxon origin, since the Saxons and Normans tended to favour different saints: St Cuthbert, St Lawrence, All Saints, St Benet, and St Etheldreda. In addition two, believed to be St Michael and St Edmund on the basis of tradition, are confirmed as pre-Conquest from archaeological investigation. Finally, the Domesday Survey refers to an unnamed church owned by the abbot of Bury, and this is probably the church of St George, close to the nunnery site, although as this saint was popular with the Normans that may not have been its original dedication.

There are thus eight churches known with certainty, and a further six for which a Saxon foundation seems reasonable. It is still very doubtful if the dedications attributed to most of the sites by tradition, and by the 18th-century historians, can be accepted without serious reservation, as the case of St Martin's at Red Castle shows. St Edmund, St Michael and St Benet/Benedict are to be considered especially doubtful, while which church was dedicated to St Martin is, as a result of Alan Davison's work, now unknown.[14] A major problem is that other churches may have existed of which all visual, documentary and archaeological trace is at present lost, while we have no reason to be certain that the list of dedications which we have is complete. For example, excavations at the priory of the Holy Sepulchre revealed what is perhaps a hitherto unrecorded Saxon parish church beneath the medieval priory.[15]

The economy of pre-Conquest Thetford

As the town developed, so its trading role and its function as a collection and distribution centre grew. It has been suggested that this reached its climax in the more settled political and economic conditions which followed the accession of Cnut in 1016. Thetford was prominent in the flourishing trade within the Anglo-Scandinavian empire, and the destruction of that empire, following the Norman Conquest of England and the subsequent hostility between England and Scandinavia, had a serious effect upon the trade of the town.

Evidence for east–west trade routes is provided by the presence in the town of pottery manufactured at Stamford and St Neots, while Thetford ware has been found in both these places. Links with the rest of England are suggested by querns of mill-stone grit from the Pennines, and of sandstone and limestone from the uplands of Leicestershire and Northamptonshire. Abundant fish and mollusc remains indicate a regular trade with the coastal regions of Norfolk and Lincolnshire. Overseas trade is represented by finds such as querns of Rhineland lava and hones of Norwegian rag-stone, but these are not uncommon in East Anglia and until more unusual or specific evidence emerges the exact pattern of international trade is unclear.[16]

The location of Thetford as a river port which acted as a trading centre for a wide rural hinterland bears some resemblance to that of other prosperous towns of Anglo-Saxon and Danish England: London, Ipswich, Norwich and York, for example. Despite the lack of archaeological evidence it can be presumed that by the end of the 10th century there were riverside commercial and mercantile areas, and probably districts occupied by groups of immigrant traders, as these are well known from other, comparable, towns. At this period the region of which Thetford was the focal point extended as far north as the coastlands of the Wash, eastwards to Diss and south into Suffolk, as well as including a sizeable tract of Fenland marshes. There must have been a market place: its situation within the town is unknown, although since the greater part of the built-up area lay on the south bank it is likely that the market place was there too, perhaps where the roads converged near the present Town Bridge.

Industries developed in the town, although the extent of our knowledge of most of them has depended again upon the rather limited amount of archaeological excavation. The manufacturing of pottery seems to have begun in the middle of the ninth century, and continued for about 300 years. A hard, grey and sandy pottery was produced, and is given the name 'Thetford ware'. The style of the ware was apparently modelled on Rhenish types, pointing to the cultural influence of north Germany in the Middle Saxon period, and is closely related to the Stamford and St Neots wares, implying that cross-Fenland trading and social links were of considerable significance. Similar wares were produced in four other places in East Anglia — Norwich, Ipswich, Langhale and Grimston — as well as in Lincolnshire and Leicestershire. The potteries were the only industry of pre-Conquest Thetford for which there is, as yet, clear evidence of large-scale output. There was a notable concentration of kilns just inside the defences, adjacent to the modern Redcastle Furze school: here there were six single-kiln ovens grouped around a yard which would have been used for the stacking of pots. Another concentration seems to have been in the Dane Close area, and there may well have been others which have been missed by the archaeological coverage. In the Icknield Way area were found vast quantities of ash, which cannot be connected with the destruction of Thetford by the Danes and which perhaps indicate that the pottery industry was on a much greater scale than has previously been realised. In producing such quantities of waste the industry would have created a great deal of pollution, and it has been argued that this was responsible for its deliberate location right on the edge of the town, segregated to some extent from the residential areas.

Limited evidence of other industries is varied and widespread. At the Dane Close site crucibles for silver-smithing were found, and copper working is also attested by the discovery of crucibles, chalk moulds for casting metal bars, and a sandstone mould in the shape of a cross. The town probably had a mint from the later ninth century, and certainly from the middle of the tenth. Iron-working must have been important since large amounts of slag were used as road material, and metal-working tools such as hammers, chisels, punches and files have been found. Unfortunately no trace of hearths or furnaces has been revealed as yet. Two glass linen-smoothers might imply a local glass-manufacturing industry, but although the district, with its unlimited supplies of sand, would have been most appropriate for this there is no archaeological confirmation in the form of hearths, crucibles or glass slag. Needles, combs, handles and pins of bone have been found, as well as raw material and debris from a bone-working trade: cattle, horses and sheep provided the materials, although antlers were also used. These implements, as well as the linen-smoothers and other discoveries such as spindle whorls and weights, point to the existence of a cloth industry, but how large or important this was is unclear. All the equipment found to date could have been used in domestic production, but in view of the significance of the medieval cloth industry, and the numbers of sheep recorded in west Norfolk and Suffolk at the Domesday Survey, the manufacture of cloth on a larger scale seems likely. Similar uncertainty concerns the leather industry, the presence of which is unquestioned, both because of its great importance in the daily economy and because the woollen and bone-working trades indicate that considerable quantities of skins and hides would have been available. Archaeological investigation has not yet revealed the location or actual size of the industry, but as a major group of tanneries lay on the north bank of the river upstream of Town Bridge from early medieval times this could have been the site of the Saxon trade.[17]

By the Norman Conquest agriculture was comparatively insignificant in the urban part of the district, roughly that area within the southern and northern defences. The density of housing development, the industrial concentrations on the fringe, and the use of land beyond the ditch for suburban expansion, imply that at the peak of prosperity all the open space within the defences was used up. The only exception is likely to have been the wet riverside belt. However the boundaries of the town were much wider than the defended area: the church of St Helen was three miles from the centre, and it is probable that the present area of the borough has been unchanged since before the Conquest. There are very ancient boundary ditches and banks on the Suffolk side, and there is no reason to suppose that these are later than the 10th century. There was therefore an urban defended area of some 200 acres, surrounded by extensive tracts of agricultural or waste land still within the borough. This remained characteristic of Thetford as late as the 1950s, and even today, after the great expansion, there are substantial amounts of undeveloped land within the ancient boundaries.

This land was available for agriculture, supplying foodstuffs for the town and grazing for its livestock, as well as fuel, thatching materials and timber for building. In the Domesday Survey it was noted that the Borough rendered goatskins, oxhides and honey as tribute, and it is likely that these came from the rural parts of the town, the urban residents having to make monetary payments. It is of incidental interest that the emphasis upon skins and hides could further indicate the importance of the leather and tanning trades.[18]

Political history

Because East Anglia was for several centuries the scene of repeated warfare and foreign invasion, and because of the size and strategic significance of Thetford, it is not surprising that on a number of occasions the town was the object or location of military action. It is from this that our scanty knowledge of the political history of Thetford derives. The earliest written reference to the town relates to one such event. In 870, the Anglo-Saxon Chronicle records, the Danish host rode southwards from York across Mercia, and under Ivar Lothbroksson invaded East Anglia from the west. It 'took winter quarters at Thetford; and the same winter came King Edmund and fought against them and the Danes won the victory, and they slew the King, and overran the entire kingdom'. The battle took place at Hoxne, not far south of Thetford, and the death of King (later Saint) Edmund marked the end of the ancient East Anglian dynasty.[19] The Danes clearly occupied Thetford for some months, using at as a base for raiding operations elsewhere in East Anglia, and it has been suggested that the earth-work at Weevers Close which was apparently still visible in the early 18th century could have been a camp dating from this Danish military occupation, rather than an earlier Saxon work. The Chronicle is irritatingly unspecific about whether or not Thetford was by this time regarded as a town, but it is reasonable to suppose that urban development was at least under way. The dead king was quickly revered as a saint, and in the late 880s a memorial coinage was issued to commemorate him. The stylistic evidence suggests that Thetford was one of the minting places for this coinage, although the absence of identifiable mint marks on most East Anglian issues earlier than the mid-10th century makes it difficult to be sure. No Thetford coins are known with certainty until the reign of Eadgar (959-75) but then there is a continuous sequence until the reign of Henry II (1154-89), and four moneyers were recorded in the town during the reign of John (1199-1216). The importance of Thetford, both commercial and political, strongly implies that there must have been a mint here well before 959.[20]

The next reference to Thetford occurs in the Anglo-Saxon Chronicle for 952, when King Eadred 'ordered a great slaughter to be made in the borough of Thetford in vengeance for the abbot Ealdhelm whom they had slain'. The likelihood is that 'they' were Danish residents, for by this time Thetford was an Anglo-Danish town under English political control, and acts of aggression by the English against the Danes were not uncommon. The reference is of interest in that it refers to an abbot, and so suggests that the known pre-Conquest monastery at Thetford dated from the early 10th century or even earlier. It also describes Thetford as a 'borough', and although the meaning of the word in this context is unclear it does imply that it was a substantial and important place.[21]

Not long after that, however, a reference in the *Liber Eliensis* provides a considerable amount of additional information on this subject. The book states that in the time of Abbot Brihtnoth of Ely (970-? 96), Cambridge, Norwich, Ipswich and Thetford 'were of such liberty and dignity that if anyone bought land there he did not need witnesses'. Such freedom to buy and sell land within a town was crucial to the concept of the borough as a place with special privileges and a greater degree of self-government than that available to other towns and to rural areas. It later became the basis of 'burghal tenure', the jealously guarded form of land ownership which was fundamental to medieval borough status. The *Liber Eliensis* thus confirms that by the later 10th century, only just over 100 years since it began to grow into a town, Thetford was one of the four most powerful and sizeable towns of East Anglia, in possession of extensive and noteworthy rights and privileges.[22]

At some point in the 10th century the defensive ditch was greatly strengthened, so that it formed a formidable barrier 42 feet wide at the top and 12 feet deep with steep sides and a flat bottom, and in the vicinity of Red Castle its course was altered to run slightly to the east of the original line. This may have been in response to the renewal of large-scale Danish raids upon eastern England in the 980s. As the wars continued Thetford once again suffered very severely. In 1004 Swein of Denmark landed on the east coast, sacked Norwich, and breaking a truce marched across Norfolk to Thetford, 'and remained inside there one night, and ravaged and burnt the borough'. The next morning the East Anglians, under Ulfcetel, arrived and fought the invaders just outside the town: they fought valiantly, but the Danes eventually triumphed and, in the poignant words of the Chronicle, 'many fell slain on both sides. There the flower of the East Anglian people was killed'.

The Danes returned in 1010, landing at Ipswich and marching across country in the direction of Thetford. They met the same Ulfcetel and a large force of East Anglians and men of the Fens in a great battle in which many of the English nobility were killed: they included the son-in-law of King Ethelred. The location of the battle is not given in the Anglo-Saxon Chronicle but other sources make it clear that it was near Thetford. The name is given as *Hringamere* which is usually identified with Ringmere, a lonely spot on Wretham Heath about five miles north of the town. An alternative is even closer: part of Barnham Common was until recent times called Ringmere. As yet there is no evidence for deciding between the two possibilities. After defeating the English the Danes ravaged the countryside between the Fens and the heart of East Anglia, burning both Thetford and Cambridge. In 1013-4 Swein became *de facto* King of England; when tribute and supplies for his armies were demanded in 1013 Thetford served as the collecting centre for all of west Norfolk.[23]

With its geographical centrality, its size and its importance as a trading centre Thetford was in this period effectively the capital of East Anglia. Ulfcetel, whom some sources call the earldorman of East Anglia, may have had viceregal powers in the region to conduct its administration and organise its defence. It seems quite probable that he carried out his work from Thetford: he seems to have used it as a military base and thus it was to Thetford that the Danes marched in 1004 and 1010. In the forty years before the Norman Conquest Thetford was one of the chief towns not only of East Anglia but also of England. During the reign of Canute II (1040-2) it was one of the nine English boroughs which had six or more moneyers working at the same time, and in the same reign a charter refers to a house in the town owned by the Abbot of Ramsey, one of the richest monasteries in the country.[24] That a leading religious house found it worthwhile to maintain a town house in Thetford, presumably as a base for commercial, political and ecclesiastical dealings, points to the high importance of the pre-Conquest town.

By this date there were probably about 4,500 people in Thetford, meaning that it ranked in size with Norwich, Oxford and Lincoln, and slightly behind York, as one of the five chief provincial towns. It had easily overcome the setbacks posed by the sacking and burning of 1004 and 1010, and had risen swiftly from obscurity to a place almost at the top of the urban hierarchy in only two centuries. Just before the Conquest its size and population were greater than they were to be at any time until the 1950s, and its relative importance was never again to be surpassed.

The decline of Thetford

The rise of Thetford was swift, but so was its decline. By the end of the 15th century it was merely a small country market town, of no national significance, whereas those towns which had been its equals in the 11th century had retained and augmented their status, wealth and magnitude. This change was remarkable, and must be considered as one of the more significant features of the urban history of medieval England. The decline probably began in the 1050s, rather before the Conquest, accelerated later in the century and became very rapid during the 12th century, when the town also experienced drastic geographical change.

Initially, however, the importance of Thetford seemed confirmed when it became the seat of the bishops of East Anglia. In the early 10th century, probably in response to the Danish wars, the dioceses of Norfolk and Suffolk were reunited, with a cathedral at 'Elmham'. This was most likely North Elmham, Norfolk, which has the remains of what has long been called the Saxon cathedral, although South Elmham near Beccles, another ancient religious centre, also claims the title. Whichever Elmham *was* the seat of the bishop, it is apparent that this was located in a small village. William I followed a policy of replacing Saxon bishops by loyal Normans, and in 1070 deprived Aethelmar, Bishop of Elmham, of his see, and appointed Herfast in his stead. Another policy of the new regime was to remove diocesan seats from villages to towns — the transfer in the Sussex diocese from Selsey to Chichester being an example — and in 1071 Herfast accordingly abandoned Elmham and established his cathedral at Thetford.

He took possession of the church of St Mary and elevated it to cathedral status. It thus ceased to be a parish church, and as a substitute Herfast built a small new church, Holy Trinity, immediately to the north. Both lay approximately where the Dominican friary was later established, on the site now occupied by the Thetford Grammar School. It might have been supposed that, as the cathedral city for East Anglia, with the prestige, economic benefits and administrative importance consequent upon that, Thetford was assured of a bright future, but this was not to be the case. Herfast had no intention of remaining long in Thetford, for his real aim was to acquire for his cathedral the large, wealthy and powerful abbey of Bury St Edmunds, an aim which depended upon the defeat of its abbot, and which would not be realised without a hard-fought struggle.

Herfast enriched the diocese of Thetford by the careful gathering of estates and manors, a policy continued after his death in 1084 by the second bishop, William Beaufo. In the Domesday Survey the Bishop of Thetford is recorded as possessing more than 70 manors. Bishop William died in 1091, and his successor, Herbert de Losinga, soon removed his throne from Thetford to Norwich, the formal transfer taking place in April 1094. After only 23 years Thetford ceased to be the location of the cathedral of East Anglia. It was now smaller and less wealthy than Norwich, and had begun to experience acute economic difficulties. The move to Norwich, the new commercial, political and military capital of the region, was logical.[25]

But there was another reason for the move. Herfast, as part of his scheme for securing the abbey of Bury and all its wealth, had picked a quarrel with Abbot Baldwin by claiming jurisdiction over the abbey, which in the reign of Edward the Confessor (1042-66) had been granted exemption from episcopal control. Baldwin appealed to William I for the protection of his liberties and privileges, and at Christmas 1081 the King, in a judgment with far-reaching consequences, not only upheld his plea but granted him extensive new economic, judicial and administrative powers over the wide area which later became West Suffolk, the Liberty of Bury. This region extended to the border of the borough of Thetford, but in the southern part of the borough, on the Suffolk side of the Little Ouse, Baldwin and his successors enjoyed considerable influence and were also major landowners. The bishops of Thetford had not only been defeated by the abbot of Bury, who was henceforth freed from episcopal control, but their own cathedral now fell within the territorial sphere of the abbey. A move to Norwich was thus doubly desirable.

The Thetford of the mid-11th century is described in some detail, although often ambiguously, in the Domesday Book.[26] Since this was a return of lands and taxes, great caution has to be employed in considering its data, but nevertheless much valuable information can be derived. Thetford was situated in two counties, straddling the border between Norfolk and Suffolk which followed the course of the Little Ouse. There were three major landowners in the town, each of whom had property on both sides of the river: King William I, Bishop William of Thetford, and Roger Bigod, a companion of the King and lord of the manor of Thetford.

As has been mentioned, the Domesday Survey gives important information about the churches of the town, and names six of them. The abbot of Ely owned three churches in the town, one of which can be identified as St Etheldreda. This dedication — she was a Saxon princess whose relics were kept at Ely — was shared by the minster, later cathedral, there. At Ely and at Thetford the name was frequently corrupted to St Audry, and today it is often quite erroneously known as St Ethelred. The abbot of Bury, the great enemy of the bishops of Thetford, owned one church, presumably connected with his own religious house, and therefore in the vicinity of the nunnery site. The Archbishop of Canterbury had two churches and Roger Bigod one. A curiosity is that the Bishop of Thetford owned half a church, which may perhaps have been Holy Trinity, built by Bishop Herfast in the 1070s: the other half-share would probably have been held by the parishioners.

The Domesday Book reveals the extent to which most of the Borough — as opposed to the defended town in its centre — was agricultural. It refers specifically to 34 acres of meadowland and pasture, and sufficient arable land to support 10 plough-teams, and this represents only a small proportion of the total, since a large area was not subject to tax. Reflecting the importance of agriculture the Survey refers to seven or eight mills, implying a thriving corn trade. Four of these were on sites known to have been occupied by later medieval mills: Melford Bridge (the name of which is a corruption of Mill Ford), the Bishops Mill (now the site of the moulded products factory), the Pit Mill, and the Castle Mill, upstream from Nuns Bridges on the Thet. The other sites have been lost.

Perhaps the most significant information in the Survey concerns the population of the town. The figures for this are, by the standards of the time, unusually detailed: in the time of King Edward, c. 1065, it states, there were 944 burgesses, but in 1086 there were 720 burgesses and 224 vacant properties. The fact that the two figures add up exactly is suspicious, and smacks of arithmetical convenience, but the message conveyed is striking and undisputed. Modern demographic analysis suggests that to achieve an approximate figure for the population at the time of Domesday, one which includes not just the burgesses — free, adult males — but also women, children and bondmen, it is necessary to multiply by five. For Thetford, this gives a 1065 population of about 4,750, with a remarkable, indeed astonishing, decline to only 3,600 by 1086, a fall of almost 25 per cent. in only 20 years, and evidence of a disastrous change in the fortunes of the town.

Reductions in population between the Conquest and the Domesday Survey are not uncommon, although they are rarely of such proportions. The 'harrying of the North' by the Norman armies in the early 1070s produced widespread physical and economic damage, while in some towns — Norwich is an example — the construction of a castle involved the clearance of residential property. But in the case of Thetford the decline was so great, and of such long duration, that more fundamental causes must be sought, and in turn related to a remarkable change in the shape of the town, which not only shrank as might be expected, but also shifted from the south bank to the north bank of the Little Ouse.

A castle was built at Thetford, almost certainly in the period 1067-9 immediately after the Conquest and simultaneously with the first castle at Norwich. It comprised a huge artificial motte and ditch erected within the oval ramparts of the Iron Age and Icenian hillfort. The Normans deepened and strengthened those ancient defences, utilising both the natural advantages of the site and the works of their remote predecessors. On the summit of the motte wooden buildings and a stockade were erected. At the other end of the town a ringwork, a circular enclosure 220 feet across surrounded by a ditch at least six feet deep and forty feet wide, was constructed at Red Castle. This substantial earthwork lay across the line of the Saxon town ditch and bank, which were levelled for the purpose although they may well already have been abandoned. The town was thus defended at its eastern and western extremities, allowing control of the routeways running along the Little Ouse valley and north to south along the low ridges. The construction of these defences was probably connected with the continuing unrest in East Anglia, exemplified by the semi-legendary exploits of Hereward the Wake in 1069-71, and the uprising by Ralph Guader, Earl of East Anglia, in 1075. Thetford may have been used once again as a military base, for which it was well-situated by its proximity to the troubled Fenland district, while the danger of attack from rebels makes the additional defences at Red Castle seem a wise precaution.[27]

The construction of the motte of Thetford Castle on such a grand scale suggests that initially the plan was to have a permanent stone building: the ambitious earthworks are surely too substantial to be merely a temporary base for a short-term military expedition. That the castle was not made permanent, and seems never to have been reconstructed in stone, was probably due in part to the lessening need for such strongholds as the region was pacified, in part to the development of Norwich Castle as the centre for military and political power in East Anglia, and partly to the preference of the manorial lord, Roger Bigod, for his other castles at Framlingham and Castle Acre.

In 1173 the castle was dismantled, according to an entry in the Pipe Rolls which states that 72s. was paid 'for the Custody of the Castle of Thetford from Palm Sunday until 15 days after Pentecost before it was pulled down'.[28] In July 1173 Henry and Richard, two of the sons of Henry II, rebelled against their father and were joined by Earl Bigod. He brought an army from Framlingham towards Thetford, heading for the Midlands, but it was defeated by the forces of the king at Fornham St Genevieve, between Bury St Edmunds and Thetford. The slighting of the castle was almost certainly connected with these events, probably to prevent it falling into the hands of the rebels, and archaeological investigation has confirmed that there was no occupation of the site after the later 12th century.

Why Thetford declined

Saxon Thetford, as has been seen, was situated mainly on the south bank of the river, the Suffolk side. Here were the major industrial areas, the short-lived Norman cathedral, and presumably the first market place. The north bank settlement, although by no means inconsiderable, was definitely lesser in importance, and was only one-quarter of the size — a suburb and a bridgehead. The decline in population might have been expected to produce a straightforward shrinkage towards the original core area, with the fringes and suburbs being abandoned, but this was not so. The south bank was progressively depopulated, and turned over to agricultural use and the grounds of religious houses, while the north bank town survived. In a reversal of rôles the suburb became the town, and the old town became a tattered appendage. Not until the years between the two World Wars did any substantial development again take place south of the river, in the process destroying the evidence for its Saxon forerunner.

The decline was very rapid, and so was the abandonment of the south bank. Excavation has shown that even in the early 13th century the sites of houses and streets, which had been a flourishing town only 200 years before, were being used for agriculture. The churches lasted longer, but by the 14th century, instead of being surrounded by the bustle and buildings of a town, were isolated amid the fields and in some cases were sufficiently remote to be used as leper hospitals. The speed, scale and duration of the decay mean that a cruel combination of powerful and hostile factors was involved. These range widely, from the changing economic geography of Eastern England to the vindictive dispute between the Bishop and the Abbot (map 5).

During the 11th century, even before the Conquest, the hitherto unchallenged position of Thetford as the chief town and market centre of west Norfolk and Suffolk

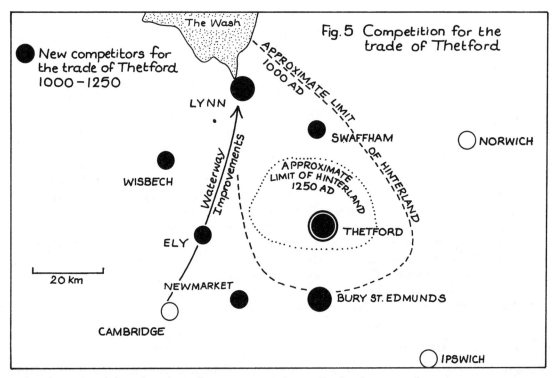

Fig. 5 Competition for the trade of Thetford

New competitors for the trade of Thetford 1000–1250

was threatened by the rise of two competitors. In both cases the newcomers were sponsored by ecclesiastical lords, the bishops of Norwich and the abbots of Bury, and by the end of the 12th century each town — Bury itself and Lynn — had carved large new market areas from the former hinterland of Thetford. The growth of Bury St Edmunds after 1044, when Edward the Confessor granted the abbot extensive privileges, and more especially after the extension of these privileges in 1081, was especially dramatic, and was directly connected with the equally dramatic decline of Thetford. As one grew the other shrank, for the two towns were only 12 miles apart, and fierce competitors for trade and influence. The misfortune of Thetford was that it lacked a powerful and determined lord, and could not survive the deliberate attacks of the abbot of Bury.

To the north, Lynn became a prosperous market town, capturing the trade of Thetford in the northern Breckland and the Marshland district, but even more important was its meteoric rise as one of the leading English ports. As a newer, more convenient and more privileged centre for the import and export of goods, Lynn deprived Thetford of a great deal of river and road trade. Access to Lynn improved, and the difficult navigation of the shallow and winding Little Ouse became an unattractive proposition; once the upgrading and straightening of the Fenland waterways had commenced, Lynn was assured of a large and wealthy catchment area. This additionally benefited towns such as Wisbech and Ely, which were on major waterways, leaving Thetford a disadvantaged, awkwardly-placed and remote river port.

Locally there was other competition. In the south the Abbot of Bury ruthlessly suppressed markets within a wide radius of Bury St Edmunds, and doubtless attempted to reduce the size of Thetford market, with the result that Bury market soon reigned supreme within half a county. In contrast, the early medieval period in west Norfolk saw a proliferation of local markets, granted charters by manorial lords with the aim of increasing their own income from tolls, customs and dues. Eventually this resulted in an over-provision, but at the peak, around 1350, there were 12 markets within a 12-mile radius of Thetford on the Norfolk side, and the larger of these — Methwold and Feltwell for example — drew a great deal of local trade away from Thetford.[29]

These economic disadvantages were exacerbated by changing agricultural patterns in the locality. Pollen samples from former lake beds in Breckland suggest that the fertility of the 'open country' belt north and south of the town was gradually reduced during the later Saxon and early medieval periods, as the soil became exhausted. The yields of arable agriculture diminished and the pastoral and grazing systems of farming began to predominate, with cattle on the damper meadows, and sheep and rabbits on the drier sandy areas. The heath-type vegetation which was so characteristic of Breckland until the First World War became ubiquitous during this period, although its origins dated back to before the Roman occupation.

In contrast, the central plateau of East Anglia, from Fakenham and Aylsham south to Stowmarket and Sudbury, was cleared of much of its remaining forest cover in the middle and later Saxon period, and became rich agricultural land, ideal for wheat and cattle. Towns such as Diss and Dereham grew prosperous as the agricultural wealth of the East Anglian heartland increased, but Thetford suffered as its surrounding country-side became relatively poorer. Already at the time of the Domesday Survey Thetford was in the centre of the least densely-populated part of East Anglia, while the belt between Norwich and Ipswich was the most populous district in the whole of England. In later years, as the plateau maintained and increased its wealth, and the Fens became prosperous with reclamation and land improvement, Breckland, with Thetford at its heart, was an impoverished and thinly-populated territory between two rich and flourishing regions.

These large-scale economic changes, which deprived Thetford of trade and prosperity to the benefit of competitors to the north, south, east and west, were made much more serious by the failure of the pottery manufacturing trade during the late 11th and early 12th centuries. This removed a mainstay of the traditional economy of Thetford, and left it a town without a staple industry. Thus a peculiarly powerful group of unfavourable circumstances combined to devastate the economic base on which the old prosperity of Thetford had been built. As a result its trade declined, its markets contracted, it became a geographical, political and social backwater, and its population fell sharply. In 1066 it had been the fifth or sixth town of England. In 1130 it had sunk to 15th place, according to a list of borough 'aids' or tax payments. In the list of aids of 1156 Thetford did not even appear; this might have been because the list was incomplete, but it is symptomatic of the decline of the town.[30]

Chapter Three

MEDIEVAL THETFORD

THE DOCUMENTARY EVIDENCE for the history of Thetford during the Middle Ages is limited. The muniments of the borough have been scattered or destroyed over the centuries, and in comparison with the volume of material which must once have existed only miscellaneous fragments remain. In the late 18th and early 19th centuries George Bird Burrell, a member of the Corporation and an enthusiastic amateur antiquarian (a plumber and glazier by trade), collected and preserved all the documents which he could locate, and to him Thetford and its historians owe a great debt.[1] But even Burrell could only find a random assortment of medieval deeds, a few mayoral account rolls of the early 14th century, and a collection of 16th-century petitions, letters and miscellaneous items. All else has been lost, probably destroyed deliberately at different times.

Administration and authority in medieval Thetford

Because the records have been lost there is little detailed evidence for the way in which the town was governed before the reign of Edward VI (1547–53). There are glimpses of the organisation of administration from the 12th century onwards, but no really adequate means of telling how important were the different officials, what they did, and how they were appointed or elected. It is therefore necessary to rely upon circumstantial evidence, casual references in deeds, rentals and the records of central administration, and upon what is known of administration in towns with better-preserved records.

The foremost difficulty is that no charter seems to have survived earlier than the charter of incorporation granted by Elizabeth I in January 1574. This cannot possibly have been the first charter granted to Thetford, and it must be presumed that its medieval predecessors were lost centuries ago. The 17th-century volume known as the Thetford Town Book, containing constitutions of the Corporation, refers vaguely to the liberties granted to Thetford by medieval kings, but gives no detail, probably because the earlier charters were even then lost.[2] That Thetford did have royal charters well before 1574 is consistent with the little that is known of its medieval liberties. These included certain legal and financial privileges which could only be granted by the sovereign, in contrast with market charters which could be issued by a manorial lord. In 1286, for example, the town was said to be exempt from tolls and customs throughout the kingdom, and from the jurisdiction of any other authority except for crimes and misdemeanours which affected the royal writ and so had to be tried at the county Assizes. The clear implication is that Thetford had at some point before 1286 received a royal charter, and as Thetford was one of the Assize towns for Norfolk, sharing that status with Norwich, such an assumption is further justified.[3]

The relationship between the privileges granted by the sovereign and those granted by the manorial lords is quite obscure, and may well have been confused even at the time. For long periods the Crown, represented by the Duchy of Lancaster, held the lordship of the manor of Thetford — the smaller manor of Halewyk in Thetford being held by the priory of St Mary — and so the distinction was scarcely apparent. Of the origin of market rights nothing is known. There were undoubtedly market privileges laid down by charter and, until 1574, when the borough took over the administration of the market, the clerk of the market was a manorial official: in matters affecting the regulation of the market and its trade the mayor and burgesses were answerable to him. This obviously represented the manorial origins of market administration, since if a royal charter had granted market rights the town officials would have been given this authority. As late as 1786 the lord of the manor claimed and exercised rights to certain rents, tolls and leases in Thetford market. As will be seen, the manorial market charter almost certainly dated from the century after 1173.

After the Conquest the town was governed by a royal official with the assistance, voluntary or otherwise, of local people of commercial or social standing.[4] His main tasks were to levy and collect royal taxes, to ensure that law and order was maintained, and to act as viceroy in the issuing of proclamations and writs. He may have been called 'provost', a term long obsolete in English local government but still in general use in Scotland. Roger de Scherdestona and one Fulchard, the first two officials in Thetford of whom there is any reliable record, were described as *praepositus*, or provost, in 1139 and 1140.

At some stage in the later 12th century the office of provost was apparently replaced by that of bailiff. In 1197 Richard de Reifham was described as Bailiff of Thetford, but there is no indication of whether he was the first to hold that position. Martin suggests that he was, and also that Richard I made the change, but this seems to be mere guesswork based on the supposition that the earliest written reference to the term can be equated with its introduction. The bailiff was also a royal official, and probably had powers and duties similar to those of the provost. The names of the bailiffs suggest that they were often Norfolk, but not Thetford, men: as elsewhere the people of the town began to select some of their number as local representatives to deal and negotiate with the bailiff and other royal appointees. The leader of this group of townspeople soon became an important figure in the administrative process, and his role was formalised into the office of mayor.

John le Forester (1272) is the earliest mayor of Thetford of whom there is written record, but as with the offices of provost and bailiff there is no reason to suppose that the first record corresponds with the establishment of the position. Almost certainly Thetford had mayors for many years before this date. The mayoralty later became an annual office, but in the 13th and 14th centuries does not seem to have been so strictly limited: Adam Cokerel, for example, was mayor from 1329 until 1333. Before the late 14th century the mayor was the leading townsperson, but only third in order of precedence and authority within the town. The bailiff had overall authority, and beneath him was the chief legal officer of the Borough, the coroner, who was appointed by the Crown for an indefinite term and was not necessarily a local man.

Not until the reign of Henry VII (1485-1509) was it ordained that nobody could serve as coroner who had not already served as mayor, thus ensuring that outsiders could not become coroners for the Borough.[5]

In 1373, according to Martin, John of Gaunt, as Duke of Lancaster and Lord of Thetford, changed the order of precedence so that the mayor became the superior authority within the borough, with precedence over the bailiff and coroner. Such a change can only have been made with the authority of the Crown, and it is a least a possibility that it was Edward III rather than John of Gaunt who granted the privilege. By the end of the 14th century, by this means, the citizens had established significant authority within their town, ensuring that their voice would be heard. Just as important was the effective separation from the jurisdiction of both Norfolk and Suffolk which had been achieved in the previous 200 years. The relationship between the town and the two counties is quite unclear until the early 13th century, but the appointment of separate coroners for Thetford, certainly from 1272 and probably well before then, shows that *de facto* autonomy had been gained. The town then had its own legal officers and courts, operating quite independently of the county sessions and of the hundred courts.

Full self-government was not finally achieved until incorporation in 1574, when Thetford gained possession of the fee-farm — the right to collect taxes on behalf of the Crown and to remit only a fixed annual sum, so that any profits were retained for the use of the town. Until 1574 Crown officials collected taxes, to the great dissatisfaction of the townspeople who regarded the presence of these men as an insult and a burden. Until 1574, too, the mayor was sworn into office by the Steward of the Manor, acting on behalf of the Crown. These symbols of subordination, and the conflict between local and Crown officials, produced constant complaint and dispute. In 1539, for example, the mayor and burgesses, when petitioning for the grant of a charter of incorporation, protested that the town had

> 'a mayor, a coroner, a baylyf of the fraunches and his deputye, which ys under baylyf and jaylour ther; also ther ys the kyngs baylyf, the whiche gathereth the rent of assyse, and his deputye, which is a serjeant, whose offyce ys to attache by ther bodyes and goodes for det ... ther haithe bene great dyscencyon, sute, and debate, betwene the saide offycers, for the occupacion and usyng of ther several auctorytes'.

It was suggested that the grant of a charter would be the best way to 'end all stryffe and devysyon and to bryng concord, peas and unyte emong the inhabitaunts'.[6] Their words were not heeded.

Alongside the development of the various town offices was the evolution of the 'council', although it was never given that name. The informal grouping of leading citizens which had led to the development of the mayoralty also produced, at least as early as 1249, the recognition that such a body should exist continuously, to help the mayor with his work and to provide future mayors. How they were chosen is not known. If the practice in many other towns was followed there would have been some element of popular participation in the choice of burgesses and mayors until perhaps the second quarter of the 15th century. After that time the few most powerful families and trade groups would probably have taken steps to close ranks and to exclude the inferior sections of Thetford society from the making of decisions. Such restriction of membership and influence to a small group was usually done with royal encouragement, as a means of limiting popular and radical expression.

By the end of the 15th century it was recognised that there were eight principal burgesses, the 'most honest and discrete men of the town', who were often known as aldermen. As early as 1291 Richard de Bungeye had used that term to describe himself on a deed.[7] Beneath the aldermen were the common councillors, who in the middle of the 16th century numbered 30, although this was not necessarily the case in previous centuries. Together these groups constituted the council of Thetford. They acted, more or less willingly, to assist the royal officials and to negotiate with them to secure privileges and liberties for the town. The mayor and burgesses had the right, subject to the observance of manorial privilege, to hold a Saturday and a Wednesday market and four annual fairs, on the feast of the Invention of the Cross (3 May), St Mary Magdalen (22 July), St John the Baptist (29 August) and the Exultation of the Cross (14 September). They had rights over Bromehill Fair, and rented all bridge tolls upon the Little Ouse between Honington and Brandon from the king. They also drew tolls, rents and dues from market stalls, fairs and traders.[8]

The only important documents which survive from the medieval administration of Thetford are various mayoral account rolls of the period 1318-40.[9] These list the income and expenses of the mayor. Since there was no corporate government, with a perpetual existence separate from the identity of its individual members, the mayor had to account personally for all financial transactions. The rolls are too few to allow an assessment of the general pattern of incomes and outgoings, but do give glimpses into the activities of the mayor and burgesses. Entertainment figures prominently: in 1335 John le Forester spent sixpence 'for the Mayor, and divers Vintners, at the Tavern, when taking Tolls',[10] while in the previous year Peter Markaunt meeting the Constable of the Hundred of Shropham had spent a mere 14½d. on general needs but no less than 6s. 0d. on bread and wine.[11] Other miscellaneous expenses included visits to Norwich on government business, the testing of weights and measures, and the payment of compensation for the withdrawal of false pennies.

Perhaps the most interesting aspect of the business revealed by these accounts is the involvement in military matters, for Thetford was responsible for raising its own militia and for finding and equipping soldiers for the royal armies. During the 1330s England and Scotland were at war and, in 1334, 2s. 0d. was paid 'to elect or appoint one Person as a Bowman to be sent into Scotland', and 1s. 0d. to send him to Lynn to join the forces.[12] The following year saw a total of £5 7s. 4½d. spent on sending two light horsemen into the army to march against the Scots, including the provision of gowns, uniforms, horses shod and harnessed, a lad to care for the horses, pay for the two men, and 6d. 'allowed a Boy, for carrying a letter to Lynn for the Captain conducting the expedition'.[13]

Manorial history

The manorial history of Thetford is comparatively simple: in many places manors were bought and sold, seized and forfeited, with great frequency, but here there was stability for long periods. William I granted the manor to his son-in-law, William, first Earl de Warenne, a fortunate individual who eventually accumulated 139 manors in

Norfolk and more than 100 elsewhere, so did not attach any particular significance to his manor of Thetford. His family held the manor for almost 300 years, until the death in 1347 of the last Earl Warren, as the title had by then become. Thetford was then annexed by the Crown and granted to Henry, Duke of Lancaster, a cousin of Edward III, passing eventually to his daughter Blanche and her husband John of Gaunt, who was created Duke of Lancaster in her right. When their son became King Henry IV the estates of the Duchy of Lancaster came into the possession of the Crown once more, and the manor of Thetford thus became a royal property although administered as part of the Lancaster estates. It retained that status until 1548.[14] The manor of Halewyk was granted by the Conqueror to Roger Bigod, who gave it as part of his endowment to the new priory of St Mary in Thetford, which he founded in 1104. It remained the property of the priory until its dissolution in 1539.[15]

The manor of Thetford included most of the eastern part of the Borough, while Halewyk comprised much of the southern and western parts. The monks of Thetford priory also owned the manors of Croxton and Lynford, contiguous with Halewyk, while the manor of Sibton in Croxton, which included some land within the Borough, was owned by the abbey of Sibton near Southwold. Included in Halewyk were three areas which were originally distinct, but important, manors: Norwick, which was the outlying farm also known as Croxton Park, in the extreme north of the Borough; Faverton, on the border with Santon Downham; and Westwick, in the area of Thetford Warren.

The manor house of Thetford was traditionally said to have been on the site of the Kings House, on the north side of King Street immediately east of St Peter's church,

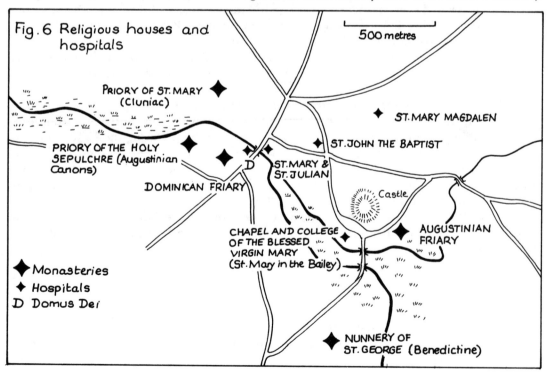

Fig. 6 Religious houses and hospitals

500 metres

PRIORY OF ST. MARY (Cluniac)

ST. MARY MAGDALEN

PRIORY OF THE HOLY SEPULCHRE (Augustinian Canons)

ST. JOHN THE BAPTIST

D

ST. MARY & ST. JULIAN

DOMINICAN FRIARY

Castle

CHAPEL AND COLLEGE OF THE BLESSED VIRGIN MARY (St. Mary in the Bailey)

AUGUSTINIAN FRIARY

◆ Monasteries
✦ Hospitals
D Domus Dei

NUNNERY OF ST. GEORGE (Benedictine)

and since the present house does have vestiges of medieval work in its cellars this seems a reasonable assumption. The location beside the church implies that this site was of considerable importance from an early date. The grounds of the manor house seem to have extended north and east as far as Earls Street, formerly known as Earls Lane — a street name which in this context assumes a great significance for it presumably relates to the Earls Warren, lords of the manor. Medieval documents contain occasional references to land and buildings called Earls Barn and Earls Yard, situated near to the present market place in the angle formed by King Street and Earls Street. For most of its history the manor itself was owned by absentee lords, and the steward of the manor would probably have lived there, acting on behalf of the lord in a wide range of dealings with the townspeople, the mayor and burgesses, and the tenants of the manor.

The religious houses

The monks of Thetford priory were among the leading landowners of west Norfolk, and exerted a tremendous influence within the town as employers, property-holders, purchasers of goods and services and bringers of trade and travellers. Medieval Thetford, which had shrunk from a leading provincial centre to a country market town, was small enough to be dominated by the religious houses which were established there, and when the Dissolution swept them away the town and its economy suffered severely. In the early 15th century Thetford, with a population of perhaps 1,500, had no fewer than five religious houses and several other monastic hospitals and hostels (map 6).[16]

There had been religious houses in the town well before the Conquest, and it appears likely that one of them had a continuous existence into the medieval period. In the reign of Cnut (1016-35) the abbey of Bury St Edmunds founded a daughter-house in the town, and from the evidence of the Domesday Survey this was endowed with churches. It seems to have decayed and allegedly to have been left with only two canons, probably in the middle of the 12th century. To avoid abandonment and deconsecration the two monks were withdrawn and the house was refounded as a Benedictine nunnery, being populated by nuns moved from an existing foundation at Lyng near East Dereham. It is thus possible that there was continuous occupation from about 1020 to the refoundation in about 1160, and then on to the final suppression in 1537.

The nunnery was eventually endowed with the churches of St Benedict, All Saints and St George, and with other Thetford properties of Bury Abbey. It retained close links with the abbey which, for example, supplied it with most of its food and beer. The abbot of Bury, who as part of his extensive privileges was allowed to hold Assizes for west Suffolk, on several occasions held them at the nunnery in Thetford.[17] The nuns were assisted by wealthy benefactors and acquired substantial endowments, but a taxation in the reign of Henry VI was met with claims that mortality and serious flooding had reduced their wealth and income. At visitations in the early 16th century no important claims were made concerning the conduct of the nuns, but the poverty of the house was noted and when it was suppressed it was valued at only £40. The buildings formed the basis of The Place, home of Sir Richard Fulmerston.

The first post-Conquest foundation was the priory of St Mary, established in 1104 by Roger Bigod, allegedly in atonement for his manifold sins and in preference to undertaking the long and dangerous pilgrimage to Jerusalem which was the alternative way to achieve salvation. The priory was a Cluniac foundation and was originally settled by 12 monks from Lewes Priory in Sussex, the first English house of the order. Its original site was in the town itself, on the south bank of the river, incorporating the church of St Mary the Great which had been the cathedral until 1094 and was now in effect redundant, Holy Trinity church having taken over its parochial functions. By 1107 there were 20 monks and it was felt that the site was becoming too cramped, so in that year Prior Stephen obtained approval from Roger Bigod for a removal to the much more spacious site on the western edge of the town, north of the river, where the beautiful ruins are today. The foundation stone was laid at the beginning of September 1107 by Bigod himself, but he died only a week later and, despite his expressed wish to be buried in his priory church at Thetford, his body was seized by the Bishop and interred in Norwich cathedral.[18]

The new church was consecrated in 1114, and construction of the cloister and other buildings continued throughout the 12th century. In the original Thetford cathedral there had been a statue of the Virgin, later moved to the priory church and then replaced by a more modern image. The statue was recovered, cleaned and decorated after it had apparently worked miracles through dreams, and it became an object of veneration and pilgrimage.[19] The priory grew rich as a consequence of this pilgrim traffic and its considerable endowments of property, and in the 13th century the whole east end was rebuilt and a large Lady Chapel was added. It also benefited from close association with the dukes of Norfolk. In 1524 the second duke was buried in a magnificent tomb before the high altar, and in 1536 Henry Fitzroy, illegitimate son of Henry VIII and son-in-law of the duke, joined him there. Despite this personal connection with the king the priory was dissolved in 1540.[20]

It was, in its heyday, a very wealthy house, with land in 53 parishes in Norfolk and 25 in Suffolk, as well as in other parts of the country. At the Dissolution its estates were valued at almost £420, and the income from rents, tithes, its extensive flocks of sheep, corn-mills, timber and urban property was sufficient to give an annual profit of £316. Its prosperity contrasted with the poverty of the other religious houses in the town: this was no accident, for the existence of such a rich and powerful house, owning large tracts of land in and around Thetford, militated against the expansion of its neighbours.

The priory of the canons of the Holy Sepulchre, later absorbed into the Augustinian order, was established in 1148 by William, 3rd Earl Warren, on the south bank of the river immediately opposite the priory of St Mary, from which it was easily visible and its bells audible. When, in the 14th century, the Dominican friary was founded just upstream, there were three large monasteries within a quarter of a mile of each other. The site of the priory was formerly occupied by houses and streets, part of the Saxon south-bank town. When it was excavated in the 1950s the foundations of a smaller and earlier building were revealed: the archaeological evidence suggested a late Saxon or early Norman date, and its size implied that it was not a temporary church built after 1148. It may therefore have been a previously unknown late Saxon parish church, abandoned between the Conquest and the foundation of the priory of the Holy Sepulchre.[21]

The Saxon town had evidently shrunk very considerably by 1148, so that the site of the priory was completely or partly depopulated. If this had not been so it is hard to imagine that this land would have been available, because to build the priory would have meant clearing houses and closing streets. Thus the abandonment of the south bank left large areas of cheap vacant land close to the river and the town centre, and the religious houses took advantage of this to extend their precincts. The priory was endowed with property by Earl Warren and by King Stephen, who became its patron and transferred to it his rights over churches and tithes in the town. These, and the comb of St Thomas à Becket which it later secured as a precious relic, gave it a substantial income until the later 14th century, but thereafter its revenues declined as a result of the falling value of its tithes and its agricultural land. A particular problem was that rents from tenements in Thetford also declined, as the town and its economy suffered stagnation and contraction. It retained extensive sheep-farming interests, but at its suppression in 1539 the priory and its estate was valued at only £83.

Three smaller religious houses were founded between 1100 and 1300. The earliest was the hospital of St Mary and St Julian, which was said to have been established under the patronage of Henry I (reigned 1100-35) and was on the north bank of the river immediately above the Town Bridge, where the *George Inn* formerly stood. Its ruins were demolished in 1777, when it was said to be a nuisance. The hospital was intended to serve travellers, and in particular pilgrims visiting the priory: it was therefore a hospice rather than a hospital in the modern sense of the word. On the opposite side of the river was the Domus Dei, also known by the French form of its name, Maison Dieu, which was founded by Earl Warren during the reign of Edward I (1272-1307). It was endowed with extensive lands in the Suffolk part of Thetford and in the rural area north of the town, but did not long enjoy a separate existence, for in 1335 it was conveyed by Earl Warren to the new Dominican friary, into which its lands and buildings were absorbed.

The third foundation of the 13th century had a much longer and greatly more profitable existence. This was the chapel of the Blessed Virgin Mary in the Bailey End, adjacent to the old market place. It was founded by Sir Gilbert de Pickenham in the early 1280s and quickly became a fashionable and influential house because it was run by the Gild of St Mary the Blessed Virgin, the preserve of the elite in Thetford society. The chapel purchased and was given extensive endowments of property and money, so that it was eventually a major landlord in the town: it owned, for example, shops and tenements in the Grassmarket next to St Cuthbert's church, nine shops in Bailey End, three in Nethergate, market stalls and cottages. It also owned the Guildhall, which stood where its modern successor now stands, in the centre of the town. The most generous of all benefactors was Lady Isabella Galion (died 1472), who gave as gifts in her lifetime and as bequests over 1,000 acres of land, mainly in the parish of Barnham in Suffolk, but also in the open fields and closes of Thetford itself. She was buried in the chapel, at the entrance to the choir, and gave for its decoration and the enrichment of its coffers rich jewels, plate and vestments, including 'a crosse of Silver & gilte, ii small Candelsticks of silver & gilte, ii basons of silver, ii cruetts of silver, one holywatr stoppe with a sticke [stopper] of silver . . . iii vestments of silke, one of redd color, one other blew, ye third of black to ye worshippe of God'.[22]

The Gild of St Mary was also known as the College, in the old sense of the word as 'a body of men', and membership of it was *de rigueur* for those who wished to succeed in Thetford social or business circles. It was exclusive and socially desirable, a combination of religious society, society club and political meeting place. The mayor and burgesses were members of the Gild, and so by the late 15th century it had acquired a vital secular role, with its purely religious functions being almost incidental. Such exclusive Gilds were a common feature of medieval towns, for they were bodies in which social, political, economic and religious power were concentrated and where the elitism of late medieval town government could be practised. Many towns had similar quasi-religious organisations for individual trades, but although these may have existed in Thetford — and the manner in which the traders were organised in the later 16th century would suggest that this was the case — there is no documentary evidence.

In Thetford the lack of a corporate council meant that the mayor and burgesses could not easily extend their power and influence by overt means, and so worked through the agency of the Gild, with the added advantage that by doing so they by-passed all elements of popular participation. The Gild bought and sold property and goods, which the mayor and burgesses could not legally do except as individuals, so that much of the accumulated wealth of the chapel and Gild was regarded as belonging to the burgesses. This is strikingly illustrated by events in 1539 when the mayor and burgesses sold the plate and jewels from the chapel to fund an expensive bribe to Henry VIII, in the hope that he would grant them a charter of incorporation. Although the attempt failed, the mayor and burgesses evidently felt that the Gild property, nominally that of a religious body, was in reality theirs to sell.[23]

During the 14th century four more religious houses were established. In the 1330s the Hospital of St Mary Magdalen, intended primarily as a leper colony, was founded by John, Earl Warren and Earl of Surrey. It was outside the town near the Norwich road, in a relatively remote and isolated location typical of the contemporary policy of segregating lepers well away from the more populous areas. The Hospital used as its chapel the former parish church of St Mary Magdalen, which had probably been the last parish church to be founded in Thetford (in about 1200) and the first to be abandoned. Endowments made to the Hospital included the profits from the fair on the feast of St Mary Magdalen, and also 870 acres of pasture, heath and arable land. A second leper colony was said to have been at the Hospital of St John the Baptist, but this is more doubtful. Some sources say that the Hospital was on the south-west side of the town and used the abandoned church of St John as its chapel, but recent research suggests that it was located within the block of land bounded by Earls Street, King Street and St Giles Lane, and that the crypt beneath the Chinese restaurant at the top of King Street may have been associated with the Hospital. Previously this was thought to have been the only surviving feature of the church of St Lawrence, but the identification of St Lawrence's church with this site now seems to be incorrect.

During the early 14th century the several orders of mendicant, or begging, friars came to England. Initially, and in theory, they were not permitted by their rules to have extensive property and had to derive their income from gifts and alms rather than from investments and rents. This meant that locations in the centre of towns were particularly advantageous. In 1335 a Dominican friary was founded in Thetford by Henry, Duke of Lancaster. It acquired as part of its foundation the Domus Dei and the parish church of Holy Trinity, as well as the decayed buildings of St Mary the Great which had been the cathedral 250 years before and briefly the site of the priory of St Mary. All these were incorporated into the friary buildings or demolished, and in 1370 with the permission of Edward III the friars further extended their property by annexing and demolishing the derelict and vacant houses between their church and Bridgegate, the present Bridge Street.

The Dominican friary was protected from 1380 by a royal decree that no new mendicant order should be established nearby, and that the mayor and burgesses of Thetford should safeguard the friars from oppression. The first order was intended to prevent competition from other begging orders, and the second to stop the hostility which all these orders often encountered from other religious houses, who saw them as theologically dangerous, and from town authorities who saw them as subversive. The dukes of Lancaster, and the Crown as Duke of Lancaster, continued to take a close interest in the affairs of the Dominican friary, and this was reflected in a special arrangement whereby the lord of the manor could nominate its priors. In the later 15th century, when the original enthusiasm for their lifestyle had waned, the mendicant orders experienced severe economic problems and at the Dissolution only six brethren remained.

In 1387 John of Gaunt, Duke of Lancaster, founded a second friary in the town, for the Augustinian (often abbreviated to Austin) order. To conform with the royal decree of 1380, he bought land at the other side of Thetford, granting them a site formerly owned by Thomas Morley and Simon Barbour at the eastern end of the market place. The Austin Friars in time found the site cramped, and in 1408 obtained licence to demolish a house to make way for extensions to the church and cloister. The latter was well-placed according to George Burrell, who noted in about 1800 that it 'opened towards the Market, & the high Road, being at that time a very publick situation, for this Road at that time was the chief or high road by the Ford, the situation of this monastery was peculiarly adapted to answer their purpose'.[23] Despite this choice location the friary was always small and impoverished, perhaps because the market was already peripheral to the built-up area of the town. At the Dissolution the Visitor who reported to the king was most contemptuous: 'there is no earthly thing here at all but trash and baggage'. The buildings were quickly demolished, and the stones used for other houses and walls in the area: today the site is occupied by Ford Place and Friars Close.

By the middle of the 15th century the religious houses dominated Thetford physically and economically, as the greatest landowners, employers and purchasers of goods and services. Their pilgrims and visitors provided a constant and lucrative passing trade, and the robed figures of monks and friars were a familiar sight in the streets of the town. A series of accounts from the priory of St Mary has survived from the late 15th and early 16th centuries, long after major construction projects had ceased; the lists of purchases and expenses thus give a picture of how just one of the monasteries affected the ordinary economic life of Thetford.[24]

The accounts show that the priory regularly bought goods and services within the town to provide for its many and varied needs and responsibilities. Thus, loads of timber, nails, stone and glass were purchased frequently for the routine maintenance of the priory itself and of the numerous properties which it owned in and around

Thetford. In 1482–3, for example, 7s. 8d. was spent on repairs to the *Angel Inn*, while in 1498–9 the accounts record the payment of £1 4s. 0d. 'for the repair of the wheel at the Bishops Mill and for the making of both water ways'. The town benefited in other ways, since the priory undertook tasks which were later the work of the Corporation: in 1504–5 £1 1s. 4d. was spent 'for pathyng in Bryggegate'. As an employer the priory made much use of casual labour, and so further assisted the local economy: in 1499 John Mannyng was paid a shilling 'for skerying of rooks' and in the same year it cost 8s. 0d. to have Henry Crow bring a load of herrings from Southwold. The priory, as the greatest and wealthiest property in the town, far eclipsed the manor house and so, despite the latter being a Duchy of Lancaster possession, it was the prior who was host to Henry VII when he stayed the night in Thetford en route to Norwich in 1499. The priory accounts record: 'In divers expenses and costs when the Lord King was entertained here, £0 16s. 6d.'.

Parish churches in medieval Thetford

As stated in the previous chapter, there were probably 14 pre-Conquest churches in Thetford, and another, Holy Trinity, had been added by the time of the Domesday Survey (1086). In spite of the contraction of the town, which was by then well under way, several other churches were founded in the following 150 years. This was a period of particular enthusiasm for the founding of small churches, often as an act of individual or family piety. These churches were not really intended to be parochial, and even at the time of their foundation had tiny congregations and inadequate incomes, but the ecclesiastical authorities eventually adopted most of them and carved out very small urban parishes to serve them. The result was that by 1300 many of the larger English towns had too many churches; the next three centuries saw a reversal of the process and the abandonment of considerable numbers.[25]

In Thetford five new parish churches were founded between 1086 and 1200. One of these, St Mary the Less, was in the south bank town close to the convergence of the several radial routes focusing on the Town Bridge. The area remained built-up even after most of this district had reverted to agriculture, and there was only one other parish church in the vicinity, that of St Etheldreda: Holy Trinity had been absorbed by the Dominican friary. St Mary the Less survived the Reformation and the suppression of small churches which accompanied it, and was one of the three parish churches of Thetford until modern times. In the early 1970s it was declared redundant, but in 1980 was rescued and reopened, with a neat turning of the circle of history, as a Roman Catholic church.

The three post-Conquest north-bank town churches reflect the much greater relative importance of that area as the south bank town shrank: all of them, however, have disappeared today. These were the churches of St Nicholas, in the angle between St Nicholas Street and Minstergate, and only about two hundred yards from the existing St Peter's church; St Giles, on the north side of King Street halfway down the small hill from St Cuthbert's, and again very close to St Peter's church; and St Andrew, which stood at the junction of White Hart Street and Earls Lane, at one of the main entrances to the town. Remains of all three are scanty — a few dressed and carved stones from St Giles' and St Nicholas', and merely a space (now partly occupied by a modern house) which was the churchyard of St Andrew. The construction of three new churches meant that by 1300 there were no fewer than five tiny parishes in the area bounded by the river, the modern A11 and the present market place.

Then, in the late 14th and 15th centuries, the process of abandonment began, and by 1500 only nine of the perhaps 20 churches which had existed still survived. Four were on the south bank and five on the north. Several, such as St Mary the Great and St Mary Magdalen, had been annexed by religious houses as they ceased to be viable as parish churches. Others, such as St Lawrence and St Margaret, had simply been abandoned as their congregations dwindled and disappeared with the shrinking of the south-bank town. The continued existence of others owed more to their having alternative sources of income than to their supplying a parochial need. The church of St Etheldreda, for example, was the proud possessor of the miraculous smock of St Etheldreda, 'as a greate jewell & precious relique. The vertue of this smock was mighty & manyfold, but specially in putting away the tothach & ye swellyng of ye throte': the resultant income from the many common people who flocked to the church ensured its survival until the Reformation swept away such Popish practices.[26]

The disappearance of the churches was inevitable as Thetford was unable to support such a number, with its declining population and diminishing wealth. At the taxation of Pope Nicholas in 1291 only five churches in the town (St Cuthbert, St Giles, St Edmund, St Nicholas, and an unspecified St Mary) are listed, the remainder being too small and impoverished to pay tax. In 1369, when an inventory was made of the goods in each church in the diocese of Norwich, St John, St Martin, St Helen, St Margaret and St Benedict had apparently been abandoned as they do not appear. When application was made in 1548 for the closure of St Nicholas' church and the union of the benefice with that of St Peter it was stated that 'the sayde churches be not distant one myle the one from the other & that neyther of the sayde Churches of St Nicholas & St Peter is not above the yerelye valewe of VI£ as anye of them is rated', reasons of poverty and proximity which go far to explain the disappearance of no fewer than 17 of the 20 churches in the town between 1300 and 1550.[27]

Geography of medieval Thetford

The town as it existed until the years immediately before the First World War was largely a product of the medieval period: its size, shape and plan differed little in substance from the Thetford of 1500, and significant numbers of buildings survived. Modern development, redevelopment and expansions have radically altered those characteristics, but there is still enough of medieval Thetford for us to gain some fair impression of its geography. Analysis of the plan of the medieval town, insofar as this can be established from maps of the very early 19th century, and from interpretation of documentary evidence, immediately points to several interesting features, and it becomes apparent that the evolution of the town was far from straightforward.

On the south bank several roads focused on the Town Bridge including the present Bridge Street-London Road, Bury Road and Star Lane. Brandon Road is deflected somewhat to the south, to join the London road near the church of St Mary the Less. It is clear from the 1807 map drawn by George Bird Burrell that the original course

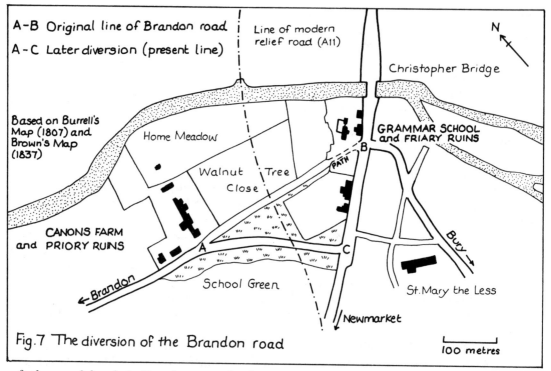

Fig. 7 The diversion of the Brandon road

100 metres

of the road headed directly towards the junction of Bury Road and Bridge Street, and so also pointed to the convergence immediately south of the Town Bridge.[28] The old course headed across the site of the Dominican friary, and this lane is still evident today, immediately south of the Grammar School but truncated by the modern relief road. When the diversion took place is not clear, but it is likely that it was in the 14th century when the friary is known to have been expanding its territory. By moving the Brandon road southwards on its present course the friary could have added new land to its site, although it is apparent that the route remained in use as a minor lane or footpath for centuries afterwards (map 7).

On the north bank the road pattern within the area of the Saxon defences consists of a cross which meets at St Peter's church, a Saxon foundation which is immediately adjacent to the site of the medieval manor house (map 8). The four roads — Minstergate, White Hart Street, Bridge Street and King Street — perhaps pre-existed the Saxon town; it is possible to visualise a village settlement with its focus at the church, crossroads and bridge or ford, around which the later town developed. It appears very possible that St Nicholas' Street and Tanner Street were subsequent additions to the basic network: it is clear from the plan that they join the main roads some distance back from the crossroads, as though doing so behind the line of existing buildings. They are also tangential to the basic arrangement of the cross, which could also point to their rather later origins. If this is the case is is probable that Minstergate was the main route eastwards from the north bank Saxon town until blocked by the development of the medieval priory beyond Water Lane. The St Nicholas' Street exit would then have become more important, and was perhaps at this point carried through as a north-east exit to the town to join the Mundford road. If there was any element of planning the north-bank town it might have involved the laying out of the long narrow-fronted blocks of land known as burgage plots, but cartographic and archaeological evidence for these is minimal as yet.

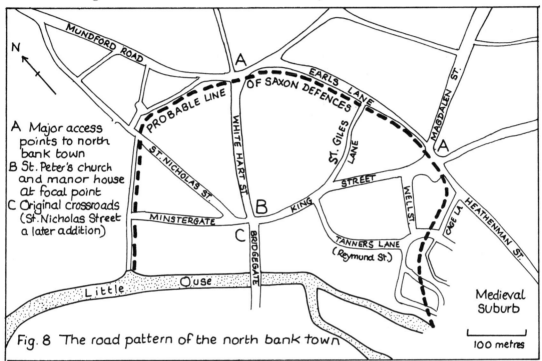

Fig. 8 The road pattern of the north bank town

A Major access points to north bank town
B St. Peter's church and manor house at focal point
C Original crossroads (St. Nicholas Street a later addition)

100 metres

The entrance to the town from the north was at the top of White Hart Street, and the eastern entrance at the present market place. There were other minor entrances at St Nicholas' Street, Minstergate and Raymond Street–Tanner Street. None of these five was ever a gateway, as far as is known, since neither the Saxon town nor its medieval successor was walled, and at a comparatively early date the defences must have ceased to have any military significance. It is indicative of the failure of medieval Thetford that there is no evidence, documentary or archaeological, for any attempt to build a stone wall.

The two main entrances became foci for roads and lanes approaching the town, but there is no means of establishing the antiquity of most of these routes, and their relative importance prior to the 18th century. Medieval documents make many references to the pilgrimage road, the 'Walsingham way', and this appears to be the present Mundford road or another closely corresponding to it. It was certainly west of the Croxton road, which ran along the eastern slope of Gallows Hill, since a document of 1338 refers to land 'inter Walsingham waye et Croxton waye'.[29] The turnpiking of the Mundford road in 1792 reduced the importance of the Croxton road, while the closure of the latter north of Croxton Heath when the Battle Area was imposed during the Second World War, has left this route as almost a cul-de-sac. The modern Station Road, which until the construction of the A134 diversion was the main road to Mundford, follows the line of an old route north-westwards from the town, and may lie along the axis of one branch of the Icknield Way.

The third major road to converge on the White Hart Street entrance was the Norwich road, and despite the construction of the A11 relief road this is still the case. There is however a puzzle in this, since a glance at any map, even a modern one, shows that as it approaches Thetford from the north east the Norwich road is exactly aligned upon the present market place, and the Magdalen Street entrance to the town is its logical extension. All the older maps show that Magdalen Street began boldly enough but soon petered out into a small lane which ended in a field. However, until recent alterations its continuation was marked by field boundaries and the boundary between the parishes of Thetford St Cuthbert and Kilverstone. There is no doubt that this is the original course of the Norwich road, and that the route which leaves it at a tangent and heads for the White Hart Street junction is much later. Not least, this heavily-trafficked road entered the town at an awkward right angle, which suggests that it was an afterthought (map 9).

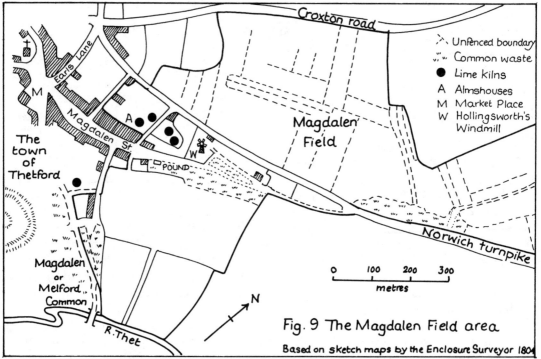

Fig. 9 The Magdalen Field area

Based on sketch maps by the Enclosure Surveyor 1804

The reason for the abandonment of the more direct alignment is not entirely clear, but is probably associated with the turnpiking of the Norwich road and the enclosure of the open fields which lay on either side of it. When the road between Attleborough and Thetford was turnpiked in 1766 the length covered by the Act of Parliament extended only as far as 'the chalk pits in the Borough of Thetford': the stretch thence to the Town Bridge was never subject to the turnpike trust. There was probably an earlier lane across the open field, and upon turnpiking this seems to have been adopted as the main road, so that through traffic avoided the congested area at the top of

King Street. In the last 20 years of the 18th century there was a considerable amount of piecemeal enclosure on the southern edges of Magdalen Field, between the two roads, and it is likely that the old road was closed at this time. It is unfortunate that the closure of rights of way was achieved by an order of the Justices of the Peace, who were in the case of Thetford the mayor and coroner, since the road orders which must have been part of the borough records have not survived.

Since the idea of north bank defences was first advanced in 1963 it has been assumed that these extended from Earls Street south-eastwards along the line of Guildhall Street, to meet the ramparts of the Castle beside the junction of Guildhall Street and Pike Lane.[30] Superficially this is an attractive idea because there is a rough coincidence of the line on either side of the market place, but in detail it can be seen that Earl Street is not aligned on Guildhall Street. This could be due to changes in the sites of buildings and streets over the thousand years and more since the ramparts were constructed. An alternative explanation is however possible, and this is linked to the evolution and plan of the district between Cage Lane and the Nuns Bridges (map 10).

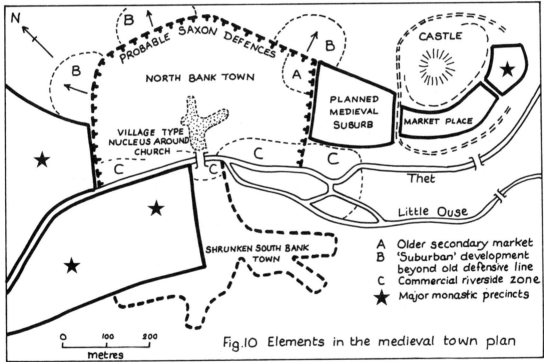

Fig.10 Elements in the medieval town plan

Among the most remarkable features of the plan of medieval Thetford was the location of the market place. This lay at the eastern extremity of the built-up area, on the very edge of the town and in an awkward position sandwiched between the Norman castle and its prehistoric ramparts and the river to the south. It was always on the edge of the town, and never acquired the role of urban focus which is often associated with market places. Throughout its existence as a market it had virtually no buildings to the east and only a few, in single rows, to the north and south.

The market place was certainly in this location by the second half of the 13th century: a deed of 1290 mentions it and provides the latest possible date for its establishment.[31] It seems reasonable to suppose that the main market of the Saxon town was somewhere on the south bank — the convergence of roads towards the bridge might have provided a site — but it is also possible that there was a subsidiary market place in the north-bank town. From a comparatively early date there was a market, called the Grassmarket, along the roadway between St Cuthbert's church eastwards to the Guildhall Street junction. This market was referred to in deeds as early as 1379, and the road here is still perceptibly wider as a result of its former rôle. This market was quite distinct from the Bailey End market because the deed of 1379 describes the present Guildhall Street as the way leading from *le Gresmarket ad mercatum Theffordre.*[32] The Grassmarket may have been Saxon in origin: certainly its location beside a known Saxon church would suggest this, and it is also significant that the Guildhall was close to the site at least as early as the middle of the 13th century.

The Bailey End market therefore probably postdates the Grassmarket. It lies across the outer defences of the Iron Age hillfort and Norman castle, and so is unlikely to have been laid out until the castle was abandoned in 1173. Subsequent development has obscured the line of these defences, but the area south of the castle has always been known as Bailey End, so the outer bailey must have encircled the castle. It crossed the site of Ford Place, and in the early 19th century Burrell noted that 'the Austin Friers churchyard land [was] close where the Rampart is cut away by the Market Street'.[33] He also describes its existence to the west of this, although mistakenly believing that the ditches were a moat in the medieval style: 'the water formerly ran

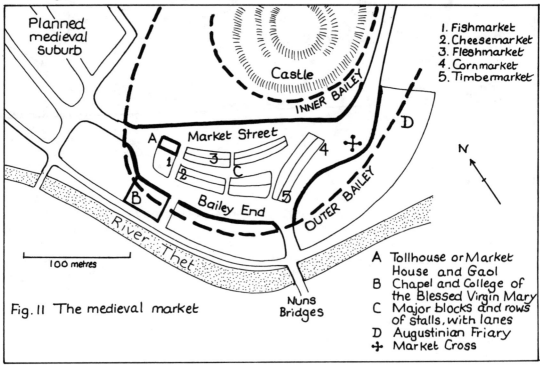

Fig. 11 The medieval market

1. Fishmarket
2. Cheesemarket
3. Fleshmarket
4. Cornmarket
5. Timbermarket

A Tollhouse or Market House and Gaol
B Chapel and College of the Blessed Virgin Mary
C Major blocks and rows of stalls, with lanes
D Augustinian Friary
✝ Market Cross

round the Castle Hill so as to incircle ye same with a deep ditch, and the outlet therefrom was near the Gaol & Burnt Lane as I have seen from the form of the ditche, in a great excavation about 24 feet deep'.[34] The line of Ford Street, with its gentle curve, was dictated by the shape of the rampart, and until the early 19th century this was even more apparent since the edge of the market place continued along the same line just north of the present Ford Place (map 11).

The new market place was therefore laid out — probably in the century after 1173 — with its southern edge following the line of the rampart and its northern edge roughly aligned with the inner defences of the castle. Many markets laid out at this time had a more definitely quadrilateral shape but the constraints imposed by existing features precluded this at Thetford. There are hints from the maps of 1807 that it may originally have extended as far west as the junction of Pike Lane and Nether Row. The market began as an open space but, as explained in Chapter Four, soon became infilled with more or less permanent stalls, so that today there is little open ground.

To the north-west of the old market place is another distinctive area which is closely connected with the development of the market place. There are four streets, today called Pike Lane, Guildhall Street, Raymond Street and Nether Row, which form a roughly square block of land with Cage Lane along its northern boundary. Guildhall Street and Raymond Street are the two, roughly parallel, central roads, while Pike Lane and Nether Row are narrower back lanes. The property boundaries in this block, although altered in modern times, show that originally there were long narrow plots extending back from Raymond Street and Guildhall Street to Nether Row and Pike Lane respectively. The regularity of the street and property plan in this area contrasts very markedly with the pattern in the Saxon town to the north-west, and indicates that this is almost certainly a planned suburb dating from the early medieval period.

The development of such suburbs was a widespread phenomenon of the three centuries from 1100, and was frequently associated with the granting of a new market charter and the provision of a market place. It is probable that in Thetford the new market was given a charter by one of the Earls Warren in the late 12th or early 13th centuries, its site being determined by the existence of the castle land which was in the ownership of the Earls as lords of the manor. This suggests that the entire length of the town between Cage Lane and the Castle Lane–Ford Street junction was a deliberately planned manorial creation, a new early-medieval suburb with a market place and a block of regular streets linking it to the existing town. That the new suburb was not entirely regular in plan was, as in the case of the market, because existing features such as the castle ditch presented obstacles (map 12).

The implication of this theory — which, it must be emphasised, is based on analysis of the plan of the town and circumstantial evidence, but which appears to be a valid interpretation of these — is that the defences of the Saxon town did not in fact extend as far as the old market place, but turned south-west across the corner of the present Guildhall and then roughly along the line of Cage Lane towards the Small Bridges. Since the Saxon defences on this side of the river are in any case only postulated this alternative route deserves the most serious consideration.[35]

The medieval planned settlement clearly did not prosper as much as might have been hoped. Thetford was a declining town, and although the development of the new market would perhaps have stabilised its trade the location was neither convenient

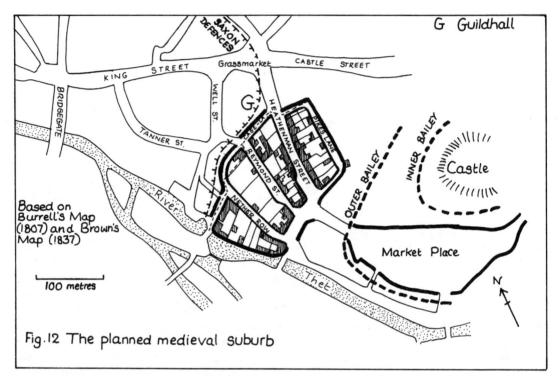

Fig.12 The planned medieval suburb

nor well-suited to growth. The site was cramped, with the river and the castle preventing expansion north and south of the market place and, after 1408, the Augustinian friary blocking eastward growth. The market place lay off the main road network of the town since the Nuns Bridges route already had secondary status, and the real focal point of Thetford continued to be King Street, with St Peter's church and Bridgegate at one end and the Grassmarket and Guildhall at the other. Another problem of the site was described by Burrell, who said that in former times (i.e. before the market was removed in 1786) people could only 'with some difficulty go to the Market, by reason of the Water being so high on the roads & Causeways leading thereto'.[36]

Nevertheless the new market place was provided with certain facilities as befitted its manorial sponsorship. The Chapel of the Blessed Virgin Mary was on the south side, and was built in the 1280s. A' striking feature of the distribution of medieval churches in the town is that there was none in the area south-east of St Cuthbert's church. The whole of the Bailey End district was without a parish church, and this can be attributed to the lateness of its development. By the time it was laid out the enthusiasm for church-building had waned, so the chapel of St Mary, although non-parochial, was held to be sufficient. A 15th-century Gild Certificate said of the Gild that it 'supported 3 chaplains who celebrated in a chapel ½ league away from the parish church for the benefit of those Who flocked to the town on market day'.[37] According to some sources the Guildhall in the present market place also had its own chapel: a document of 1446 refers to the 'Capella Sci Barthlii', or chapel of St Bartholomew.[38]

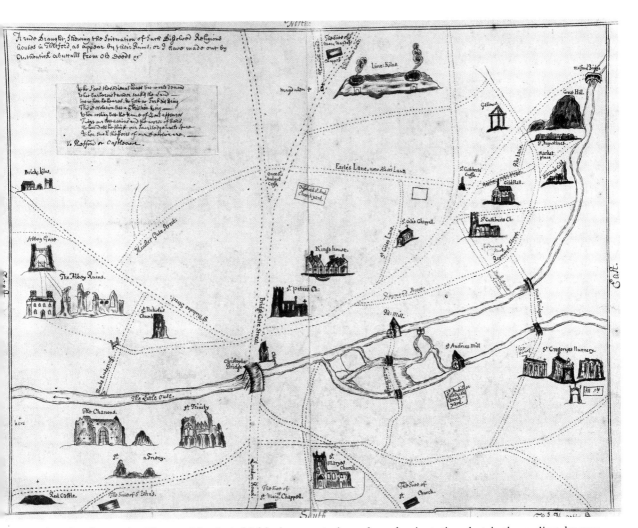

1. This sketch-map by Thomas Martin is highly inaccurate in scale and orientation, but is the earliest known plan of the town. Martin made small drawings of notable ruins and public buildings, and in several instances these are the only representations of these features in existence. Note the lime-kilns and brick-kilns on the northern edge of the town, the gallows on Melford Common, and the sketch of the Kings House before it was rebuilt in the 1760s. The map was prepared in about 1760, when Martin was collecting material for his *History of Thetford*: his signature is at the bottom right-hand corner.

2. (*above*) In the early 1820s the Vicar of St Mary's, Rev. Joseph Wilkinson, made a set of valuable if occasionally fanciful drawings of Thetford ruins and buildings, and as in this example they provide an important record of those of which all trace is now lost. In 1820 the east window of St Giles' church, towering over the sagging roofs and lean-to sheds which were typical of 19th-century Thetford, was sketched not long before its demolition. Dressed stones from the church, which was closed at the Reformation, can still be seen in adjacent walls and buildings.

3. (*left*) Wilkinson also drew St Peter's church, shown here with the jettied corner of the *Bell Hotel* to the right. The church was extensively restored and the tower rebuilt in 1789, after the latter had shown signs of imminent collapse. A new churchyard wall and railings were erected at the same time. Much of the expense was borne by James Mingay K.C., Mayor and (briefly) M.P. for Thetford. A rusting plaque on the wall opposite the *Bell* reads IAC. MINGAY ARM. DOM. REG. CONSIL. ET HUJ. PAROCH. INDIG. SUMP. EXTRUCT. A.D. 1791 (James Mingay Esq., K.C., a native of this parish, paid for these works, 1791).

4. Castle Hill was raised in the late 1060s within the ramparts of the Iron Age fort: it is one of the two highest Norman mottes in England. In the 1820s Leonard Shelford paid for trees to be planted on the summit to beautify the mound. Lady Cecil leased the Hill and the Castle Meadow to the Corporation in 1905, and in September 1908 the area was opened to the public as a park.

Thetford Grammar School, (before 1879).

5. This early photograph shows the original building of the Grammar School before the major alterations and new buildings of the late 1870s. It was built in 1612-15 within the grounds of the Dominican Friary, the ivy-clad ruins of which can be seen to the left of the schoolhouse. In the foreground is the footpath linking School Green with the Town Bridge, and following the ancient route of the Brandon road, which had for centuries been diverted to its present course well to the south.

6. The Guildhall as we see it today is essentially an Edwardian reconstruction of a jerry-built 18th-century predecessor, itself incorporating parts of the late 17th-century building erected by Sir Joseph Williamson (which may in turn have had medieval fragments in its structure). The Guildhall was rebuilt in 1798-9 by the corporation as part of its attempts to retain the Lent Assizes in the town. The work was so shoddily done that various rooms soon became unsafe. Another rebuilding in 1901-2 incorporated features of the old Guildhall including the statue of Justice and the bulk of the cupola. This view was taken in about 1895: on the right is the Market Shambles of 1837.

7. (*above*) The first proper hospital in Thetford was built in Earls Street in 1897-8. This photograph shows the original building with the balcony which was added in 1907, and was taken in 1913. Funds for the hospital and its upkeep were raised by public subscription and donations, but the land and £400 of the initial cost were provided as a gift by Thomas Shelford Bidwell.

8. (*below*) In 1910 a new Citadel for the Salvation Army was opened in Magdalen Street, and, as can be seen from the photograph, the occasion was the excuse for large celebrations. The old flint cottages of Magdalen Street are clearly seen. The low-roofed cottage next to the Citadel towards the Market Place was demolished in 1911 and the Y.M.C.A., opened in 1912, built on the site. Both the Citadel and the Y.M.C.A. were largely financed by Joseph Vavasseur of Kilverstone Hall.

9. (*above*) This drawing of the old Town Bridge (also known as Christopher Bridge) was made by Joseph Wilkinson in about 1820. Nine years later this bridge, which was rebuilt in 1796, was pulled down and replaced by the present cast-iron structure. The old bridge was made entirely of wood, and although only 12 feet wide had to carry all the traffic on the main Norwich road. Beyond the bridge are the roofs of the maltings and in the foreground coal is being unloaded from small lighters.

10. (*below*) Lighters, the characteristic barge of the Fenland waterways, are tied up in a train along the Navigation in this view taken in 1886. At that time the river had a small but steady trade in coal, fertilisers, manure and grain, and the banks and haling path were kept in good repair. On the left of the picture are the chimney-pots of Bridge House and the sheds of Burrells works, while in the distance the roofs of the maltings and their oasthouse-like kiln rise above the treetops.

11. (*above*) From the dimmest historical past there has been a ford on the Little Ouse, about half a mile below the present Town Bridge, at the site now occupied by the footbridge. The ford was known in the medieval period as Inselford, and later as Ditchingford or Redcastle Ford. This photograph dates from about 1905 and shows what was probably a street-watering cart, a large barrel on wheels drawn by a horse. In the distance is the First Staunch of the Navigation, and on the right bank the haling path.

12. (*below*) The Third Staunch was situated on a remote reach of the river between the Abbey meadows and Two Mile Bottom; it was also known as Turfpool Staunch. In this view, looking downstream, the structure and mechanism can be clearly seen: a weir and sluices are to the left, the lock section to the right. A single gate dams the flow and is raised or lowered by chains wound by the great wheel to the right. The lifting of the gate allowed the water to rush through and to carry the vessels downstream or to be hauled up. To judge by the accumulated weeds and debris against the gate, it had not been used for some time before the photograph was taken in about 1910.

13. (*above*) The 23 human and two animal employees of the Great Eastern Railway Company who worked at Thetford station posed in a somewhat unnerving place for this photograph, which was probably taken about 1900. They are sitting on the level-crossing at the western end of the station, on what used to be the main Mundford road. The two horses would have been used for shunting in the goods yard at the other end of the station.

14. (*below*) The two phases in the building of the railway station are shown clearly in this picture. On the left is the small flint Station House which dated from the opening of the line in 1845, while on the right is the larger and more imposing red brick extension of 1889. The *Railway Tavern*, a fine 'Jacobean'-style flint building, was built shortly after the railway station and survives almost unchanged. In 1900, when this photograph was probably taken, it was owned by Bidwell's Brewery.

15. This superb photograph of the workers at the Bidwell's maltings was taken in 1909, 15 years before the associated brewery was to close after being taken over by Bullards. The brewery and maltings were in Old Market Street. Of particular interest are the various tools which the men are holding, including broad wooden shovels and forks, brushes and brooms, and a sieve. The closure of the brewery brought to an end an industry which had flourished in the town for over 500 years, and on the proceeds of which—as well as the profits of political office—the Bidwell family had grown prosperous and powerful.

16. Another ancient local trade which died out in the early years of this century was warrening, the catching of rabbits for meat and fur. This faded photograph shows a group of warreners with their hunting dogs, ferret cages and at least six dozen dead rabbits. It was probably taken at the turn of the century on a local estate. The warreners are dressed in their traditional long smocks. They usually lived with dogs and ferrets in temporary huts on the heath during the killing season.

17. Although a relatively small town, Thetford supported a wide variety of shops and traders. Henry Goddard, whose fish, fruit and vegetable shop was in Magdalen Street, had his own curing and smokehouse, where bloaters were prepared daily in the season from fresh fish brought from Lowestoft and Yarmouth. This view shows the fish strung on long racks ready for light smoking to make bloaters. It is from an advertising postcard printed in the early years of this century.

18. Castle Street, formerly Little Magdalen Street, c. 1903. The line of the street was dictated to some extent by the shape of the ancient ramparts of Castle Hill, and this may help to explain the widening of the street to form a broad central strip which merges into the Common. In 1902 trees were planted to commemorate the Coronation of King Edward VII and Queen Alexandra; in this picture they are still very young.

19. (*above*) Every one of the buildings in this photograph of Well Street, taken just after the First World War, has now been demolished to make way for the redevelopment of the town centre. In place of the attractive and varied cottages and small shops are large concrete and steel buildings, out of keeping with the scale, character and appearance of the old town.

20. (*below*) Since the early 18th century King Street has been the main shopping area of Thetford. In the century before the Second World War, Bridge Street and White Hart Street were also important for retailing, but they are now very much peripheral to the commercial centre. The shift in the focus of commerce from the inconvenient old market place was completed in 1786 when the market was transferred to its present site. Despite modern changes, including the unfortunate abundance of plate-glass and plastic shop-fronts, King Street still retains some of its old country town air, although nowhere near as much as in this view looking eastwards in about 1910.

21. (*above*) This picture was taken before the First World War, on a quiet summer morning. To the left is the flint wall of St Cuthbert's church, which had been virtually rebuilt in 1853, and in the distance is the tower of St Peter's. The road surface is in a 'semi-improved' state, with a smooth and unrutted finish, a result of the efforts of Thetford corporation since 1870. The provision of a pavement and kerb in King Street had been a priority, but it took almost 10 years to complete the stretch between the two churches.

22. (*below*) One of the leading shops in Thetford from 1900 until its closure in 1962 was Savage Brothers. Its advertisements in the 1900s refer to ladies' clothing, boots and shoes, millinery, gentlemen's outfitting, carpets, rugs, linoleum, groceries, wines and spirits. This photograph was taken in 1910, when the window, with its fine wrought-iron supports, was filled with an impressive array of summer millinery.

23. In the years before the First World War the great empty heathlands around the town were regularly used for military exercises and training, a foretaste of the permanent military occupation of the Breckland which was to come 30 years later. Soldiers of the regular army and the reserve usually arrived at Thetford Bridge station and then marched through the town to the vast tented camps on the heath. This column passed along King Street in the high summer of 1911, and evidently excited much local interest. On the right is the *King's Arms*, demolished in 1927 although it was a very old timber-framed building of great charm.

24. The north range of the *Bell Hotel*, at the corner of Bridge Street and King Street, is one of the best and oldest buildings in Thetford, first mentioned in 1493. It is a late 15th-century timber-framed structure, but its internal details are puzzling: there have been suggestions that it was once divided into a series of stall-like units which were perhaps shops.

25. (*above*) The muddy and rutted road surface as late as the First World War is apparent in this photograph taken in about 1910. This view looks south from the Bell Corner across the Town Bridge to the London Road. On the left were small shops and behind them a large area of maltings. All have now gone, and in their place are the sympathetically-designed *Bell Hotel* extension, and the less appealing Riverside precinct.

26. (*below*) Another view of Bridge Street, taken at about the same time, shows that mud and ruts were not the only hazard to be faced when crossing the road. The narrowness of the road, the overhanging jetties of the *Bell Hotel*, and the prominent landmark of St Peter's tower, are all well seen. Note the chimney sweep with coal-black face, hat, and clothes, crossing the bridge with his pony and trap.

27. (*above*) Heavy commercial carts were the only traffic on the main London to Norwich road when the picture was taken in 1912. The trees on the right were beside the bowling ground which belonged to *Peacock's Commercial Hotel*, and which covered the site of the Domus Dei, a medieval religious hospice for travellers. The hotel and the adjacent *Anchor Inn* had superseded the famous *Christopher Inn*.

28. (*below*) To the north of the old town the area between the Norwich road and the railway remained as open fields until the 1880s, when new building began and a suburb started to take shape. The area grew in a piecemeal and fragmented fashion. Vicarage Road, linking the Norwich and Croxton roads along the line of an old field track, was built up over more than 50 years. In this photograph, taken in about 1905, the practice of selling small plots to different builders is revealed by the presence of five quite distinct house types and designs in a continuous row of only 16 properties.

29. The late Victorian and Edwardian houses in Croxton Road are larger and more elaborate than their neighbours in Vicarage and Station roads. The houses shown here (1916) indicate their superior character by such embellishments as turrets, balconies, iron railings with spiked finials, and panels of flintwork in facades and garden walls. The road slopes uphill to the railway bridge, but before it reaches that the pavement stops: the town has ended.

30. A view of Bury Road c. 1910. The Corporation had provided a footpath as far as the last house in the road. Since then three short rows of houses had been built but the pavement had not yet caught up. The large chimney belongs to Thetford Gaswork, opened in 1848 when this site was well beyond the edge of the town. In the distance is the workhouse of 1836, like the gasworks an undesirable establishment, so placed far away from the town itself. Because of these two features the Bury Road had an inferior status and its population was mainly working class.

31. This working class character was reinforced by the development of the large Newtown council estate between the Bury and London roads in 1911-13 and 1919-23. This photograph shows part of the second phase of the estate. The houses were substantially built and the design was influenced by the Garden City ideals of the 1900s. The development of the estate wrecked much of the archaeological heritage of the town, for under these new houses was the long-abandoned Saxon settlement on the south bank.

There was also a market house, where the administration of the market was conducted. It was often called the Toll House, or *tholondo*, and appears to have been converted from a shop as the business of the market expanded. In 1290 Margaret, widow of Alan de Kilverstone, sold 'a shop in the Market of Thetford, now the Toll House'.[39] The same deed describes its location as 'near the Prison of our Lord Earl Warenne': that the manorial lord should have had his prison in the market place is another indication that he was responsible for the market charter. The gaol may well have been on the site of the Old Gaol that exists today and was used as the Borough Gaol until 1891. At the opposite end of the market place was the cross, which stood on land incorporated into the grounds of Ford Place in 1805, when the enclosure of Thetford was in progress.[40]

The economy of medieval Thetford

As with so many aspects of its history, the economy of medieval Thetford remains a subject shrouded in obscurity. There is circumstantial evidence but little detailed information. The background to the economy was of course the declining size and population of the town, which was diminishing in relative importance as it faced economic competition from Lynn, Bury and the larger village markets of the district. Later in the period the remarkable prosperity of the East Anglian woollen industry benefited Thetford, so that in the 15th century there was some economic revival.

The population of the town declined sharply after the Conquest, when it had been about 4,500, but unfortunately there are no reliable and accurate figures until the first census, in 1801. Estimates based on the partial census of 1549 give a figure of about 1,500, and on the 1664 Hearth Tax one of the 1,250 (see chapter 4): the figure of 700 suggested by Patten for the mid-16th century seems to be a serious under-estimate.[41] No figures are available between 1086 and 1549 apart from very incomplete taxation lists, such as one of *c.* 1326 which gives 123 names and so implies a population of at least six hundred.[42] It is, however, quite certain that the Black Death (1348-51) must have resulted in a rapid fall in numbers during the second half of the 14th century. It is significant that this period saw the acquisition of derelict properties close to the Town Bridge and the market place by the Dominican and Augustinian friaries respectively, and it may well be that the Black Death completed the abandonment of the south bank town which earlier economic and political changes had begun. The social distress and discontent produced by these economic problems probably contributed in large measure to the tension and lawlessness which were evident in the district for much of the 14th century. In 1331 a group of rioters attacked the priory of St Mary and killed some of the monks, while during the Peasants' Revolt of 1381 a band of rebels occupied Thetford briefly and were given 20 or 28 marks by the mayor for not burning down the town as they had threatened.[43]

In general terms, therefore, the population levels may have stabilised, perhaps at about 2,000, during the later 13th century, and then started to increase with the economic recovery associated with the new market, only to suffer a further catastrophe with the devastation wrought by the pestilence of the 1350s. A period of recovery in the second half of the 15th century seems to have culminated in relative prosperity during the years from 1490 until about 1520, but there was then a very serious setback, as general economic difficulties were exacerbated by the Dissolution, which had a very damaging impact in a town so heavily dependent upon the monasteries for its trade and commerce. This was certainly the view of contemporary Thetfordians, as the first section of the next chapter shows. In relative terms Thetford fell further behind the other leading towns of Norfolk as the centuries progressed. In 1334 the town was assessed at £16 in the taxation known as the 'Tenths and Fifteenths'; this compares with £95 for Norwich and £68 for Lynn, and meant that Thetford was only 16th in a list of Norfolk towns and villages, behind such places as Heacham, Snettisham and Swaffham. In 1524 Thetford was assessed at £30, compared with £713 for Norwich and £96 for Lynn, which implies that a revival of fortunes had taken place in relation to Lynn but that the enormous prosperity of Norwich had quite eclipsed the other towns in the county.[44]

The wool industry never dominated Thetford as it did some of the Suffolk towns, but it was undoubtedly important, particularly since the religious houses, especially the two priories, were actively involved in large-scale sheep-farming until the Dissolution. Financial assessment of its value to the town is impossible, but the probability is that sheep and wool provided the income which allowed some Thetford merchants to build large and impressive new houses in the late 15th and early 16th centuries. Several of these survive, most of them hidden behind later façades of brick and plaster — The Chantry, in White Hart Street, and the antique shop at the town end of Castle Street, are excellent examples.

The finest is of course the Ancient House, also in White Hart Street, which was at that time the most fashionable street in which to live. The house, which has been described as 'one of the best examples of an early Tudor house in East Anglia', was rediscovered beneath later plaster in 1867, and was carefully restored in 1921-4 as a museum for the town. It was probably built soon after 1500, and was originally detached although it is now built into a terrace.[45] Other late medieval and early Tudor buildings survive, of which the most prominent is the north wing of the *Bell Inn* opposite St Peter's church. This building has a complex history, but the single jettied range which exists today is probably that referred to in an indenture of 1493 which describes a property 'lying in St Peter between the House of the said Andrew [Carter] called the Shop, late parcel of the said Messuage on the East, and the Hospital called the Bell on the west, one head on the North in a way leading from the Bridgegate towards the Church of Saint Cuthbert'.[46] A deed of 1510 describes another inn, on the north side of the old market place, 'callyed of old tyme the Dolphyn now the Gryffyn; whych parcell of grownde forseyd conteynyth yn lengthe xlvii fotes and in brede xxv fotes'.[47] The rebuilding and new building of all these houses and inns from the later 15th century into the reign of Henry VIII argues for a period of increased prosperity.

Several documents refer indirectly to the cloth industry. In 1347, for example, one of the properties in the parish of St Etheldreda listed in a deed was that of 'John, son of Richard le Fuller', a fuller being someone who cleaned cloth before it was finished.[48] There appear to have been tenters, the wooden frames on which the cloth was stretched, on the land between Castle Street and Pike Lane. A deed of 1324 describes 'a court walled round the two tenters in the ditch called *Le Tendedyk*, each 6 score feet in length, lying between the messuage of Hugh de Thetford and the highway leading to Middlegate',[49] while in 1379 a property was said to lie between 'the messuage of Walter Pycard and the high road leading to the Middlegate, abutting on *Le Tentedych* at one head and on the high road from the Grassmarket to the market of Thetford on the other'.[50] An old story, repeated by Martin, is that the vicinity of Pike Lane was once known as 'le Fantditch', said to mean 'muddy ditch', but in fact this is a misreading of 'tentedych', the ditch where the tenters had their frames. Pike Lane, it may be added, perhaps derives its name from Walter Pycard. A borough account roll of 1403–4 includes a note that William Striker paid 5d. for a one-year licence to have 'one pair of tents standing on the Common of Thetford against the tenement of Reginald Fermers'.[51]

Many other trades and occupations existed, but very few have documentary evidence. Often the casual references in deeds and leases, and in place-names, hint at economic activity: thus there is a 14th-century reference to 'lymburners street' and one of 1514 to 'calk pit yeerde', both indicating a substantial chalk-digging and lime-burning industry. Only from later centuries is there more information about either of these. Much of the medieval town seems to have been pitted and riddled with shallow quarries and mines, and occasionally the subsidence of one of these brings them into the public mind rather dramatically.[52] In later maps of the town the lime-kilns were concentrated around Melford Bridge Common and the Norwich Road area: six are marked on the 1807 map, for example. The earlier habit was simply to dig wherever was convenient for the user, and this provoked frequent and ineffective ordinances from the town authorities: those of 1547 and 1555, for example, banned indiscriminate digging on the commons, and especially upon Magdalen Green, at the far end of Magdalen Street. As this was the exercise ground for the militia the safety of the town may have been at stake! A 1598 ordinance stated that all chalkpits had to be fenced if they lay within 30 yards of the highway, 'for preventing of such dangerous mishaps as otherwise might follow either unto the Inhabitants of the . . . Borough as unto her Majesty's leige people in the daily and nightly travails by & alongest each of the chalkpits'.[53]

Not until the 16th century is it possible to make a more substantial analysis of the economy of Thetford, but there is no doubt that the economic structure of the medieval town was broad-based. There were industries such as wool and cloth, leather and tanning, and brewing. There were services provided to pilgrims, the monasteries and the passing travellers on the Norwich road. The market, despite its inconveniences and the vicissitudes of economic fluctuation and competition from other towns, was still the largest in south-west Norfolk. In addition, Thetford had a considerable agricultural sector to its economy.

Rural Thetford and its agriculture

The river valleys of Thetford were, as to some extent they still are, marshy and badly-drained. Even in this century there has been some serious flooding in the town centre on several occasions, and in the 15th century both the priory of the Holy Sepulchre and the nunnery of St George suffered from their proximity to the river. The valley floors were in general unsuitable for building and too wet for arable agriculture or sheep-grazing, so that the pasturing of cattle was the chief activity, together with the cutting of reeds for thatch and hay for fodder. The amount of riverside pasture was limited and its use was carefully regulated. Much of the land was common pasture, available to the townspeople for grazing their cattle or gathering reeds and grass for certain periods of the year. Although no contemporary accounts of the customs survive there is ample evidence from the 16th century to confirm that there were strict rules and that these were already old by then. In 1573 some of the common rights were disputed and the mayor and burgesses called evidence from John Valle, 'burges of the age of 80 yeres and more', who stated on oath that 'all ye lands aptaynynge to ye late monasterye of ye monks in Thetford from ye gattes entoe Hallewyke meer & from thence unto Pykes valye are comon when they lye unsowne for all maner of catell, all ye tyme of ye yere, accordynge unto ye ansyent custome of ye sayd towne & borough of Thetford'.[54]

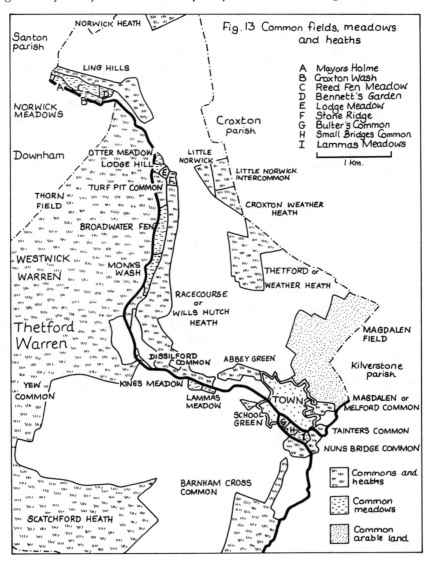

Fig. 13 Common fields, meadows and heaths

A   Mayors Holme
B   Croxton Wash
C   Reed Fen Meadow
D   Bennett's Garden
E   Lodge Meadow
F   Stone Ridge
G   Bulter's Common
H   Small Bridges Common
I   Lammas Meadows

1 Km.

Commons and heaths

Common meadows

Common arable land

The land between the two rivers west of the Small Bridges and the meadows on the south bank from the priory of the Holy Sepulchre downstream to Red Castle were available from July until Lammastide in February for common pasture – hence they were known as the Lammas Lands – and for private haymaking between Lammas and the end of July. Below Red Castle a series of marshy islands, fens and wet pastures extended to Two Mile Bottom, most of them being common. Thus Mayors Holmes, a 2½-acre islet, was the property of the mayor and burgesses, and later of the Corporation, its revenues being employed to defray the expenses of the mayoralty. Kings Meadow near Two Mile Bottom was one of the main sources of osiers, used until the late 19th century to make baskets and mats. A regulation of 1564 states that 'no Inhabytance within the Towne of Thetfforde shall mowe . . . any grasse or fother In the Common fenn a fore the common daye yt ys now & have been the Tuysdaye nexte be fore mydsomer day & every inhabitore to be gyne at vi of ye clocke in the mornyng & to have but one sythe a pece yt day'.[55]

The drier land above the riverside flats was used for arable agriculture. Here there were the common fields of Thetford, unhedged and unenclosed and divided into numerous strips (map 13). Over the centuries piecemeal enclosure had reduced the extent of these fields very considerably so that by 1804, when parliamentary enclosure was begun, there was only one large tract, Magdalen Field, still open and farmed in the traditional way.[56] Magdalen Field was named after the Hospital of St Mary Magdalen at its southern edge, and was alternatively called the North Field. Similarly the South Field was also known as St Margaret's Field after the long-abandoned church of that name, which had stood on a small knoll in the middle of the field, and latterly as St Mary's Field. Parts of it were still open strips in the middle of the 18th century, since a deed of 1744 refers to 'seven severall peices or parcells of infield arable land . . . situate lying and being dispersedly in the severall feilds belonging to the parish of Saint Mary in Thetford'.[57]

There were other open fields, which had probably vanished by the 16th century: East Field lay between Melford Bridge Common and Redgate Lane, while Westwick Field was on the edge of Thetford Warren just beyond Red Castle. In all these fields the monasteries and parish churches had extensive holdings, often bequeathed by benefactors. Thus in 1509 John Judy, burgess of Thetford, left to the churchwardens of St Cuthbert 'iiij acres of land arable called Pykys land as they be lyeing in the feilds of Thetford for seyd nere ye clay pitts'.[58] The revenues from leasing the land would be used for church repairs and ornamentation, and to pay the priests: a rather similar procedure is seen in an order of 1538 which required the mayor and burgesses to pay their share of the upkeep of the Nuns Bridges with the profits from eight acres of land in the South or St Margaret's Field.[59]

Beyond the fields were extensive tracts used mainly for sheep-pasture, although some of them had arable use for some of the year. The list of lands owned by the priory of St Mary in the late 15th century includes a parcel of 29 acres 'which lyeth in Sheldhowe towards Croxton which sometyme was arrable and now is shepespasture', illustrating well the process by which the great monastic sheepruns were taking over other agricultural land and putting it under grass.[60] The local agricultural economy in the late medieval period, and until the 19th century, involved the complicated system of foldcourses, whereby it was the right of the lord to order his tenants to put their sheep to graze upon his land and thus to manure it, and the right of the tenants to graze sheep upon the manorial waste, and upon the arable land after harvest when they ate the stalks and haulms. The regulations governing the foldcourse system defined who could graze which animals on which lands, and at which time of the year, and laid down penalties for transgression. The rights of foldcourse were jealously guarded by the proprietors of arable and pasture lands alike, and when they were extinguished in the early 19th century detailed accounts were made so that compensation could be established.[61]

Typical examples are given in the papers of the Enclosure Commissioners. Thus, 'Upon the Infield land called Maudling field the Abbey farm hath a right of sheep feed from Holy Rood day unto the third day of May following', or at Norwick Farm in the far north of the Borough, where 'Ling Hills is common to the town of Thetford for horses and cows but the Sheepwalk is several to Norwick Farm ... but in all the ploughed land belonging to the Norwick Farm the Town of Thetford (after the Corn crops are harvested) have a right to shack or feed cattle and swine'. A similarly complex set of rules governed the collection of bracken, heather and furze (gorse), brushwood for fuel and various sources of fodder. The aim was to minimise the amount which any individual could collect, so that everybody had a 'fair' share, and to prevent resale so that a profit was not made from common property. Thus 'the inhabitants of Thetford have a right to take Furze off Wills Hutch Heath, Thetford Heath & the Norwick but to carry it away no otherwise than by bundles upon their back', while an ordinance of 1560 required that nobody was to 'gather reeds or wracke [bracken] upon the Commons to sell ... and none to buy reeds for resale, only to mend their houses'.[62] This was doubtless frequently ignored, as was another order of 1598 concerning the behaviour of those who took too much, to the prejudice of the poor: 'much of the poore of the towne in the tyme of winter are ordinarily very much distressed for want of fewell, by reason of the immoderate cause of some who seeking their owne benefit leave nothing for the reste' and it was ordered that householders could gather turves for fuel only on three days in September, and then could take only as much as one man might carry.[63]

Beyond the common heaths were the warrens, which until the late 19th century played a most important rôle in the local economy. In 1627 a writer described the land between Thetford and Barnham as 'the Champion' (i.e. open country) with an economy based on corn, sheep and rabbits. Breckland, with its sandy soils and extensive tracts of uncultivated heath, was an excellent location for large-scale exploitation of the rabbit, and eventually there were eight major warrens in west Suffolk and Norfolk, centred upon Thetford. Rights of free warren were granted by royal charter: in return for monetary payment the holder was awarded exclusive rights to rabbits, hares and game birds. In the medieval period the rights of free warren were usually granted to monastic lords, such as the prior of Thetford, who owned Thetford Warren.[64]

Most warrens covered several thousand acres and each was commanded by a fortified lodge, intended as a base for acting against poachers — a well-nigh impossible task — and for the conduct of operations in the killing season.[65] The warrens were surrounded by banks and in the winter the rabbits had to be fed artificially with hay and other fodder. Sheep grazed the same area, eating lichens and long grass while the rabbits nibbled the short turf. Although in general the two animals co-existed there were some shepherds who felt that the rabbits had the better side of the bargain, but the effect was a concentrated and intensive grazing which in some parts of the warrens produced tracts of bare sand, the source of the notorious 'sand blows' which were often reported by travellers and agricultural analysts.[66]

Chapter Four

THETFORD 1540–1700

The Dissolution and its consequences

FOR THETFORD, a small town crowded with religious houses, the Dissolution was a traumatic event. Within four years the foundation of its economic and social life, its greatest landowners and its most splendid buildings had been swept away. The local economy was already in some difficulty: there had been stagnation and depression since the early 1520s. In 1527 Henry VIII had sent a Commission to investigate the 'great ruyne and decay' which was afflicting the town. It had instructions to ascertain the causes of the political struggles between the mayor and some of the burgesses, but also in its brief was consideration of the reasons why 'divers houses within the same town have ben wilfully let fall down . . . to our great damage and dysheryson, but also to the great molestacon and inquietans of our tenaunts and inhabitants'.[1]

The Dissolution exacerbated and accelerated this decline. In 1539 the mayor and burgesses petitioned Thomas Cromwell, the Lord Chancellor, for assistance in over-coming the distress caused by the recent suppression of the monasteries. Although it was perhaps an exaggerated account to reinforce the claimants' plea, the petition is an eloquent testimony to the damage which had been experienced by the town. Thetford, it said,

> 'hath ever ben grettly mayntaynyd relevyd and preservyd by the resort and trade of pylgremys ther passyng thorowe, a goodly nombyr of peopyll ther inhabytyng hath ben well preservyd wyth . . . a grette nombyr of fayer howsys yn the seyd towne well beuylded and upholdyn, but now the pilgrims are abhorryd, exesepulsyd and sette apart for ever, wherby a grett nombyr of peopyll by idyllyd and lyke to be browght ynto extreme beggarye'.

The mayor asked for permission to make some 'good provysschon and remayde' to alleviate poverty and unemployment, by selling land in the parish of Croxton belonging to the town and lending the proceeds to traders who could then 'the better thereby be enabyllyd to sette a work all the seyd idyll peopyll, and to expulse idylnes, and be a mene to contenue them yn honest and queyett levying . . . a very semyng way to preserve the pore peopyll'. This unexpectedly modern idea, a subsidy to employers who would agree to take on unemployed workers, was rejected by the government.[2] Economic distress and decline continued. As late as 1564 there were vacant and derelict properties in the market place. A lease of that year refers to a 'Tenement wastyd' in the Bailey End, belonging to William Baste, tallowchandler.[3]

Ruin and decay was to be the fate of most of the monastic buildings, to the detriment of the architectural heritage. In 1539 the privy council contemplated retaining the priory church and reconstituting it as a collegiate parish church, a plan enthusiastically

56

supported by the Duke of Norfolk, many of whose family were buried there. The king soon lost interest in this laudable project and the tombs of the Howards were desecrated, while the beautiful church, potentially such an ornament to the town, was stripped of its valuables and used as a quarry for building materials.[4] The prior's lodging eventually became the farmhouse for the Abbey estate, a more honourable fate than that of the priory of the Holy Sepulchre, which was turned into a barn, with the domestic buildings making grandiose hen-houses.

The Reformation presented an opportunity for the further amalgamation of tiny urban parishes and by 1550 there were only three churches in use in the town where once there had been twenty. Several of the deconsecrated buildings were demolished but others lingered, given over to more prosaic uses. The ruined steeple of St Nicholas remained for almost 300 years after the closure of the church in 1548, but the churchyard was used as waste-ground where pigs roamed and dung was piled in heaps. St Giles' church, according to Martin, was first turned into a barn, became a magnificent dog-kennel, and in the mid-18th century housed a wheelwright and his shop. Today dressed stones from both churches can be seen built into walls and doorways in the streets which bear their names.

The monastic lands were sold or granted to private individuals. Eventually the Howard family gained possession of almost all these properties. In 1539 the Duke of Norfolk was granted the most valuable prize, the priory of St Mary, its manor of Halewyk in Thetford, and its estates in 11 counties. Sir Richard Fulmerston was the other beneficiary. He was a protégé and close associate of the Duke, and held minor government posts. By being in the right place at the right time, and by cultivating suitable friendships, he managed to secure grants of most of the lands and and buildings of the Augustinian and Dominican friaries, the nunnery of St George, the priory of the Holy Sepulchre, the Domus Dei, the hospital of St John and the chapel of the Blessed Virgin Mary in Bailey End. In 1546 all the properties of the Duke of Norfolk were seized by the Crown when he was sentenced to death. The Manor of Halewyk and its lands were annexed to the Duchy of Lancaster manor of Thetford; in June 1548 both manors were granted to the Duke of Somerset and less than two months later the entire estate was sold to Sir Richard Fulmerston, who thereby completed the acquisition of all the lands, properties and lordships formerly owned by the various religious houses of Thetford.

Fulmerston had thus become a very wealthy man indeed, while the town and people of Thetford had gained almost nothing and had lost a very great deal. But Fulmerston's ownership was of short duration. In 1554 the Norfolk family estates were restored, and by a deed of 1558 Fulmerston acknowledged that his title to the priory lands and the manor of Halewyk was based on illegal forfeitures. He therefore returned all that part of his extensive estates to the Howard family, keeping all the properties granted to him outright in 1539. When he died in 1566 his lands passed to his daughter and her husband, Sir Edward Clere. From then until Sir Edward died in 1616 the greater part of the Borough of Thetford was owned by the Howard and Clere families, who exerted powerful economic, social and political influence. Nevertheless, since Clere was a supporter of the dukes of Norfolk as his father-in-law had been, the over-riding control was exercised by the Howards.

When Clere died his Thetford inheritance passed to his son, another Edward, who in fulfilment of a previous bargain almost immediately sold the entire estate to the

Howard family, so uniting once more the former monastic lands. It was by a descent through a junior Howard line that the lordships of Thetford came into the possession of Lord Petre, the chief landowner at the Enclosure Act of 1804.[5]

Trade and economy

During the 150 years to 1700 Thetford declined perceptibly in its economic importance relative to Norwich, Yarmouth, Lynn and Bury, towns which had larger populations, more prosperous agriculture hinterlands, and greater social or administrative significance. Locally Thetford retained its status as the main market town for south-west Norfolk, and indeed the gradual decay of the smaller markets such as Methwold and East Harling reinforced that particular rôle. But the entire region was thinly populated in comparison with most of lowland England, and with its extensive rabbit warrens and infertile heathlands was agriculturally less productive.

There was almost certainly a continuing decrease in population, a process which had been apparent since the early medieval period. A census of households was taken in Thetford in 1549, and although the returns have been damaged there were probably about 300 heads of families in the original list, implying a population of about 1,500.[6] The 1664 Hearth Tax returns list 164 taxable households and 98 exempt, which would suggest a further decline, although inevitably all such figures must be treated with caution.[7]

The major trades of Thetford did expand during the 17th century, but this was only sufficient to compensate for the great depression of the early and middle 16th century, and did not allow a real increase in size, wealth or population. All the industries made use of agricultural products, and were thus dependent upon the hinterland of the town. The woollen industry was in its last phase of prosperity, and had given rise to clothing and apparel trades. The local sheep-farming and rabbit-breeding were the basis of the extensive leather and tanning industry, and this too had spawned subsidiaries such as glove-making and shoe-making. Brewing, the third major industry, drew its grain supplies from the corn districts of central Norfolk and Suffolk.

Thetford Corporation pursued policies designed to encourage people from the surrounding countryside to buy at the market and to purchase goods made in the town, but to discourage the sale of many categories of goods brought from outside Thetford. It was thus a protectionist policy, using price controls, tolls and customs to penalise 'outsiders', and with strict regulations as to when and where they could offer goods for sale. All businesses conducted within Thetford were licensed, and whenever possible non-residents were excluded. Even natives of the town had to be freemen of the Borough before they could trade. None of this had the altruistic aim of benefiting the inhabitants at large. Rather, the intention was to protect the interests of a small group of traders. The Corporation was composed largely of gentlemen (usually wealthier merchants), small traders and shopkeepers, and the elaborate regulatory system was designed to reinforce their influence, standing and share of the market. The constitution of 1668 expressed these restrictions in detail: 'No body living in Thetford shall conduct any kind of occupation, mystery, science or trade, or keep any shop, cellar or other place open for the sale or utterance of his wares and merchandise, or sell any bread, beer, ale or other victuals without being a freeman of the borough, and those disobeying can be distrained'.[8]

The creation of freemen was at the discretion of the Corporation, the office enjoying its greatest influence in the 150 years from 1570. Since only the Corporation could create freemen (usually from the ranks of apprentices or the sons of existing freemen) it could exercise direct control over those permitted to work or trade in the town. Not unexpectedly, there were continual and often successful attempts to evade such unpopular and discriminatory restrictions. Partly to counter this, the traders were organised into groups similar to medieval trade gilds, and perhaps originating in the Middle Ages. Between 1569 and 1599 there are references to the following trades being so organised: butchers, cobblers, shoe-makers, millers, bakers, brewers, inn-keepers, tipplers or beerhouse-keepers, glovers, tanners, flannel-makers, clothiers, haberdashers, drapers, leather-workers or cordwainers, fishmongers, and tallow-chandlers.

The Corporation often negotiated with these groups rather than with the individual traders, as in 1577 when the butchers agreed to lease some town-owned market stalls, and it also had to issue ordinances concerning working practices and their demarcation. In October 1578, for example, it was ordered that 'noe shoemakers shall medle with, or take to mende, anie olde worke, neither shall anie Coblers make anie newe worke of theyre owne, but shoemakers to make their newe worke, and Coblers to doe all olde worke'.[9]

Many 16th- and 17th-century documents refer to the cloth industry. The 1549 census lists, among others, fullers, and shearmen who trimmed the long nap from the woven cloth. A deed of 1573 refers to the Castle Mill as 'ye fulyngmyll', indicating that at some stage it had been converted from the grinding of corn.[10] Clothiers and flannel-makers had their own 'gilds', drapers were numerous, and the 1549 census included a hatter. The main centre for tanning and related crafts was along the north bank of the Thet, between Pitmill and the confluence with the Little Ouse. Here the names Tanner House and Tanner Street recall the trade, which survived until the First World War on this site. The tanners of 16th- and 17th-century Thetford were a pros-perous group: John Snelling, who died in 1602, called himself 'gentleman' in his will,[11] and both he and his son Robert were mayors of Thetford and prominent members of the Corporation. The trade was always unpleasant, and gave rise to com-plaints because of its smell and the noxious effluent which was produced. A further problem is revealed in an indictment of 1558: Robert Sendall and Robert Retham were fined by the local court because 'they have hanged their sheep skins & other things in persuing their occupation of Glovers in the Common & open street to the nuisance of the King & Queene liege people'.[12] The finished leather was sold on Thetford market, or was made up locally into gloves, bags, shoes and harness.

From the mid-1570s Thetford had a small community of Flemish immigrants, as did several other East Anglian towns. This was not the first foreign community in Thetford, for in the 12th century there had been a Jewish colony. It must have been shortlived, since there are no records of Jewish surnames in later medieval documents, but it was of some significance. When aliens were taxed in 1158-9 the Jews of Norwich paid £44 6s. 8d. and those of Thetford £30, indicating that the local group was not much smaller than the well-known community in Norwich.[13] The Flemings in the 16th century seem to have been few in number and poor: the tax of 1586 lists only nine households with a total payment of only 5s. 8d.[14] and by the end of the century they seem to have been absorbed into the existing population and to have lost their separate identity. The Flemings were weavers, and although the Corporation tolerated their presence it exacted a levy upon their cloth to protect indigenous workers: in February 1580 it was recorded that 'the duchemenne are aggreed to paye to the use of the towne for everye warpe of yarne that shalbe made or uttered by them to sale ½d from this day forthe'.[15] They were also given facilities for worship, the Corporation agreeing in 1578 'with the assent of the cheife ducheman that they shall have the Guyldhall for to use as theyre Churche, untill they shall have a more convenient place for them appoynted'.[16]

Brewing was the other major trade of the town, and throughout the period from 1574 to 1835 the brewing and malting interest was the largest 'bloc' within the Corporation. In 1574, the first year of the new Corporation, five of its 10 members with identifiable trades were publicans. In 1834, just before its abolition, the mayor owned 10 of the 19 public houses in Thetford. The protection of the brewing industry was thus particularly careful. All alehouses had to be licensed by the Corporation: in 1682, for example, no fewer than 51 ale and beer houses were approved at the annual licensing session. It was inevitable that many tried to evade the restrictions. The 1668 bye-laws observed that 'great inconveniences result from the common brewers selling strong ale in unlicensed alehouses, where there are many disorders and many poor people do extravagantly spend their money to the ruin of their families'.[17]

The market and its regulations

It is only from the middle of the 16th century that detailed information on the geography and government of Thetford market becomes available. The market-place was subdivided into sections devoted to the sale of particular commodities, a practice found in all but the small village markets. In Thetford there are documentary references to markets for butter, cheese, timber, meat, fish, corn, hay, leather and kiddier (smallwares), and this list is certainly not exhaustive. A fishmarket is first mentioned in 1462 and was located next to the market house, but according to ordinances of the 14th century this area could only sell fish brought from outside the town. Locally-caught fish had to be offered for sale at the Bell Corner, and in 1489 a deed refers to one Thomas Roberdys, fishmonger of Bridgegate.[18] By the early 17th century this custom had fallen into abeyance, and in the reign of James I the Bell site was called the 'oldfyssh market'. The earliest reference to a subdivision of the market-place is in a deed of 1391, when a property in Ford Street was described as being 'in the common way leading from St Mary in the Bailey to the Corn Market'.[19]

The market-place was initially open, but stalls soon became a permanent feature as in Norwich market today. They were arranged in two pairs of parallel east to west rows, with a wide central lane and very narrow passages between the rows of each pair. Narrow lanes also ran north to south, with a wider one separating the prison and tollhouse from the fishmarket. A lease of 1564 gives the dimensions of a fishmarket stall (seven feet wide and 12 feet long) while a lease of 1577 confirms the arrangement of the stalls. It refers to 'three and Twentie stalles, called butchers stalles, situate and being in the common market place of the . . . boroughe aforesaid, in Two Rowes Rebuilded in four partes'.[20]

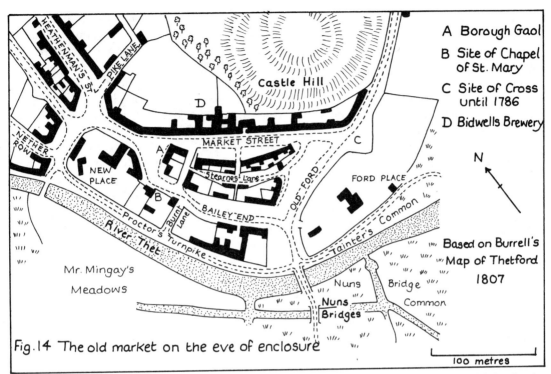

A Borough Gaol

B Site of Chapel of St. Mary

C Site of Cross until 1786

D Bidwells Brewery

N

Based on Burrell's Map of Thetford 1807

Fig.14 The old market on the eve of enclosure

100 metres

Stalls were regarded as any other property, to be bought, sold, leased and inherited. When the market was moved to its present site in 1786 their sites were used for housing and maltings, and the old market-place was thus permanently infilled. There are, however, traces of the original layout. The western lane, beside the fishmarket, is the unmade track which links Ford Street and Old Market Street next to the Old Gaol. At right angles to it can be seen the truncated remnant of the former east to west central lane. This and other passages were taken into gardens or built over after the 1804 Enclosure Act (map 14).[21]

The regulation of market business prior to 1574 was the responsibility of the clerk of the market, an official of the lord of the manor. After that date the mayor of Thetford was also clerk of the market, and controls over trading standards and market customs were a matter for the Corporation. This ended the irritating and demeaning submission to the manorial lord, exemplified by a summons of 1569 issued by Robert Wright, Clerk to the Duke of Norfolk, ordering the mayor, his officers and 24 'discrete, sober and honest men of the best and substantyalest wyrth' to appear before him for the examination of their weights and measures.[22] After 1574 similar inspections were carried out by the mayor using a set of standard measures owned by the Corporation: in October 1577 these were themselves checked when 'Mr Sheringe did assay ye brasen measures viz. one gallon & one pynte & various weights of brass & iron'. A later set may be seen in the Ancient House Museum.[23]

To check the quality of goods, 'searchers and sealers' were appointed: they gave the seal of Corporation approval without which, at least in theory, nothing could be offered for sale. Thus in February 1591 men were sworn 'to search for flesshe in ye market yf anie be corrupte', and on other occasions unfinished and finished leather, woollen cloth, pewter and fish were subjected to searches.[24] The most frequent assizes were upon beer and bread, the two basic commodities, and tables of permitted prices and weights were published. Outside bakers had to give more weight for the same price: in 1597 for example a penny white loaf baked locally was to weigh 12 ounces, but one brought from elsewhere 13 ounces. The 'foreign' loaf, being larger, was better value for money, and was presumably more popular with the consumers, a fact which betrays poor contemporary understanding of economics.[25]

Other market regulations tried to prevent forestalling – the purchase of goods before they reached the market – and regrating, the resale at higher prices of goods bought in the market-place. In January 1579 the Corporation heard that 'strangers and diverse persons have secretly and continually do use to buye hides or skins coming to this market and not in the same market'. It was ordered that in future 'no person shall neither bringe nor yet sell any hides or skins but in open market in the place for that purpose there set and allowed & appoynted as it have been heretofore used and not before such time as the market bell shall ringe'.[26] Thomas Cowye and the widow Goffe, outsiders, were reported in May 1579 to have come to Thetford 'bringing certain eel-fish, in number 13, to sell at the market and sold them to Walter Beets, fishmonger, at 12d. each'. Beets was fined for regrating, as he subsequently resold the eels at a higher price in his shop. He was a persistent offender, on later occasions being fined for regrating candles and for using false weights. As he had been mayor of Thetford in 1575 he really should have known better![27]

Local government to 1660

Until 1574 Thetford, as has been seen, was not a corporate borough, and the mayor and burgesses who governed the town did so technically as a group of individuals, not as a council with its own identity distinct from that of its members. There were certain legal restrictions upon them, in such areas as the ownership of property, but of greater importance was the irksome subordination to royal and manorial officials. Pressure for incorporation, which could only be granted by royal charter, grew from the late 15th century. However, there was frequent internal division among the burgesses, and this on several occasions provoked royal intervention, at the same time damaging the case for greater independence.

In 1532, for example, a Commission was sent to investigate 'diverse discords and variaunces as well of & for the yerely elecon of the Mayre'. It was laid down that the burgesses should follow strict new rules for the conduct of mayoral elections, while they and the commoners were instructed to behave properly towards the mayor, to 'accepte hym, love & favour him & use suche assisstens & good obedyence towards him as apptyenythe'. The King agreed to the recommendation of the Commission that the number of principal burgesses should be increased from eight to 10, and instructed that the mayor should be chosen from among this number and not from outside. In June 1532 he additionally granted the ceremonial privilege of having a sword of office and a sword-bearer. But he refused to grant a charter of incorporation.[28]

The town tried again in 1538, sending a petition to the Earl of Southampton, Chancellor of the Duchy of Lancaster. He turned down the request for incorporation:

as the manorial lord the Duchy had a vested interest in maintaining the status quo. When the matter was raised again in 1539 the mayor and burgesses tried a different approach: bribery. They seized the valuables from the chapel of St Mary, sold them for £54 15s. 5d., and offered the money to the King in return for a charter. Henry replied that not only was the amount too small, but that the seizure of goods from a religious house was sacrilegious, a fine example of royal hypocrisy since he was then in the middle of ransacking the monasteries himself. The plea was withdrawn.[29] In 1549 more internal squabbles led the Protector Somerset to reaffirm the rules of election and good government drawn up in 1532, and to emphasise that Thetford was still a Duchy borough by reasserting the requirement that the new mayor be sworn into office by the manorial steward.[30] Approaches to Philip and Mary in 1555, asking for incorporation and economic assistance, were as fruitless as all previous attempts.

In 1572 the Duke of Norfolk, lord of the manor of Thetford, was executed for his treasonous intriguing with Mary, Queen of Scots. As soon as he was dead the mayor and burgesses took advantage of the temporary absence of a powerful lord and landowner by reviving their demands for a charter of incorporation. The strength of the manorial control had been a major factor militating against success in earlier petitions, and so the circumstances were now auspicious. The burgesses sent a delegation to London to ask the Queen in person to grant a charter: accounts survive listing their expenses, which include 'gifts' to leading figures at Court. Entertainment was not forgotten — 5s. 0d. was given to 'My Lord of Leceisters Players' — while a respectable appearance was ensured by the 12d. 'for washing our Shirts &c'. The total cost of the visit was £15 17s. 11d., but it was a worthwhile trip, for the Queen agreed to the request, and in January 1574 Thetford was finally granted its charter of incorporation.[31]

This provided that the town should henceforth be governed by a Corporation consisting of a mayor, 10 burgesses ('the most discrete and honest men of the town') and 20 common councilmen, the commonalty. The first 31 members were named in the charter, which also laid down rules for the appointment of the recorder (the chief legal officer) and for the election of the mayor. Liberties and privileges were granted or confirmed, including the right to hold a Saturday market and a two-day fair at the feast of St Mary Magdalen (22-23 July). The most important provisions were financial. In return for the payment of fixed sums to the Crown and the manorial lords the Corporation was empowered to levy tolls and dues on the bridges under its jurisdiction, and in the markets and fairs, and also to have the fee-farm on the royal taxes. In other words, instead of collecting these and handing them over in entirety to the Crown, the town could now send a set sum to the Exchequer each year and then keep all the surplus moneys. It had secured its financial and jurisdictional independence.

The commonalty were normally chosen from the freemen of the borough, the principal burgesses from among the commonalty and, as before, the mayor from among the principal burgesses. Democracy was almost entirely absent. The sole occasion at which popular choice played any part was the election of a mayor, when all adult males were entitled to vote: they did so by a 'show of hands' in the Guildhall yard. By the early 18th century such demonstrations of popular choice were a rarity, since the public was well aware that the Corporation was by then an irrelevance. At all other stages in the choice of members the Corporation was a self-perpetuating body which filled its own vacancies by nomination, so that the population had absolutely no part in the selection of its councillors.

For the first 80 years of its existence the Corporation enjoyed a calm and harmonious life and during this time it undertook its most useful work. Since it appointed its own members it could easily follow consistent policies by the careful selection of like-minded and suitable replacements. Powerful patrons often saw that their protégés were admitted, as in 1615 when Robert Shales was sworn in as a burgess following a request from Thomas Howard, Earl of Arundel and Surrey. Even the Civil War and the political turmoils of the 1650s scarcely disturbed its proceedings. The Corporation was solidly puritan and parliamentarian throughout the period, and there was no change in its membership, except as a result of death or voluntary resignation, between 1640 and 1659. This was in pronounced contrast to the experience of other boroughs, such as Norwich, where the puritan ascendancy in the late 1640s led to the wholesale ejection of Anglican Tory councillors. Many Thetford men sat on the Norfolk Committee of the Eastern Association, which had the task of raising men, money and supplies for the Parliamentary forces. They included Sir Framlingham Gawdy and Sir Thomas Wodehouse (M.P.s for the Borough in the Long Parliament 1640-53), Henry Kettle (Mayor 1640 and 1656) and Thomas Lincoln (Mayor 1638, 1641 and 1646). Thetford was an important rendezvous for militia forces heading westwards to join the armies, and was also regarded as a possible defensive site in the event of Royalist troops invading Norfolk. A letter survives from Oliver Cromwell to the Constable of the Hundred of Holt, in March 1643, ordering him to send cuirassiers to join a militia force at Thetford.[32]

In December 1651 the Corporation subscribed to the yearly payment of a salary to support 'the ministry and preaching of our well loved in Christ Charles Frank of our town & borough', a firm statement of strong puritan views since Frank was a celebrated nonconformist minister. Six years later the Corporation was enthusiastic about the scheme of the Trustees for the Maintenance of Ministers, to unite the three town parishes and Santon to form one large parish with its 'meeting place' at St Peter's church. The scheme was implemented, with the personal approval of Cromwell, and the organisation of the Anglican church in Thetford was thus destroyed, but in the 1660s the old order was restored with the national re-establishment of the Church of England.[33]

The Corporation 1660-1700

For Thetford Corporation, as for many other borough councils, the 40 years from 1660 were a time of major and continual upheaval. During most of his reign Charles II was identified with the Anglican Tories, and a series of measures was passed with the aim of destroying the power and influence of the Whig Dissenters. These included the Corporation Act of 1661, which required members of corporations to acknowledge the supremacy of the Church of England and to receive Holy Communion at least once a year. In the General Election of 1679 the anti-Government groups gained a majority, and to prevent this happening in future many borough charters were withdrawn between 1679 and 1685, to be replaced by new charters giving the King far greater influence over the political composition of the corporations, and thus over the M.P.s which they returned to parliament. James II, a Catholic, swiftly reversed these policies, by trying to forge an alliance with the Dissenters in order to crush the Anglican Tories. He used the very clauses which had been designed to exclude the Dissenters as a means of excluding their opponents, but in 1688 he went further by attempting direct 'regulation' or purging of those corporations where the Anglicans were still powerful.

Thetford Corporation experienced bitter internal disputes after 1660 as the powerful Whig Dissenter faction suffered constant attack from the Anglican Tories who, with central government support, were attempting to gain control. The municipal records for the period 1659-82 seem to have been deliberately destroyed, and it is therefore difficult to identify the detailed events of that quarter century. According to allegations made in 1681 the Corporation Act was ineffective in Thetford, because successive Dissenter mayors refused to administer the oath of supremacy, and submitted false returns to the privy council. There is also evidence of a violent disagreement between the town clerk, Thomas Cropley, and the mayor and several burgesses, in 1664. This led to the intervention of the Lord Lieutenant and the imprisonment of the mayor and six of his colleagues: it is reasonable to suppose that the quarrel related to the political and religious troubles.[34]

From 1681 evidence is more abundant. A key figure in Thetford politics between 1670 and 1700 was John Mendham, an implacable opponent of the Whigs and Dissenters: for 20 years he passed information and reports on events in Thetford to the privy council. The first to survive concerns his own election as Mayor, in October 1681. He had been chosen by his group of burgesses, but the Dissenters elected a different man, whom they swore into office, and kept the common purse. Mendham sought government help, took his case to court, and on the instructions of the privy council the decision went in his favour. In November 1681 he reported that the previous mayor, John Crymes, had deliberately evaded the provisions of the 1661 Act, and the Corporation was therefore full of Dissenter opponents of the government.[35]

The privy council sent a royal writ to the Corporation in December, ordering it to deliver the charter of 1574 into the hands of the king, an instruction which could not possibly be refused. The charter was sent to London in February 1682, and in March a replacement was granted. This reiterated most of the provisions of its predecessor, but one clause entitled the king to nominate the mayor, the recorder and the 10 principal burgesses. In consequence the king could be much more confident of the loyalty of Thetford Corporation, especially as it was stated that the 12 nominees had authority over the unnamed commonalty. The Corporation, as a self-perpetuating body, should therefore have maintained its Anglican majority in the future. Mendham was named as mayor, and wrote to a friend in January 1682 that he could 'have the major part of the body to make any act here . . . they [the Dissenter opposition] still threaten a revenge to myself and my friends but, though I be ruined, I will never yield to them'.[36]

He continued to act as informant, reporting conversations which he had overheard in the *Bell Inn*, chance remarks made by his colleagues, and the apparently treasonous views of William Harbord, M.P. for Thetford, who had spoken of armed rebellion against the king. The accession of James in 1685 produced political disruption nationally and locally. The Corporation immediately declared that the 1574 charter had been surrendered illegally, and in the spring of 1686 abolished the customary declaration of loyalty to the Church of England. The Anglican Tories, led by John Mendham, fought hard to retain their position, and the affairs of the Corporation degenerated into unseemly disorder, with both sides struggling to seize and keep control.

In April 1688, when the Dissenters had the upper hand, a loyal address was submitted to the king, assuring him that the Corporation would do its 'utmost Endeavours to chuse such members to represent us in the Insueing Parliament as shall concur with your Majestie in such your Royall purposes',[37] but in the summer the agent sent by James to test the loyalty of the Corporation recommended further purges of Anglicans. John Mendham had clung to his place as mayor in 1686 and 1687, but in 1688, just before the mayoral election, he read to the Corporation a letter which purported to be from the King, requesting that he should be re-elected for a third time. The Corporation refused, saying that it was not 'well satisfeid of the realitie thereof (out of the sence we have of our dutie as obleiged as well by the Charter as also by the auntient customes of this Burroughe) . . . notwithstanding being desirous so far as in us lie to observe the aforemenconed mandit (saveing our rights and priviledges)'.[38] The rival candidate, John Seabrooke, was then chosen. Mendham seems to have forged the royal letter in a clumsy and desperate bid to retain power: it was a naïve attempt, since James would scarcely have asked for one of his most determined opponents to be re-elected.

The mayoral election of 1688 split the Corporation irrevocably, and the result was anarchy. There are no entries in the Assembly Book between February 1689 and September 1696, apart from one meeting in January 1693. This was attended by the mayor, the mayor-elect, six members of the Corporation and seven 'cheife Inhabitants' who were unconstitutionally co-opted to make up the numbers. This group of 15 appointed solicitors to recover the 1574 charter and to secure the cancellation of its 1682 replacement. When the Corporation met next, in 1696, only six men remained from the 1686–7 Corporation. From other sources we can obtain some idea of what was happening. Both factions claimed to represent the legal Corporation and to exercise its authority, the Whig Dissenters under the 1574 charter which they said was still in force, and the Anglican Tories under that of 1682, which they held to have been legally issued. From the autumn of 1688 the two factions each functioned as a separate Corporation, with their own mayors and burgesses, with parallel elections and with each seeking to enjoy the assets of the Corporation and the fruits of office.

The Whig Dissenters, who entered the record of their proceedings in January 1693, were ultimately successful: in the autumn of that year William and Mary issued a third charter which reaffirmed and restored that of 1574, and so gave the Whig Corporation the support of law.[39] Nevertheless the rival Tories continued to claim that the 1682 charter was valid, and exercised their hollow authority until the early years of the next century. This farcical struggle, which tore apart the Corporation, mainly benefited the lawyers. The town and its people had to endure two decades of incessant political quarrels culminating in eight years of anarchic chaos. Their loss was a long-term one, for the Corporation never again felt any concern for social and economic affairs, and for the welfare or improvement of the town. From now until 1835 politics, elections and party fighting were its *raison d'être*, and corruption became the hallmark of its activities.

Parliamentary history to 1700

Although a borough of some importance, Thetford was not represented in any medieval parliament. In 1529 it was enfranchised, probably after pressure from the Duke of Norfolk, who would be in a position to influence the results. Regular representation began in 1547; thenceforth Thetford sent two members to every parliament until 1867. From the very first it was a pocket borough, like many other small constituencies, and noble patrons exercised the privilege of nominating M.P.s, in order to increase their own influence in parliament. From 1679 Thetford elections were complicated by strong party rivalries, and many polls were the subject of petitions for invalidation when the outcome did not suit one or other patron.

Before 1574 the electorate comprised the mayor and the 40 burgesses and common councilmen. After the incorporation of the Borough the electorate was even smaller, being only the 31 members of the Corporation, which made it easy for wealthy patrons to control or influence the results. In return the Corporation expected, and obtained, financial and social benefits for its members. An excellent example of the mutually respectful relationship between Corporation and patron is provided by a letter sent in August 1606 by Thomas Howard, who had just been granted the right to nominate an M.P. for a vacant seat: he expressed his 'great Satisfacon and good contentmente' for the acceptance of his request, and said that his 'care shalbe by my choice, to recommende such a person unto ye all for his worthe, sufficiencie and respecte that he in particular shall not only discharge ye generall dutie of ye place and free from all excepcon in that behalf, but also desire your owne good opinion and allowance'.[40]

Until the Civil War patronage was exercised chiefly by the Howards, and by the Gawdy family of West Harling — between 1588 and 1669 a Gawdy sat for Thetford in all but two parliaments — and elections were not contested. After the Restoration, with the development of party political warfare, there were contests and the results were frequently disputed. In 1679 and 1681 one of the two M.P.s was Sir Joseph Williamson, an entirely loyal supporter of Charles II, to whom he was a Secretary of State, but the other was Sir William Harbord, a leading Whig Dissenter: the parliamentary representation thus reflected the split which had divided the Corporation itself.

The result of the election of March 1685 was disputed. Williamson received 29 votes, Henry Heveningham 16 and William de Grey thirteen. The mayor (and returning officer) was the same Heveningham. He declared himself and de Grey elected: Williamson appealed to the House of Commons, which overturned the result and further decided that Heveningham was disqualified by his position as mayor. It also ruled formally that only the 31 members of the Corporation had the right of franchise in Thetford.

The campaign to pack the House of Commons with supporters of James II began in the spring of 1688, when agents were sent to boroughs to report on the steps needed to 'manage' the Corporations. Thetford was stated to require a purge of remaining Anglicans, 'otherwise Sir Joseph Williamson will be chosen'. The 1688 election did not take place, but that of February 1689 resulted in the return of Harbord and Francis Guybon. Williamson claimed that he had been elected, but the House of Commons ruled against him on the grounds that he purported to be the choice of the Corporation under the charter of 1682, whereas his successful opponents recognised the 'legal' charter of 1574. The existence of two rival Corporations, both demanding the right to elect M.P.s, produced total confusion. In March 1690 both held polls, and both notified the Sheriff of Norfolk of the return of two members. The Sheriff, understandably reluctant to make a personal decision upon such a complex matter, found a simple solution. He issued writs for all four M.P.s to take seats at Westminster. The House of Commons then had to determine who should sit for Thetford. As before, it decided that the 1574 charter was the valid basis for the Corporation, and recognised Harbord and Guybon as M.P.s for the Borough, rejecting the claims of Williamson and Adam Felton, who had been returned by the 'illegal' Mayor, John Tyrrell, under the 1682 charter.[41]

Disputes continued, despite the re-establishment of normal Corporation government in 1696. It became increasingly difficult to understand Thetford elections, and in this unsettled climate blatant financial corruption became general. The name of Thetford was a byword for corruption and dishonesty, a state of affairs which was to last for another 150 years.

The work of the Corporation

Politics and elections became the main business of the Corporation, but until 1660 there had been concern for the administration of the town. In this the Corporation continued the work of its predecessors prior to 1574, promulgating ordinances and bye-laws in an attempt to ensure 'good government'.

Environmental action was rudimentary, but some effort was made to apply minimum standards. In 1547 it was ordered that nobody should leave muck or compass (manure) in the vicinity of St Nicholas' churchyard, a regulation notable mainly for its lack of effect.[42] Disposal of waste was always troublesome, for, despite the extensive gardens, backlands and disused chalkpits, most people were happy to throw rubbish in streets and lanes. The offenders were from all classes. In 1564 Walter Beets, already seen infringing trading laws, was fined because 'he dothe a noye hys neybores with castyng & layeing so moche meynor and compase at hys bake syde upon our common be twene the common ryver & his ponde yerde'.[43] Householders were obliged to remove refuse from the streets in front of their houses. A bye-law of 1668 states that 'filthy muck or noysome things' were to be removed before Sunday morning each week, and carried away to 'some couvement place'.

The same bye-laws order that 'for the better keeping of the Towne free from sickness as to avoyd loathsomenes to Strangers that resort to the Burgh . . . the Streets and Channells in the streets [be] kept cleane and that no noysome thing be suffered to remaine and abide there'. The 'channels' were central gutters which carried away rainwater and liquid slops. Householders had to repair the roads adjoining their properties: 'so much of Bridgegate Street and of the streets . . . as have been heretofore paved or set with stone shall be from time to time continued and kept by the owners or farmers [tenants] of the houses into the middle of the street or channell'.[44] Fines were imposed upon those who neglected such regulations, as in 1555 when John Sheringe failed to 'well & sufficientlie make ye common drain in briggegate strete agaynst ye messuage yt was of old tyme called ye Angel'.[45]

Road maintenance could be left to householders, but bridges were solely a public responsibility. The Corporation maintained five, of which the most important was the Town Bridge — also known as the Christopher Bridge, because the *St Christopher Inn* stood beside it — which was heavily used and produced a sizeable income from tolls. It needed constant repair and periodic reconstruction. The bridge, built in 1610-1, was in a dangerous condition by 1696, when it was 'agreed upon that a convenient bridge be forthwith built next the Christopher for the passage of horse men & coaches'.[46] Nuns Bridges had been the joint responsibility of the town and the priory: an agreement of September 1538 gave the former the northern arch 'on the kinges water and ryver runninge from the Castell mille toward the Pytmell ... annexte the markett'.[47] After the Dissolution the town took over the southern arch as well, and used the rents from land in St Margaret's Field to pay for its upkeep. Melford Bridge, straddling the borough boundary, was jointly maintained by the county justices and the Corporation, but the Corporation alone had the ownership of, and toll income from, the Suffolk bridges at Brandon, Euston and Honington.

The Corporation provided communal arms for the trained band — the town militia. Armour was kept at the Guildhall: in 1578 it included three staves, 'one sheaf of arrows and an old case with three arrows', two swords, two 'hed pecs' (helmets), a pike, three suits of armour, two touchboxes, two powder flasks and two moulds for bullets.[48] Militia exercises were held on Magdalen Field, and on important occasions the mayor would review the troops. It was agreed in 1626 that the 'train of souldiers ... should be paid by the Chamberlins ... after the rate of xiid a day for their travail besides powder & munition', while in the following year the militia was given new equipment: 'the repayring & amending of the town armor byeing of new pykes powder match and shott'.[49] It is clear that in a real emergency the town militia was quite inadequate to defend Thetford. In 1553 Princess Mary was lodged at Kenninghall during the brief rebellion which attempted to put Jane Grey on the throne. Thetford seems to have been the scene of some fighting, but the town forces could not cope: the privy council noted 'a lettre resceyvede from the Mayre of Thetforde requyeringe the Queen's aide againste the rebells'. The reply was not helpful: the mayor was sold that 'the pryde of the enemye shall soon be abated' and that there was no need to fear.[50]

The preservation of the peace also involved the issuing of public proclamations. In 1568 the mayor ordered that 'for the mayntenance of artillerie & debarring of unlawfull games ... as dysing, carding, bowling, tennys, coyting & such like ... every man above thage of xvii yeres & under thage of lx yeres not being lame maymed impotent decreped or spirituall pson to have a bowe & fower shaftes & they shall use & exercise shoting'.[51] National events were also announced: on 17 December 1586 'the proclamcon agaynst the Queene of Skotts was published and read by Assignment of Evans Richard maior in Thetford mkt'.[52]

Poverty, crime and punishment

Perhaps the most important area in which the Corporation became involved was the attempts to find a remedy for the twin problems of poverty and unemployment. The Dissolution had put an end to much of the charitable work in this field, although the Anglican church and private benefactors continued to collect alms for the poor:

in 1572 for example the will of John Gooch, a former mayor of Thetford, included 12d. given to the parish of St Cuthbert, 'to the poore mennes boxe ther'.[53] Economic depressions later in the century produced growing numbers of vagrants as well as town paupers, and many people felt that the very fabric of society was under threat. Government responses culminated in the 1601 Poor Relief Act, which formed the basis of the Poor Law until 1834.

In Thetford the initial concern was with vagabonds and beggars, of which the town attracted large numbers because of its position at the junction of several main roads. The authorities on many occasions tried to prevent these people from stopping in the town, but their numbers, and the inadequacy of the parish constables, made enforcement of the regulations almost an impossibility. An ordinance of 1560 insisted that shelter should not be given to strangers, and even natives of the town could be housed only if they were maimed or elderly.[54] A further resolution, of December 1578, stated that no stranger could live in the town without the permission of the Corporation.[55] As these rules were easily evaded there were occasional house-to-house searches for illegal immigrants, the feckless and the idle. In October 1582 it was decided that 'a view & search be made for the pore for those that maye worke & not goe igdle about the town to be sette at worke & for using of unlawfull games in alehouses and endes'.[56]

The 1601 Act made some differentiation between the wilfully idle or vagrant, who were to be 'corrected', and the deserving poor. The latter — elderly, helpless or unavoidably unemployed — could receive out-relief, that is, assistance while resident at home, or could be put to useful work organised by the parish or town authorities. This was the origin of the 'workhouse' system. The correction of the wilfully idle was formally approved by the Corporation in 1621, when a beadle was appointed. Resplendent in the blue cloak which was given to him as a uniform, and carrying a staff of office, he was to arrest vagrants and beggars and send them to the Bridewell (borough gaol) to be corrected, which usually meant a savage whipping. The idle were to be given work, and the deserving poor travellers were to be 'assisted' out of the town. The beadle was appointed by the Corporation, but paid from rates levied by the overseers of the poor of the three parishes. This sharing of responsibility, whereby policy was administered by the Corporation but the costs were borne by the parishes, was awkward and reduced the effectiveness of the work.[57]

In April 1630 the Bridewell keeper, Ralphe Steggall, was told to convert part of the building into a workhouse. Between then and 1633 he had responsibility for the deserving and feckless poor, as well as for criminal offenders. The arrangement was unsatisfactory, and in March 1633 a low-cost solution was found in the conversion of the lower room of the Guildhall to form a separate workhouse. A small yard at the end of the building was walled-in, and partitions made in the room itself. The cost of the conversion was met from income due to the Corporation as trustees of the Fulmerston School and Hospital. This avoided the need for a special town rate, although the impropriety and illegality of diverting charitable funds from what was, in law, a completely separate body seem to have been completely ignored.[58]

The conversion was completed in the autumn of 1633, and the poor were set to work downstairs from the Council Chamber. In July 1635 the new Governor was offered a salary of £5 per annum if he agreed 'to have his dwelling in the workhouse, and also that he shall have delivered into his hands threescore pounds of stock with which he shall employ fifty poor families with such work as they can best make'.[59] In fact the poor had no choice in the work they did, for the spinning of coarse yarns was the only employment offered, and little attempt was made to cater for other skills. In 1649 the Governor was told that his chief task was 'to find work for all such persons as are sent to the workhouse that can spin well'.[60] Some efforts were made to provide the basic comforts for the inmates. Coal was bought in 1631 for the 'relief' of the workhouse occupants, and when the lower room of the Guildhall was being fitted out orders were placed for 'boarded beds with cover & blanket & pillow for lodging' the poor people. In addition most paupers continued to receive out-relief at home, and several benefactors bequeathed money to the town for the provision of staples for these people: cloth and shoes, corn and coal.[61]

None of these efforts to remedy the problem of poverty was effective. Illegal immigration was as serious in the 1660s as it had been in the reign of Elizabeth, and most people of Thetford did nothing to prevent it. Particular condemnation was reserved for local residents who leased rooms to poor newcomers, a practice described by the Corporation in 1668 as 'the only ruine and decay of all Townes where liberty and a negligent regard gives way to owners to stuffe their houses and tenements with people of all sorts only to the enriching of themselves . . . making their houses more like hospitalls and spittalls than habitacons for tradeing and commerce'.[62]

It was widely suspected that much crime was committed by the poor, and this again required action on the part of the Corporation. During the 16th century the rôle of local courts became more clearly defined. The 1574 charter confirmed the right of the Corporation to hold the long-established market court, and the Borough Court of Record, which was equivalent to a petty sessions. Thetford also had its own Borough Sessions, meeting two or three times a year, and alleged to have been held since medieval times, although the earliest surviving records of this Court date from 1610. The maintenance of law and order was shared between the parishes and the Corporation. In 1564 it was decided by the Court of Record, which passed civil judgments and made ordinances prior to incorporation in 1574, that the town should have four constables, two for the Bridgegate ward and two for the Bailey End ward, each serving a yearly term.[63] In the early 1630s the parishes began to elect two constables each, and this six-man volunteer police force continued, only slightly changed, until 1857. The constables dealt with vagrants and the indolent, helped to collect the parish rates, and assisted the authorities in the regulation of church attendance, market trading and other trivial civil matters. Crime was infrequent and usually minor in character.

There was a rudimentary form of night-watch, and an incident connected with this in June 1579 must have afforded the inhabitants great entertainment. The night-watch constables had been negligent, and had 'suffered straungers in the night to mysverste the inhabitants here in putinge downe ther tubbs of water yt stode at ther dors and all to bracke them'. As a punishment, the constables were put in the stocks![64] The stocks and the cage, or lock-up, were rebuilt in 1578 beside the Guildhall in Cage Lane; they may still be seen, moved to the other side of the road and incongruously set in the concrete of a car-park wall. A new pillory was provided in 1582, some of the money being raised by levying fines on 14 people who had been found guilty of 'playing allnyght at unlawefull games'.[65] In 1578 a new ducking-stool was erected: there had been one since at least 1390, when *le Cokstole* is mentioned in a deed. It was situated on the Thet, just downstream from Nuns Bridges, and in the 1770s could still be seen, although long disused. The new stool was apparently first used in December 1578, when 'Bridget Kepas the wife of Thomas Kepas & one Baker's wife were both docstolled for skouldinge'.[66]

Far more horrific punishments were also carried out in Thetford, because as an Assize town it was a place of execution. In 1555, according to some sources, three Protestant heretics, Thomas Cobbe, Roger Cue and James Abbes, were burned at the stake in the town.[67] One case of burning which is reliably documented was in March 1608: the rector of Rockland had been murdered by his wife and curate. The pair were 'sentenced to death at Thetford: the woman was first burnt to ashes at the aforesaid place; at the same time Lowe was hanged close by in the same place'.[68]

The Corporation was extremely sensitive to criticism of its members and its policies, and frequently reprimanded or fined the offenders. This had absolutely no effect, which does not occasion much surprise. A favourite pastime of Elizabethan Thetfordians was being rude to, or about, councillors. William Stephenson, one of the commonalty, was fined in October 1578 for just such an offence, and he was a councillor himself. The Recorder of the Borough, he said, 'went with a scrippe [pilgrim's purse] and a wallet to begge breade & cheese for the devill of painge what he would spende by the way'.[69] In 1599 the privy council was informed that Thomas Osborne, attorney of Thetford, had attacked the mayor, John Snelling, in the market-place, saying that he would kill him, that 'the mayor and burgesses . . . use their Recorder as the Queen uses her hangman', that he would 'make the town too hot for them', that he would blow up the Corporation and that the mayor was a goose.[70]

Such accusations were usually prompted by a grievance — Thomas Osborne had owed the Corporation a small sum and had been threatened with arrest — but the burgesses were far from being model citizens. The townsman who was punished in 1585 for claiming that among the Corporation were 'nought but that were whoremongers and bankrouts'[71] was perhaps prompted by the deplorable case of John West, a leading member of the Corporation. In December 1583 his servant, Bridget Pitcher, came to the meeting of the Corporation and confessed that on 15 November

> 'the said West having her with him in a botte to gather ling & beinge in the midst of the streme urged upon her to have his pleasuer of her & overcoming her with strength had his pleasuer of her & agayne when he came in the ling, ther he had her downe agayne & ther he had his pleasuer of her agaynste her will as she sayth and further sayth that upon the Saturday after . . . when the sayd Wests wyfe was gone to ye market bredgitt came than her mayster agayne havinge his pleasuer of her . . . and sayth further whan she mad a noyse he stopt her mouthe & . . . sayd to her that yf she weare with child should lay it to summe younge fellow'.

Unfortunately, no verdict was recorded.[72]

The school and the hospital

One of the responsibilities of the Corporation from the early 17th century was the administration of the trust which owned the Grammar School and the Hospital, or almshouses. Writers in the 18th century, and as late as the 1960s, claimed that Thetford Grammar School could trace its origins to the reign of Alfred or even earlier, one recent account suggesting that it is 'probably the oldest school in England'.[73]

Unfortunately these claims are entirely fanciful. There was certainly a monastic school in Thetford as early as the 14th century, for in 1328 Edmund de Mendham was appointed as the master of the 'grammar scholars'. The last recorded appointment to such a post is in 1496, and there is little doubt that the school, a religious institution, disappeared at the Reformation. Although it may have included some local boys among its scholars the main purpose would have been to provide training for the church and for clerical office.[74]

The true origins of the present school lie in the bequest of £160 and some property made by the will of Sir Richard Fulmerston, proved in 1566. In small recompense for the enormous profits which he had made from the acquisition of the monastic lands of Thetford, Fulmerston provided for the establishment of a free Grammar School for 30 boys, and a Hospital for four elderly and deserving poor people. Land in the Holy Trinity churchyard and the former Blackfriars church was allotted for the construction of the school, and the almshouses were to be established in a property beside the Bury St Edmunds road. To ensure a long-term income the foundation was endowed with a large estate at Croxton, itself former monastic property, from which to draw revenue.

Although part of the plan was put into effect by the executors, and a schoolhouse was built, the momentum was soon lost, and there were moves by the executors to dispose of some of the real estate included in the bequest. In 1608 the Corporation petitioned James I to allow a new body of trustees to be constituted, with an obligation to complete the work. By a private Act of Parliament in 1610 Thetford Corporation became the trustees in perpetuity of a new charitable corporate body with the full formal title 'The Masters and Fellows of the School and Hospital of Thetford, founded by King James, according to the last Will of Sir Richard Fulmerston'. Until the 1830s, when a reform was implemented, the school and hospital were administered by a trust identical with the Corporation in its membership, but legally quite distinct from it. In practice, however, that distinction was ignored. The revenues from the Croxton estate were used as though they were an integral part of the Borough income, and in later years the destination of the money tended to be far removed from education.

A perquisite of freemen of the Borough was the right to have their sons educated at the Grammar School. Patronage was exercised by the Corporation in the selection of a master, usher (under-master) and preacher for the school. In 1490 the mayor and burgesses had been given the right to appoint to the living of Santon, and it became customary from 1612 for this to be given to the master of the School. The choice of inmates for the Hospital, which became necessary whenever an occupant died, also provided an opportunity for influence and patronage to be employed. The tendency to regard the School and Hospital merely in this light, the misuse of the considerable financial resources which were available, and the growing inclination of the Corporation to abandon its social and civic responsibilities, resulted in declining standards during the 18th century. In Martin's *History of Thetford* it was said that 'the school at first flourished greatly . . . but for many years past has been in a declining condition, without any probability of recovering its former eminence'. But as a probable former pupil Martin may have had an impaired judgment![75]

'The Quenes cominge'

A pleasant interlude in the history of 16th-century Thetford was the visit of Queen Elizabeth in the summer of 1578, during her East Anglian progress. In later years James I and Charles I made several visits to the town, staying for some days at the Kings House and using it as a base for hunting trips in the Breckland area. But their presence was never as much a cause for festivity and celebration as that of Elizabeth, which was long remembered in the town and for which frantic efforts were made to ensure a worthy reception. The Corporation was informed in May that the Queen would come in late August, and it was at once ordered that 'bridgegate strete shalbe mended & that men do trym & make fayre their howses with spede & make faire the stretes afore theyre dores'.[76]

It was decided that a ceremonial reception would be held at the Guildhall. The council chamber was cleaned and redecorated, and in June the Mayor commanded that those burgesses who had 'borne office within this Corporacon should have a redde gowne and other decent apparell agaynst the Quenes Maties coming hither ... that the Corporation may be better liked of her Majestie'.[77] Money was short, and in early July the Recorder had to advance 10 pounds in gold on indefinite loan, to pay for the preparations. In June it had been decided that the regalia should be overhauled: 'the sworde of offyce be made fayre & new skaberded & the mases be made reddy & Mr Sheringe must prepare the mase lost & Mr Beets is determined to carrye the old Mase to Bury to have a new one made'.[78]

A gilt cup filled with money was to be presented to the Queen, and was duly ordered. On 16 August, however, several members expressed concern at the cost of the preparations, the regalia, and even of the gift to the Queen: 'It is demaunded howe the Cuppe appoynted to be gyven to the Quene shalbe paide for together with the mase made for that purpose'.[79] Uproar ensued, and the two most critical burgesses, Richard Evans and Thomas Alyn, were immediately stripped of office 'for disorderlie dealings & misbehavyr', and were also fined for disrespect to the Corporation. They protested vigorously, and 'Mr Evans said in the hearinge of Thomas Mobbes and others that he would pulle him out by the eares that was chosen in his rome [place]'.[80] On the previous day there had been argument over royal security: 'at this hall for the Quenes cominge yt was talked abt what would be done at her coming, for the coausdytie of the Towne'. The record of the meeting plaintively notes, 'but nothing was aggreed upon'.[81]

Arguments over money and security, and the failure to reach a quick decision, have a curiously modern flavour. But the Queen did come, and in safety, and stopped for one night at The Place, home of Sir Edward Clere. Here, on 27 August 1578, she held a short meeting of her privy council, with Lord Burleigh and the Earl of Leicester among those present.[82] The cost of the gifts and payments to the Queen and her retinue amounted to £16 2s. 0½d., several thousand pounds at present day values, creating a debt which took years to repay. But most people of Thetford would have regarded it as money well spent. The members of the Corporation, dressed in their scarlet robes and accompanied by officials bearing the full regalia of the Borough, must have experienced a triumphant pride in their town and in their own status, firmly established as leaders of Thetford government and society. To them the expense and effort were amply rewarded.

Chapter Five

THETFORD 1700-1835

Introduction

SIGNIFICANT INDUSTRIAL DEVELOPMENT did not begin to affect Thetford until the early 19th century, but even before then the decline and lethargy which afflicted the town for hundreds of years had come to an end. There was a sense of change, even of revival, from the middle of the 18th century, quickening the pace of life. For the first time since the end of the Saxon period there was sustained population growth; a slow increase initially, but one which gathered pace until between 1821 and 1831 the growth was no less than 20 per cent. The stagnation was evidently being ended quite dramatically. The later 18th and early 19th centuries saw new industries founded and flourishing, diversifying the economy and producing a new élite of merchant businessmen who bought land and property and established powerful local political dynasties. The river navigation was improved, turnpikes were constructed, the extensive heaths and commons were enclosed and sold. The moving of the market to its present site completed the migration of the commercial centre and left the old market place as a quiet backwater. Novel architectural styles and new building materials resulted in radical changes in the physical appearance of the town.

Old features of Thetford life disappeared. After 1824 there were no longer public executions to attract the crowds, and in 1833 the Lent Assizes were transferred to Norwich. The economic regulations and the trading restrictions exercised by the Corporation were abandoned, and the Corporation itself became ever more corrupt and even less effective. This sleepy market town in a remote corner of Norfolk was the birthplace in 1737 of Tom Paine, a father of the infant United States, the author of *The Rights of Man* (one of the most powerful expressions of democratic principles ever written) and an influential supporter of revolutionary France. Nothing better illustrates the way in which Thetford remained a deeply conservative town, despite these changes, than its attitude to its most famous and most illustrious son. He was vilified in his lifetime and two centuries later attempts to commemorate his local connections met with condemnation and hostility. Even today there are many who regard his links with Thetford as a source of shame rather than pride.

The Corporation

It is in no way far-fetched to suppose that one of the examples which influenced Paine in his youth was that of the Corporation of his home town. It was exclusive, indolent, venal and undemocratic, its behaviour a source of scandal and notoriety, its affairs a synonym for dishonesty even in an age well accustomed to such conduct.

Political fighting over the election of M.P.s was the only business which attracted the real interest of the Corporation, and to that end votes were bought and sold for huge sums, while public benefit and financial propriety were viewed with a profound lack of enthusiasm.[1]

The political division between Whigs and Tories continued into the 1720s. The new century began badly with the expulsion of a Tory, Walter Salter, who was alleged to have been 'creating, encourageing & promoting divisions & breeches among the Members and Suites att Law against them, by turning Informer . . . to the total Ruin & destruction of severall . . . & their families'.[2] The real offence was that he was a Tory, and when his colleagues regained control in 1702 they reinstated him and expelled a Whig, William Caudell, in retaliation. These 'tit-for-tat' manoeuvres culminated in the seizure of power by the Whigs in the spring of 1707, and the immediate unseating of no fewer than 11 Tory members, more than one-third of the Corporation. This action was overturned when the Tories obtained a writ from the Court of Queen's Bench, a device used again by them to fill six vacant seats in 1712. During the reign of Anne the Corporation proved quite unable to govern the town, and almost all its business was concerned with these interminable and labyrinthine political dealings.[3]

By 1730 in Thetford and nationally the great political and religious divide between the two parties had been considerably reduced. Locally, also, the two factions found common ground in the need to preserve their privileged status against the demands of upstarts. Party politics was less important, but violent internal differences subsequently were due to the growing rivalry between the patrons of the Borough, and the use of lavish bribery to secure the favour of Corporation members. In the 1720s the Howard influence, already greatly diminished, was replaced by that of the Duke of Grafton, of Euston Hall in Suffolk. He and his heirs assiduously cultivated the Corporation, and for many years seemed to have secured its complete subservience. But in the 1760s there appeared a rival in the shape of Lord Petre, a relation by marriage of the Howards and the heir to their Thetford estates. He was lord of the manor, the largest landowner in the borough, and the possessor of great political ambition. Between 1770 and 1815 there was vicious competition between the Fitzroy (Grafton) and Petre families, and the Corporation divided between the two patrons with entirely predictable consequences.

Both men had powerful local allies. The Mingay and Gill families supported Lord Petre, the Coles and Sternes the Duke of Grafton, while the Burrells, a rising force, were usually uncommitted. But the Duke had the invaluable support of the most powerful of all, the Bidwell family, the remarkable dynasty which dominated Thetford politics for almost 150 years. Their political fortunes were founded by Thomas Bidwell, mayor in 1728 and 1738. His father, William, was a carpenter who was also the lessee of the market and fair tolls in the town. When Thomas died in 1750 his political power passed to a grandson, Woodward Bidwell, who had greatly strengthened his own influence by a marriage with Sarah Shelford, daughter of another local 'clan'. With the assistance of his many relatives Woodward ensured that the Bidwells became the dominating family on the Corporation. He was mayor in 1756, 1762, 1765 and 1775, and four of his seven sons were also members of the Corporation. The dynasty produced its outstanding personality in Leonard Shelford Bidwell, grandson of Woodward, who exercised an ascendancy unparalleled in the history of the town. He was a brilliant politician, shrewd and wily, and quite without scruple in his use of economic power to ensure political gain, and vice versa. His cynical, sideways gaze still observes Thetford Town Council, modern successors of the Corporation, from his portrait on the wall of the Council Chamber. Nobody had more experience of such meetings than he, who served on the Corporation for almost sixty years, and was mayor no fewer than 12 times between 1809 and 1847.[4]

As a consequence of the political rivalries, disputed mayoral elections became commonplace from the late 1760s. These culminated in the violent events of the 1792 election, when the two sides were numerically equal, and the Bidwell faction resorted to desperate measures. In an attempt to prevent his attendance at the election, Alderman Baker was intimidated and received threatening letters. When he and the rest of the mayoral party arrived at the Guildhall they were set upon by a mob; Baker had his robes torn off, and was then dragged across the road and held prisoner in *The Angel*. The mayor refused to conduct the election and withdrew, taking the regalia with him. Shelford Bidwell was then quite illegally sworn in as mayor by the Duke of Grafton, who was Recorder of the Borough.

The legal mayor, Henry Thompson, then brought a court action to unseat the usurper and to seek redress for the violence and intimidation. Sensational evidence of bribery and threatening behaviour was produced. Leonard Shelford, uncle of Shelford Bidwell (and, incidentally, a clergyman) had written to Baker telling him to stay at home, and had described the Petreite candidates for the mayoralty in most unchristian terms: they were 'obnoxious . . . the one tottering upon the verge of the grave, after having survived his integrity and the proper use of his faculties, and the other the most venal of paltry sycophants, whose honour has long been pawned at Lord Petre's Banking House, to save his Crazy Carcase from a Jail'.[5]

The case was dropped — after the public had enjoyed the evidence — when the Bidwells promised to behave properly in future: but when new elections were held in December 1792, 12 special constables and 30 stavesmen guarded the council chamber 'just in case'. Such levels of violence did not recur, perhaps both sides realising that matters were getting out of hand, but verbal battles continued. In 1807, for example, the Petreite mayor, Thomas Withers Gill, refused to swear his successor into office until compelled to do so by the courts. In 1802 the election of John Faux, a Graftonite, was challenged by the inhabitants who in a poll elected instead Joseph Gill. This rare instance of the exercise of popular choice indicates the degree to which the Corporation had ceased to represent the views of the townspeople.

Its moribundity is well illustrated by an interlude of 1809. It was reported that William Bidwell had not attended a meeting since September 1802. When asked the reason his brother, Shelford (the Mayor) admitted that in 1803 William had 'Gone into parts beyond the seas' and had not returned. For almost seven years a member of Thetford Corporation, without anybody raising any objection, had been living in Philadelphia, United States![6]

Parliamentary history

The electoral malpractices of Thetford Corporation were nationally renowned by the early 18th century. In 1708 it was being said in Norwich that the going rate for a Thetford vote was 50 guineas, and one of the successful candidates for the election of that year, Robert Baylis, was alleged to have spent £3,000 to secure his return.[7] Disputed elections continued until the end of Anne's reign, but as the Duke of Grafton concentrated the power of nomination in his own hands disputes, and then contests, became less frequent. At a by-election in February 1733 the duke's son, Lord Charles Fitzroy, was returned; this was the last contest for 70 years. Thereafter all candidates were unopposed, and at 11 of the 20 elections in the years to 1806 a Fitzroy was one of those nominated.[8] Thetford was thus a classic example of a pocket borough where a powerful patron exercised undisputed control over elections by his bribery and manipulation of the Corporation.

After 1770 that control was challenged by Lord Petre, ultimately without success. By the purchase of votes and the distribution of favours he infiltrated the ranks of the burgesses, many of whom were not sorry to see the Grafton monopoly under threat. In 1791 the Petreites secured a tiny majority on the Corporation, and in 1806 the first contested election since 1733 produced what appeared to be a triumph for Lord Petre. James Mingay, a Petreite who had been mayor in 1798, 1800 and 1804, defeated a sitting Graftonite member, Thomas Creevey. But the triumph was short-lived: the Duke of Grafton appealed to the Commons, which overturned the result despite the clear margin by which Mingay had been elected. Lord Petre was unable to command as much parliamentary influence as his rival, and Mingay was unseated. Petre had lost a vital and hugely expensive contest: his defence of Mingay in the Commons had alone cost of £1,500.[9] Exhausted and financially drained, he gave up the fight. By the early 1820s his influence in Thetford elections had been replaced by that of the Baring family, the Lords Ashburton of Buckenham Hall. The Fitzroys and the Barings agreed to divide electoral spoils, and for another 40 years Thetford was a pocket borough.

Parliamentary and municipal reforms

In Thetford, as elsewhere, the corrupt Corporation was a source of annoyance, contempt and frustration, derived from the spectacle of its financial improprieties, its arrogantly undemocratic and exclusive character, and its extreme feebleness as an institution of government. A newly prosperous section of the community, led by James Fison and Henry Bailey, was prevented from taking what it regarded as its rightful place in the administration of the town. Bailey and Fison were wealthy radicals, with a strong dislike and disdain for the entrenched conservative interests. Encouraged by the national pressure for reform of municipal and parliamentary government, they made their first challenge on the old establishment during the general election of May 1831. A Fitzroy and a Baring were, as usual, nominated at a short ceremony in the Guildhall, when the proceedings were interrupted. 'Mr. James Fison, an Inhabitant paying scot and lot [i.e. rates] at this assembly claimed the right to propose the Honourable George Keppell as a candidate to represent this Borough, and seconded by Mr. H. W. Bailey, and proposed him accordingly, and votes were tendered. The Mayor decided that the Inhabitants paying Scot and Lot had not the right to propose or to elect.'[10]

Fitzroy and Baring were elected. According to the 1685 decision of the House of Commons the mayor was quite correct, but this was the last election in which the 31 members of the Corporation were the only people entitled to vote. The new Whig liberal government at once began to implement reforms, and sent commissioners to investigate every parliamentary borough. It had already been decided to extend the franchise, but it was found that even allowing for this Thetford would have only 203 electors. The Commissioners recommended the addition of Brandon to the Borough for parliamentary elections to augment what they described as 'the present very feeble constituency', but the 1832 Reform Act in fact left the boundaries unchanged and Thetford, although among the smaller boroughs, also retained both its seats. This was generally, and with every reason, thought to be the result of political pressure from the two patrons. After 1832 Thetford was the smallest constituency in the country and was perhaps the most notorious of the surviving pocket boroughs.[11]

In 1834 the Royal Commission on Municipal Corporations investigated the town. Although its report was admittedly based on a presumption that reform was both inevitable and desirable, and so was far from objective, its catalogue of the arbitrary, undemocratic and incompetent features of the Corporation and its methods was convincing. The 1835 Municipal Corporations Act abolished all the old borough authorities, whether corrupt or honest, moribund or vigorous, and except in tiny and decayed villages established a uniform system of municipal boroughs in their places. The new councils were to be elected on democratic principles — although property and wealth qualifications meant that the franchise was still limited — and strict rules were laid down for the conduct and timing of elections, to avoid the glaring irregularities of the past.[12]

On 26 December 1835 democratic elections were held in Thetford for the first time, to choose members of the new borough council, and on 31 December such life as still remained in the old corrupt body was finally extinguished. The new council, also known as the Corporation, took office on 1 January 1836. It comprised 17 members: the mayor, elected annually by and from among his colleagues; four aldermen, elected by their fellow councillors for a four-year term; and 12 councillors, elected by the enfranchised male inhabitants for a three-year term. The electorate in 1836 numbered 259 and so was more than eight times greater than before the reforms, but it still comprised only 30 per cent. of the adult male population.[13]

The Thetford Navigation

The failings of the unreformed Corporation are clearly revealed in its mismanagement of the Thetford Navigation. From the earliest involvement in the 1660s almost until the reforms of 1835, neglect, incompetence and dishonesty were the prevalent features. This is despite the fact that the Navigation was the main source of Corporation revenue, and if properly administered it could have produced a substantial annual income: even that prospect was insufficient to stir the Corporation from its lethargy.[14]

Navigation of the Little Ouse became increasingly difficult during the 16th century. Although a petition of the mid-1550s stated that Thetford was 'invyroned with a goodly freshewater ryver, the which transporteth to and from the mayne sea by vessells of xii or xvi lodes burthen',[15] there had already been disquiet about the condition of the river. The commission of 1529 was told that among the problems of the town was that the river was 'stopped, turned and apayred' to the hindrance of trade.[16]

During the 1630s the improvement of the Fenland waterways and the associated rivers became the subject of great interest, and several schemes for navigation works were prepared. In 1636 Thetford Corporation strongly opposed a plan to make the Lark navigable to Bury St Edmunds, fearing that its own bridge and toll revenues would be prejudiced by the diversion of trade.[17] After the Civil War it joined with the landowners and mercantile interests of Thetford to promote a navigation scheme for the Little Ouse, and an Act of Parliament of 1669 authorised the improvement of the river from Whitehouse, near Brandon, upstream to Thetford Mills (map 15).

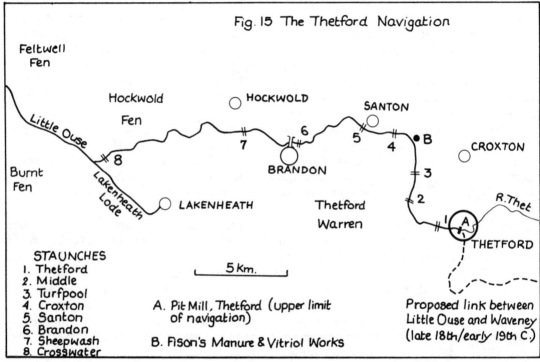

Fig. 15 The Thetford Navigation

STAUNCHES
1. Thetford
2. Middle
3. Turfpool
4. Croxton
5. Santon
6. Brandon
7. Sheepwash
8. Crosswater

5 km.

A. Pit Mill, Thetford (upper limit of navigation)

B. Fison's Manure & Vitriol Works

Proposed link between Little Ouse and Waveney (late 18th/early 19th C.)

The Corporation originally intended to carry out the work and maintain the river itself, but for reasons almost certainly connected with its developing internal warfare this plan was quickly abandoned. In 1674 it transferred all its interests in the project, including the right to charge tolls, to Henry, Earl of Arlington, who implemented the scheme in 1675-7. He dredged the river and built two new cuts to bypass narrow winding stretches between Thetford and Santon. A series of staunches — weirs with single, lifting lock-gates — was built to assist navigation. These are usually said to have been constructed in the 1740s, but there is ample evidence to the contrary. In 1729, for example, Nicholas King was authorised to build a fulling-mill 'in the Overfall of the Water near the Middle Staunch', and a house 'for a person to reside there to take care of the Locks in the said Navigation'. As payment for this planning permission he had to deliver annually 'unto the Mayor Elect at the Guildhall . . . a piece of Roast Beef or some other dish'.[18]

Arlington's daughter, Isabella, Duchess of Grafton, returned all the rights over the Navigation to the Corporation in 1696, but the latter at once leased the undertaking to a tenant. For a fixed annual rent the tenant kept all the profits and income, and the inevitable result was that successive lessees neglected upkeep of the river to reduce their costs and maximise their profits. Navigation again presented difficulties and the trade of Thetford suffered accordingly. In 1750 a second Act of Parliament was passed with the aim of revitalising the Navigation, and in a brief burst of activity the seven staunches were rebuilt, but the Corporation continued to allow tenants to take the profits and to shirk their responsibilities for maintaining the river.

In the 1760s it was noted that, considering the situation and trade of Thetford, the river carried surprisingly little traffic. Many goods were transferred to road wagons at Brandon, the limit of the toll-free section. A third Act, in 1789, authorised the charging of variable tolls instead of the flat rate of sixpence per ton charged since 1675, but the Corporation derived no benefit and continued to take £280 a year in rent regardless of the size of the profits. In 1818 the tenancy was granted to a member of the Corporation (a questionable procedure) and he not only kept the profit but also took £100 a year 'salary' from the common purse and built up large debts by borrowing from the Corporation. Net income fell to almost nothing, and all attempts to institute a proper audit were rebuffed.

Finally, in 1827, a group of councillors became so dissatisfied that they forced a thorough investigation. It was found that accounts had not been kept for years, apart from a few odd figures on scraps of paper, and the conclusion was that matters had been 'grossly mismanaged'. The tenancy was terminated, a paid superintendent was appointed, and a separate Navigation Committee established to manage the river. The Corporation borrowed £4,200 and dredged the channel, rebuilt the towpath and reconstructed five staunches. Trade, and the financial balances of the Corporation, showed immediate improvement, and the otherwise hostile 1834 Commissioners held up the recent changes in the management of the Navigation as an example of money 'judiciously and economically applied'.[19]

What is remarkable is that it had taken 150 years to discover the benefits of such efficiency. In 1834 the Navigation tolls (£955) represented no less than 86 per cent. of the income of the Corporation. Had proper administration been introduced at an earlier date Thetford Corporation would have been greatly more prosperous, and might even have been able to improve the amenities of the town. But more probably, in the light of its self-centred venality, the money would have augmented the income of its own members.

Industry, trade and commerce

Despite its inadequacies the Navigation was an important element in the gradual revival of the town after 1750. Continued dredging, widening and straightening of the Great Ouse improved the access to Thetford and reinforced its position as a trading focus for central Norfolk and Suffolk. Coal, the main import, was brought from Northumberland and Durham by coasters, and trans-shipped to river vessels at Lynn. Since overland transport of coal was extremely expensive Thetford, on a navigable river, was advantageously situated to obtain cheap fuel supplies, and also acted as a distribution centre for coal destined for the adjacent small towns and villages.

Later in the 18th century manufactured goods were brought upstream to Thetford, especially when the expansion of the canal network gave direct links to the Midlands. Timber was imported from Northern Europe, as a building material: it was scarce in the heathland areas of Breckland. The greatest export was grain, although wool, woollen goods, livestock and leather products were also sent down-river. Grain was bulky, and of relatively low value, and so it was worthwhile for local maltsters to process it in the town. Malted grain was more economical to transport and greater in value, and like many East Anglian towns Thetford developed a sizeable industry supplying local breweries and also exporting to the rest of the country and even to Germany. In the early 1790s it was reported that on some occasions – presumably during the harvest – 'upwards of 200 lasts of corn' (i.e. about 350 tons) were sent to Lynn each week, although usually the quantity was less than that.[20]

The maltings, the kilns for drying the grain, were built near the river in Thetford, and had direct access to the Navigation. In May 1725, for example, William Peirson, merchant, was given permission to 'built a Malt Kiln above the Bridge called the Christopher Bridge from the wall of the Malthouse belonging to the *Christopher* to the wall belonging to the house where he lives'.[21] By the early 19th century maltings stretched for a considerable distance up and down from the bridge, on both sides of the river. In the old market place area was a second group, served by a wharf, variously called Stone or Town Wharf, just below the Pit Mill at the farthest limit of navigation. The maltings around the Town Bridge were demolished in the 1960s to make way for the new shopping precinct and for the extensions to the *Bell Hotel*, the latter being designed in a style reminiscent of the former buildings. Two fine examples remain from the other group, one in Reymond Street and the other at the eastern end of the old market place. The last-named was owned by Bidwells Brewery, which survived until 1924 when it was taken over by Bullards and closed.

Corn-milling declined in importance, and in the early 18th century the Bishops Mill, on the Little Ouse, was converted to the manufacturing of paper. The origins of this enterprise are very obscure, and even the date of its first operation is impossible to ascertain. The earliest known reference occurs in a deed of May 1732, which describes 'the common river running from the paper mill to the Christopher Bridge' and it may be supposed that by then it was well-established.[22] Not until 1785 is there any more detailed information about the industry. In that year a visitor reported that linen and woollen rags were being used, so it is at least possible that the manufacture of paper was associated with the local wool and cloth industry. The rags were boiled and pulped, and then made into paper of various grades, both brown and white, using four vats.

The industry flourished, being listed as one of the main trades of the town in 1792. In 1806 it was said that the mill employed 'many hands' of whom over 40 lived on the Norfolk side of the town: the proposed extinguishing of the public access to the Small Bridges was held to be a serious threat to their livelihood, as it was the most convenient route to the Mill.[23] The 1845 directory reported that the mill employed 'about 50 hands in the manufacture of the finer sorts of paper'. Later owners, such as Richard Pawson and the Munn family, were among the wealthiest Thetford citizens, and were prominent in Corporation affairs. In the early 1870s, however, the mill, in common with most other small British paper-mills, was forced to close when it proved unable to compete with new large-scale production methods.[24]

In the 19th century engineering developed into the main industry of the town, but there was already a long tradition of specialised metal-working. In addition to the usual complement of smiths and toolmakers, more unusual crafts had been present. Thus in 1588 Thomas Draper, a bell-founder from Bury St Edmunds, came to live and work in Thetford. His foundry continued until 1644, when it closed on the death of Thomas' grandson, but the skilled business of brass-working survived into the 18th century. In 1737, for example, a brasier was made a freeman of the Borough.[25]

When Joseph Burrell founded his forge and workshops in the ruins of St Nicholas' church in 1770, he could make use of skills such as these. The Burrells were an old-established Thetford family, carpenters, builders and plumbers, but in Joseph and his sons they produced talented inventors with an entrepreneurial flair. At first rakes, harrows and simple agricultural tools were their main business, but in the 1790s Burrells began to manufacture new machines and implements, adapted or invented by the family. The two Josephs, father and son, patented new drilling and threshing machines which were exhibited at shows and fairs, winning prizes, medals and invaluable publicity. James Burrell established a brass- and iron-foundry, first in King Street and later in Bury Road, providing raw materials and parts for the agricultural equipment business. Already, by the 1820s, the Burrells were in charge of a thriving industry, and had — probably because they were acceptable in political and religious terms — consolidated their position as the second family of Thetford. When Joseph's grandson, Charles, took over the business in 1836, aged 19, he was able to use the strong foundation laid down in the previous 60 years as a basis for further expansion, which carried the name of Burrell all over the world.[26]

The oddity among the new industries of the town was, paradoxically, the one which flourished and prospered until, by the middle of the 20th century, its products were internationally renowned. It was an oddity because its founder, James Fison, was a late-comer to the town and never fitted into Thetford society. He settled here in 1808 after many years of trading in corn and malt on the markets of Norfolk and Suffolk. In 1809 he founded a new business which used the Navigation to export wool, corn, seeds and malt and to import cattle-cake and oil-seeds. As a by-product he began to deal in manure, and it was from this sideline that the great Fison fertiliser business evolved. Fison and his sons, Cornell and James, were perhaps the richest inhabitants of Thetford, but because of their radical non-conformism were never part of the old establishment. They were long-standing and vocal opponents of the Bidwells and their allies, and were the chief proponents of reform and municipal improvement, even in the 1880s and 1890s.[27]

Minor industries and market

There were of course many other industries and trades, since Thetford was sufficiently large to support specialised crafts. Thus Theophilus Barber, who died in 1720, was a bookbinder, using the leather industry to provide his raw materials. The fashions of the late 18th century are reflected in the presence of John Colman (died 1784) and Samuel Hudson (died 1794), who were peruke, or wig, makers.[28] A group of freemen admitted in 1737 included, as well as gardeners, blacksmiths, publicans and carpenters, an oatmeal-maker and a staymaker. The last was Joseph Paine of White Hart Street, the father of the notorious Tom.[29]

As the Corporation became increasingly the concern of the larger and more prosperous traders and 'gentlemen' it ceased to be concerned about regulating local trades and business. After 1743 no new freemen were admitted in the traditional manner and the office was used instead for honorary or political purposes. Trade regulations had largely fallen into disuse by the middle of the 18th century, and the strictly controlled economy of the town gave way to deregulated and competitive practices. Some traders made use of their new freedoms by diversification into other lines of business, now that craft organisations exerted no power. Thus in 1793 Grey Faux was listed in a directory as 'Grocer, Draper, Ironmonger, Builder, Cabinet-Maker and Upholsterer', while John Lyall combined the rôles of 'Grocer, Draper, Agent to the Royal Exchange Insurance Office, Vender of Medicines and Tallow Chandler'.[30] Directories give useful information about the range of minor industries: that of 1822 includes, among others, a gun-maker, glue-manufacturer, rope-maker and a cork-cutter,[31] while Pigot's directory of 1830 names two coach- and gig-makers, two basket-makers and a boat-builder.[32]

by the 1830s the shopping centre was developing a recognisable form, concentrated along King Street, White Hart Street and the market place. Only one retailer still traded from the old market-place. This change of location from the old commercial area to the new was inevitable. During the centuries when the Corporation controlled trading it maintained the status of Bailey End; the value of its many properties and market-stalls depended upon this. From the early 16th century, however, traders wished to move to the vicinity of the Guildhall, a far more central and convenient location. There was thus a tendency to return to the market site of the Saxon and early medieval period, and to abandon that deliberately planted in the late 12th or early 13th centuries.

During the 18th century, as the traders were freed from restrictions, they moved to the town centre, and market properties fell in value. There was rationalisation of the market areas: in 1739, for example, the butter-market was moved to the market cross in the Cornmarket, as it was no longer separately viable.[33] A petition signed by the Mayor, Corporation and principal inhabitants was sent to Lord Petre in 1782, asking for the formal relocation of the market 'for the Convenience and Benefitt of the Town in general'. An accompanying letter pointed out that the existing site had been found by long experience to be unsuitable, and that in the previous five years the annual income from stall rents had always been less than £2. In 1786, with Petre's approval, the remaining traders moved to the present site in the Guildhall yard.[34] The market cross, a hexagonal wooden building roofed with lead sheet and almost filled with stalls, was pulled down in February 1786, and in 1805 its site was incorporated in the grounds of Ford Place.[35] The old market place quickly became a quiet backwater of the town, and a desirable place to live: among its 19th-century residents were members of the Fison, Bidwell and Burrell families.

The new market place was improved by the construction in 1786–7 of a cast-iron market cross – a poor substitute for the recently-demolished medieval building – and a shambles, a timber-walled semi-circular iron building which provided a covered area for stalls and casual traders, and especially for the butchers. It stood facing King Street on the site now occupied by the *Red Lion Hotel*. When the latter was built in 1837 the shambles was moved closer to the Guildhall.[36]

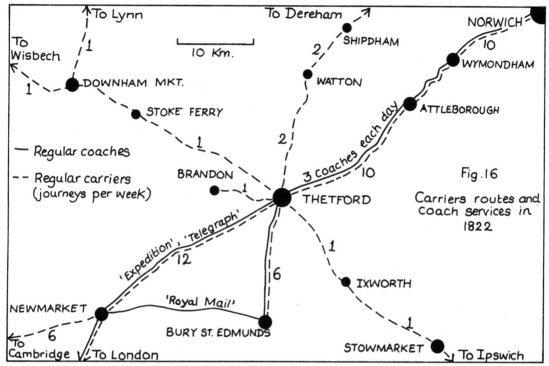

Fig. 16

Carriers routes and coach services in 1822

Associated with the market and trade functions of the town was the growth of a network of carriers' routes focusing on Thetford, where goods would be bought or sold, or transferred to and from river vessels. The 1822 directory showed daily services to Norwich, Bury and London (via both Newmarket and Cambridge), with services at least once a week to Lynn, Wisbech, Brandon, Watton, Dereham and Ipswich. There were also occasional services to more distant towns, including Peterborough and Leicester, while an unrecorded network of small private carriers served the local villages. Thetford was also a coaching town, one of the main stopping places on the trunk road from London to Norwich and also on cross-country routes such as Lynn to Ipswich (map 16).[37] In 1822 there were three coaches each day to London and Norwich, including the *Royal Mail*, which ran via Bury and stopped at *The Bell*, as it had done since January 1664. Then the Norwich postmaster had ordered that 'the Bell in Thetford . . . henceforth is to be the Common Post House for the receiving of all letters, and that William Harper there hath under taken to receive all such and Carefully to have them [delivered]'.[38]

Geographical change

The 18th and early 19th centuries saw Thetford change from a town basically medieval in character and appearance to one which more closely resembled the place which we known today. The 18th-century historian of Thetford, Thomas Martin, was unflattering in his comments upon the appearance of the town: the Suffolk side was said to resemble 'a decayed village', while on the north bank of the river the buildings were 'in general neither uniform nor elegant'.[39] Thetford appeared old-fashioned and decrepit, and to cultivated travellers on the Norwich coach was no doubt laughably quaint and depressingly down-at-heel, very much a place which had seen better days and was a faded reflection of its former glories. Antiquated and rustic buildings were untidily placed along unpaved, unlit streets of rutted mud. New styles of architecture and ordered design were absent, most buildings being constructed of chalk rubble and flint, or of lath and plaster over a timber framework, and all but a very few were thatched — even St Mary's church had a reed roof until the mid-19th century. Thetford was too remote geographically and too retarded economically to share in the new concepts of urban planning and design.

Not until the last years of the 18th century did major changes take place, even though there had been a substantial population growth for some time before then. This was accommodated by greater densities within the existing built-up area, leading to some serious overcrowding, and by infilling of vacant sites and undeveloped back-lands with small cottages, so that the overall extent of the town scarcely altered. The change was instead brought about by the 'improvement' of existing buildings. When, very belatedly, the fashion for plain, simple and formal designs reached Thetford there was still too little money for full-scale new building and redevelopment. Old buildings were newly fronted, to give a modern and fashionable appearance to a fundamentally unchanged structure.

Locally-produced greyish-yellow bricks, the 'Thetford Greys' were used, sometimes with stone quoins, and all over the town centre façades were tacked onto existing timber-framed or flint and rubble shops and houses. The solution found was thus cheaper and less disruptive. By 1850 Thetford gave an impression of a town built largely in brick and dating from the previous 75 years, a most deceptive impression. Many such refronted buildings survive today, in King Street and White Hart Street in particular. The row of shops between Lloyds Bank and the service yard opposite the Kings House shows the brick front, but where the side walls are visible it is clear that the buildings are much older, with flint and rubble construction. The former theatre, on the east side of White Hart Street (now a private house) is another fine example. Here the adjacent building has been demolished and the front can be seen in cross-section, rising well above the sloping roofline to present an impressive and exaggeratedly high façade to the street.

There are a few examples of more sophisticated Georgian architecture in Thetford. The delightful row of houses in Old Bury Road, south of the car-park entrance, has unusually attractive pillared and pedimented doorways, and displays a charming and modest use of these characteristic devices. Traditional styles were however used for the rear of the houses, and this can now easily be seen from the car-park. The most impressive apparently 18th-century house in the town is also an older shell with a later front. The medieval building on the site of the Kings House was virtually reconstructed in the reign of James I, and the King stayed there on several occasions during hunting trips. Thomas Martin drew the house in the middle of the 18th century, and although the sketch is by no means easy to interpret it seems to show a long central range with two wings, projecting at right angles across the present rear gardens.[40]

At this time the main approach was from the north, and connected with Earls Lane. In 1763 the property was bought by Thomas Wright who at once demolished the wings and constructed a new frontage, in a provincial Georgian design and built of red brick, facing King Street. The access from the north was blocked, and a new courtyard and entrance were provided to the south. The Kings House was thus greatly reduced in size, completely transformed in appearance, and reversed in orientation, to produce the building which we see today.[41]

The same period saw the reconstruction and improvement of several public buildings. In 1799-1800 the Guildhall was almost entirely rebuilt. The previous structure was largely medieval, in black flint, with substantial additions made in the 1680s. Further alterations were proposed in 1797, but preliminary work revealed that parts of the building were unsafe. As a result most was reconstructed, with the provision of a new council chamber and courthouse, and the building of the cupola and clock-tower. Only a century later, in 1901-2, it was found that the 18th-century foundations and workmanship were themselves defective, and another virtual reconstruction was required.[42] The taste for improvement also affected St Peter's church. Between 1789 and 1791 the tower was rebuilt, the interior refitted and the churchyard renovated with a new wall. On this a small plaque, opposite the *Bell Hotel*, records that the works were at the expense of James Mingay, who was born in the parish.

In the 1790s the Town Bridge was once again falling into disrepair, and despite frequent renovations threatened to become dangerous. The Corporation considered levying a rate to carry out a reconstruction, but in March 1794 appealed instead for public subscriptions. Lord Petre agreed to give a handsome sum, on condition that the Duke of Grafton would do the same; not to be outdone, Grafton accepted the challenge and between them they provided most of the money needed. A stone wharf was built along the riverbank as the first stage of the project, but although 10 guineas was paid to Mr. Byfield of London 'for his Expences and drawing a plan & design for a stone bridge' all that was eventually erected was a wooden bridge, steeply graded and only 12 feet wide.[43] Since it was on the main London to Norwich road it carried a very heavy traffic, and by the mid-1820s complaints about its poor condition were being sent to the Corporation. It was finally conceded that any wooden structure would be inadequate, and so in 1829 the present cast-iron bridge was erected. It has withstood 150 years of intensive use, and is still a pleasing feature of the Thetford riverside.[44]

All these improvements would have seemed insignificant when compared with the changes that the spa and its optimistic promoters intended. It had long been known that a chalybeate well (a spring of iron-bearing waters) bubbled up in the wet meadows between the two rivers a few hundred yards west of the Nuns Bridges. In the 1740s a long and very tedious Latin treatise extolling the virtues of the Thetford waters had been published by Matthew Manning, and local people may well have taken advantage of the medicinal properties of the spring, but not until 1818 was there any attempt to realise its commercial potential. In that year a pump-room was built over the spring, which had hitherto been simply an open-air well, and a gravelled promenade, the present Spring Walk, was laid out along the bank of the river to give an attractive approach.[45]

For a brief period people flocked to the waters, encouraged by publicity which implied that here was a universal panacea. It appeared that Thetford might yet achieve success as a fashionable spa, but the failure of the waters to produce miraculous cures, and the declining popularity of spas as sea-bathing strengthened its appeal, meant that these hopes were unfulfilled. By the 1820s and 1830s the prospect of drinking iron waters in a damp meadow in a remote corner of Norfolk was not enough to establish a flourishing resort, and in 1838 the pump-room was closed. The building, Spring House, remained as a private residence, and with the adjacent riverside walk is now the only survival from this brief period in the history of Thetford.[46]

Coinciding with the failure of the project was the demise of the short-lived theatre, opened in the early 19th century in a house in White Hart Street. An adjacent cottage was taken over and 'used and occupied by Davis Fisher as the Manager of a Company of Comedians occasionally resorting to Thetford as a dressing room for the actors there'.[47] Most business was done during the two weeks in February or March when the crowds came to attend the Lent Assizes. The removal of the Assizes to Norwich in 1833 thus deprived the theatre of its main source of revenue, and it was forced to close. Thetford then had only the visits of travelling entertainers to provide such amusements, as they had done for centuries: in 1652, for example there is a record of Richard Keele and Anne his wife, who performed 'daunceing on the ropes and other agilities of the body'.[48]

The enclosures of 1806–1810

By far the most sizeable geographical change was the enclosure of the heathlands and commons within the Borough, under the Thetford Enclosure Act of 1804.[49] As customary with parliamentary enclosure, this was promoted by the major landowners with the aim of extinguishing public rights of access or usage so that they could then be parcelled up and allocated to landowners and freeholders. The ostensible aim was the improvement of agriculture and its efficiency, but the acquisition of cheap land was a powerful, if undeclared, motive. Since so much land, within a short space of time, was changed in ownership, usage and physical character the effects of enclosure were potentially radical.

By the terms of the Act, Commissioners were appointed to carry out the work, and at their first meeting (27 June 1804) they chose Robert Chasteney as their chief surveyor. It was he who, as the designer of the new pattern of roads and boundaries, was the architect of the changes. Between June 1804 and January 1806, at nine business sessions each lasting from three to five days, Chasteney and his colleagues conducted negotiations with interested parties, drew up plans for the implementation of their proposals, and issued instructions for them to be carried out. No individual attention was given to claims for compensation or consideration by the inhabitants at large, or by the tenants of manorial land, and only the 22 freeholders whose properties were affected were given the opportunity to submit details of the rights they exercised, and for which they were to be compensated. By far the greatest beneficiaries of the enclosure were the three landowners mentioned by name in the Act, and who were its chief promoters: Sir Robert Buxton, Shelford Bidwell and Lord Petre.

Altogether the Act concerned some 5,616 acres of land, or approximately 80 per cent. of the total area of the Borough; this was composed mainly of heathland, with smaller amounts of open arable field and of common meadows. Between 1806 and 1809 most of the affected land was divided up into large regular plots enclosed by hedges and ditches, and then sold or granted to private owners. Public access was ended, and the use of the land for common grazing or farming prevented. Some small areas were set aside for special purposes. Each parish was given a small piece of land for a gravel-pit, to provide the highway surveyor with a source of road material. Some heathland was reserved for fuel 'allotments' for the poor people of the town, and was thus still accessible, while in each parish other heaths were retained for grazing and for other uses such as the gathering of furze, heather or bracken. The enclosure was therefore not complete, and some consideration was given to communal needs. As a consequence several areas of commonland, notably Barnham Cross and Melford Bridge Commons, survive as public open spaces today. The table (overleaf) shows how the affected lands were allocated, and the benefit obtained by Lord Petre is clearly seen.[50]

TO THE RIGHT WORSHIPFUL

J. B. FAUX, ESQ.

MAYOR,

AND THE INHABITANTS AT LARGE,

OF THE

City of Thetford;

AND TO THE RESIDENT PROPRIETORS

OF ITS VICINITY,

WHOSE

UNITED AND DISINTERESTED EXERTIONS IN

BRINGING THE

Mineral Spring of Thetford,

FOR ITS HEALING VIRTUES INESTIMABLE,

YET SUFFERED LONG TO REMAIN NEGLECTED AND

UNKNOWN, INTO

CELEBRITY AND USE,

AND WHOSE

CARE IN PROVIDING FOR THE

COMFORTABLE ACCOMMODATION OF THE SICK

AND INFIRM VISITORS TO THIS

Fountain of Health,

HAVE GIVEN THEM LASTING CLAIMS

TO THE

GRATITUDE OF THE PUBLIC;

THIS GUIDE

TO THE

MINERAL SPRING OF THETFORD,

IS MOST RESPECTFULLY INSCRIBED

BY

THE AUTHOR.

Title-page of Dr. Accum's *Guide to the Mineral Spring of Thetford*, 1819.

Enclosure also involved the extinguishing of a number of roads and trackways. This was not unprecedented, since in the previous century private owners had on several occasions obtained powers to prevent public access to ways adjacent to their properties. Thus in 1734 the Corporation allowed William and George Proctor to put a gate across the lane behind the market place along the river bank, provided they left 'a convenient horse way and cart way . . . which cart way is to be locked up but a key at each lock be left at the nearest house . . . for the use of such persons as shall have occasion to go that way with Carts and Carriages'. Under the 1804 Act this lane was closed completely.[51]

ALLOCATION OF ENCLOSED LANDS

	St Peter	*St Cuthbert*	*St Mary*
Gravel pits for parish .	1	1	1
Fuel allotments . . .	30	7	163
Other common land . .	7	7	108
Lord Petre	1,426	26	3,595
Other landowners. . .	107	90	47
Total	1,571	131	3,914

(All areas are to the nearest acre)

The ancient heathlands, spreading for many miles without boundaries or natural obstacles, were criss-crossed by a complex network of tracks and pathways which had developed over the centuries. In the south, for example, several main routes radiated from Town Bridge, towards Lackford and Mildenhall as well as Brandon, London and Bury. In the north, Gallows Hill was another major intersection of routeways. Upon enclosure only seven roads crossing the former heaths were selected for public use and improved, all the others being blocked off and incorporated in private grounds. In the old market place the enclosure meant the disappearance of such of the narrow lanes and alleyways as still remained, and the sale of the vestigial remnants of the open land around the central block of infilling buildings.[52]

Within five years, therefore, most of the undeveloped land in the Borough was converted from public to private ownership, the road pattern was greatly altered, and many of the traditionally-exercised rights and privileges of the townspeople were swept aside. It is thus a matter for some surprise that there was so little overt opposition, particularly since there had been some evidence of discontent over earlier private enclosures. In 1792 the issue had contributed to the mob violence which had taken place during the mayoral election. The Bidwell faction had broadcast claims that their opponents were illegally enclosing common lands and seeking to deprive the townspeople of their rights: Jonathan Lawrence, a tenant of Lord Petre, had for some years — they said — been ploughing in stubble instead of allowing gleaning and grazing.[53] Yet in the case of the parliamentary enclosure, perhaps because the Bidwells were very active supporters and beneficiaries of the Act, there was only one significant protest. Lord Petre proposed to enclose Small Bridge Common — the western end of the peninsula between the Thet and the Little Ouse — and to close the footpath across the Small Bridges. A petition objecting to the plan was signed by 167 of the leading inhabitants, both supporters and opponents of Lord Petre, and he agreed to leave the path and common untouched.[54]

It is difficult to believe that the enclosure was justifiable, on either social or economic grounds. The people of Thetford were deprived of their ancient rights with minimal compensation, and extensive areas were rendered inaccessible to the public and their grazing animals. In most of the newly-enclosed areas there was no agricultural improvement because of the extreme poverty of the soil, and so there was no compensating gain to balance the loss of popular rights and advantages. Expensive and long-term manuring and improvement might have made it possible to conduct arable farming, but such ambitious schemes were never even attempted. There was no rise in land values and no agricultural innovation, and from an economic point of view the experience was largely a waste of time and money. It damaged the interests of the poorer people while giving no great benefit to the more prosperous.

The enclosed lands — with certain exceptions closer to the urban area and in the river valleys — remained as uncultivated heath. Rabbit warrening and sheep grazing continued to be important until the later 19th century, when both became uneconomic. In the intervening period the vegetation was heavily over-grazed, and substantial tracts of the district became semi-desert, where the stripping of the grass cover had exposed bare sand to the erosive powers of the rain and, even more so, the wind. It was only with the massive afforestation programme of the inter-war period that these damaging environmental problems were overcome, and the warrens and heaths put to an economically productive use.

Poor law administration

The loss of many traditional rights came at a time when the poor were already suffering severe distress: in 1795 even the complacent and self-satisfied Thetford Corporation was moved to address a memorandum to the government asking for intervention to reduce the excessively high prices of bread and corn, and in 1816 there was an 'unruly demonstration' in the town when a mob gathered to protest about corn prices. Associated with these difficulties was the increasing inadequacy of the poor laws, which became ever more cumbersome and expensive to administer as the scale of the problem grew. In Thetford the Corporation had ceased to play any active rôle in the administration of poor laws, leaving this task to the three parish authorities. There was thus no co-ordinating body, and so muddled and wasteful arrangements were perpetuated. At no time was there a serious attempt to unite the parishes to form a single unit for poor law purposes.

Each parish appointed an overseer of the poor each year. These men collected and distributed the poor rate, which was given out in relief payments, in the provision of essential goods such as coal and shoes, or in medical bills. Much was also spent on the bureaucratic expenses of the system. Under the 1662 Settlement Act everybody had a legal place of 'settlement' derived from, among other criteria, birthplace or place of employment. If anybody having a settlement in another place was thought by the overseers to be a potential charge upon the poor rate, he could be forcibly removed to that place after approval from the local justices. It was in the financial interest of any parish to deny settlement certificates, and to obtain the maximum number of removal orders, and thus to minimise the number of resident paupers. There were three quite independent parishes in Thetford, and a great deal of time, effort and money was spent on moving paupers from one to another: approximately 35 per cent. of all surviving removal orders for the town concern such transfers, which often involved a move of only a few feet. Thus a pauper who 'belonged' to St Mary's parish might be compelled to move from a cottage on the north side of the Town Bridge to one on the south side, after the full bureaucratic procedure had been followed.[55]

Such absurdities, so wasteful of resources and so productive of human unhappiness, continued even though the three parishes joined to provide a town workhouse, and it is puzzling that the co-operation did not extend to other aspects of poor law administration. The workhouse remained in the lower room of the Guildhall until the 1760s, by which time it had become grossly inadequate. The same master ran the workhouse and the bridewell, although the two were physically separate. In October 1750, when Nathaniel Pratt was appointed to the job, his task was defined as 'setting the paupers to work' and to 'support, maintain, wash, lodge, and keep sweet and clean, all and every person and persons which shall be sent to him by the Magistrates'.[56] For this he was allowed one shilling a week for each able-bodied pauper, and 1s. 6d. for the aged, impotent [helpless] or young. The money was paid by the parishes, and they also furnished the building: an order of 1748 required them to provide 'all wheels, reels & utensils for working' and to give 13s. 4d. a year each for the purchase of beds, linen and furniture.[57]

In the mid-1760s the Corporation bought Thomas Madder's house in Magdalen Street and converted it for use as a workhouse: the use of the Guildhall basement for such an 'inferior' purpose was by then regarded as most unseemly.[58] The new workhouse was rented out to the parishes, each paying one-third of the costs. The overseers' accounts from the 1770s onwards have survived for each parish, listing in detail payments for shirts and shoes, corn and coal, lyings-in and layings-out.[59] The parishes each appointed a medical officer, who for a fee paid by the overseer would visit the poor and attend to their basic needs. Henry Best was employed by St Mary's parish for over 30 years; in 1823, when he charged 14 guineas, he listed his duties as 'any number of midwifery cases, that may appear to the Parish Officers proper objects of their Charity; together with Vaccination, Surgery, Casualties, Medicine and regular attendance in every case that may occur, in any department of the profession'.[60]

During the 1820s pressure for a thorough reform of the poor law grew rapidly, on the grounds of its complexity and cost, and also because its methods were said to encourage idleness. A greatly more efficient, rational and severe system was held to be the answer, and the 1834 Poor Law Amendment Act provided just such a remedy: it did not, of course, solve the problem of poverty or unemployment. The 1834 Act compelled the amalgamation of parishes into Poor Law Unions, run by a Board of Guardians. Each Union was to have a centrally-situated workhouse, and to emphasise the rationality which underlay the reform each was defined without reference to county boundaries. Thus Thetford became the centre of a union embracing 34 parishes, half of them in Suffolk, and which extended as far as Market Weston and Northwold. The Board of Guardians took office on 1 January, 1836, on which date the parishes lost all their poor law functions except the still-crucial task of levying and collecting the poor rate on behalf of the Thetford Union.

In 1836 the Thetford Union workhouse, a typical 1830s' institution with its severe and impressive architecture, was built on the southern edge of the town between Bury Road and the Little Ouse. It had accommodation for 300 paupers and a hospital, and during the 19th century operated a régime considerably more rigorous than that of its predecessors. In 1837 the old town workhouse was closed and sold, and the remaining inmates transferred to the Union Workhouse. This was later renamed St Barnabas Hospital, and was demolished in 1978 and its site used for housing.[61]

During the 300 years to 1835 private charity played an important although entirely haphazard rôle in supplementing public efforts for poor relief. The Corporation administered a number of charities on behalf of the townspeople, although there were persistent and frequently well-founded claims that the money was not always used for the proper purposes. Several almshouses were founded by individuals: the first was established in 1530 under the terms of the will of Edmund Heyford (died 1481), and consisted of a house in Painter Street. Better known were the Harbord Almshouses (1680) for six old men, built in Magdalen Street, and Sir Richard Fulmerston's hospital of 1610; these almshouses, opposite St Mary's church, still survive although heavily restored in the last century. Other benefactors left money, rather than accommodation, for the poor. Richard Astley, who died in 1601, left his house to the Corporation with the instruction that half the annual rent income should be used to pay a preacher for St Cuthbert's church and the other half to be given to the blind, lame and aged of St Cuthbert's parish. Sir Edwin Rich, in 1661, bequeathed £100 to be invested for the provision of coal, cloth and corn for the poor of Thetford.[62]

The most generous of all the benefactors of the town was Sir Joseph Williamson. During his long association with Thetford, as its M.P. and Borough Recorder, he contributed to numerous public causes: new regalia, books for the Grammar School, a scholarship for a Grammar School boy to go to Cambridge, the costs of the Navigation Act of 1670, and the construction of a new courtroom and Assize facilities at the Guildhall. Writing to the mayor, John Mendham, in 1681, he asked that the Corporation should remember 'to find out two poore Boys, of honest & painfull Person, to be put out Apprentices. There shall be six pounds a piece ready for them'.[63] The encouragement of apprenticeships became his greatest enthusiasm. On another occasion he gave £14 to the Corporation to invest in bonds, the money to be used for apprenticeship fees. In his will (proved 1709) he left no less than £2,000 to the Corporation, 'to buy lands for such uses as are judged expedient' which would benefit the people of Thetford.

Knowing his concern for the apprentices the Corporation bought large estates at Fornham All Saints and Great Barton in Suffolk, and rented them out to provide an annual income of £110. This money was then used to bind out Thetford boys in apprenticeships to traders and craftsmen all over the county. It still continues today, although the funds are now normally used for other purposes, and in the almost three centuries of its existence this charity has been of immense value to the town. But despite these and other charities, and the efforts of the parish authorities, there was no effective and co-ordinated action to combat the problems of poverty. Thetford, like all other towns, existed with a large section of its population in a state of permanent dependence upon poor relief and charitable doles. Once the population had started increasing in number the problem became ever more acute, with the evils of over-crowding, insanitary slum dwellings and polluted water supplies growing more apparent. In the later 19th century the result was an appalling record in the field of public health and sanitation.[64]

Crime and justice

As the Corporation abandoned its concern for the observance of bye-laws the local courts became less busy. The market court had evolved into a petty sessions during the 17th century, meeting every Monday to hear trivial cases, but it was reported in 1834 that it rarely did any business. The Thetford Court of Record, too, had almost fallen into disuse. In the early 1780s it ceased to be held although it was not formally abolished, but in 1832 the Corporation, anxious to find any useful functions with which to impress investigators into its municipal affairs, revived it. The Commissioners who came in 1834 were far from impressed, however: they noted that fewer than ten cases had been dealt with each year and that in all instances the prosecution had either dropped the suit or settled out of court.[65]

The Borough Sessions thus remained as the only regularly functioning Court in Thetford, equivalent in status to the county quarter sessions, meeting two or three times each year. The mayor was the chief magistrate, with the town clerk also sentencing in his capacity as deputy recorder, even though he was also clerk of the court. Thetford Borough Sessions could not try capital cases, but was able to transport criminals: such a sentence was passed only twice between 1800 and 1834. The Commissioners of 1834 were scathing about the procedures used by the Court, reserving particular criticism for the practice whereby the juries were chosen by the magistrates![66]

On five occasions between 1781 and 1820 Norwich Corporation petitioned to have the Lent Assizes for Norfolk removed from Thetford. Each time it was argued that Thetford was inconveniently situated, and was unable to provide satisfactory court and gaol accommodation. Thetford Corporation vehemently denounced the petitions and painted black pictures of the damage which the removal of the Assizes would do to the town. Strenuous efforts were made to improve facilities. The rebuilt Guildhall (1798-9) had a new courtroom, guardroom and accommodation for witnesses, while in January 1796 the Grand Jury and High Sheriff of Norfolk requested the Corporation to improve the gaol. This was done at once, and further enlargements were made in 1816; the ornamental plaques and inscription which are visible today were erected at that time. But the gaol was still in a shocking state when Lord Suffield visited it in the late 1820s. He described a dungeon 18 feet 6 inches long and 9 feet wide, almost without ventilation, and housing 17 people: the stench was so great that the gaoler ran away after opening the door.

In 1827 Norwich started a full-scale publicity campaign to support its case for the transfer of the Assizes, and Thetford Corporation could not compete with such superior propaganda. A parliamentary bill to effect the change was successful, and in 1833, amidst much lamenting in the town, the Lent Assizes were removed to Norwich. The last executions in Thetford had been in April 1824, when three men were hanged for sheep-stealing. Previously there had been one or two executions a year since 1795, but before that none since 1735. The gallows were situated on Gallows Hill, beside the Stoke Ferry road in a prominent position, although in earlier times there had been a place of execution on Melford Common, recalled today by the name 'Gallows Pit', and shown on Martin's map of the 1760s.[67]

Thetford had six parish constables, and in 1825 a volunteer Chief Constable — described in 1834 as 'very active and vigilant' — was appointed to supervise their activities. In normal times these seven men provided ample cover for a small and law-abiding community. Occasionally it was necessary to make emergency arrangements, as during the 1816 mob unrest when special constables were sworn, but the most serious incident of the 50 years to 1835 was the rioting at the 1792 mayoral election — and that was fomented by members of the Corporation.

Chapter Six

THETFORD 1835-1935

Introduction

THE INDUSTRIAL REVOLUTION of the 18th century had had almost no impact in Thetford, and the town waited until the 1840s before it experienced any considerable change. The railway came, and destroyed the road traffic almost at once and the river trade by the end of the century. The problems of the industrial towns — overcrowding, slum housing, insanitary and unhealthy conditions — became a growing difficulty in Thetford, and many people died before the local authorities were compelled to take remedial action. The Corporation itself was riven by party political disputes, and then sank into a more sober, perhaps complacent, tranquility. And, above all, during the middle of the 19th century Thetford became an industrial town, with the remarkable rise of Burrell's to the status of the largest traction engine manufacturers in the world.

A casual observer on the eve of the First World War might have seen in Thetford the typical English country town, with its old winding streets, its closeness to fields and meadows and heaths, and its centuries-old market, but in fact one quarter of the town was employed, directly or indirectly, in the heavy engineering industry. Thus appearances were deceptive. Just as the quaintness of the flint and chalk cottages had hidden the epidemics of typhoid and cholera, and still hid the pail-closets and privy middens which were the only sanitation in most Thetford dwellings, so the existence of an industrial community in the framework of the medieval and 18th-century town was little suspected by many. In the 1920s that community experienced the traumas of mass unemployment, when its staple industry failed and closed. Thetford became a depressed town, with a rapidly-falling population and an almost complete absence of other sources of prosperity. That was the background to the post-war expansion which has seen change in the town of a scale unparalleled in its history.

The Corporation

The early years of the new Corporation revealed a great popular enthusiasm for democracy and local politics, long suppressed by the exclusionist behaviour of the corrupt unreformed Corporation. Yet by the 1850s there had been a loss of interest and enthusiasm: apathy reigned, and the Corporation and its members were regarded with contempt. Contemporary commentators found a reason in the vigorous party politics which had dominated the proceedings of the Corporation since 1835, a period in which the old Tory Party and the newly-prominent Radicals battled for power and control, and subjected each other to savage and biting propaganda.

The election of December 1835, to choose 12 councillors for the new Corporation, proved to be a triumph for the Liberal faction in Thetford society which had hitherto been denied power. It could also be regarded as a convincing demonstration of the townspeople's support for the new reforms. Each of the 259 registered electors could cast up to 12 votes, giving a potential maximum of 3,108 votes: in the election 2,391 votes were cast, or 77 per cent. Perhaps even more symbolic of the enthusiasm of the electorate was that there were no fewer than 50 candidates for the 12 seats. After centuries of exclusion from municipal affairs the people of Thetford — or, at any rate, those who were enfranchised — were making the most of their new power. The 12 successful candidates chose four of their number to be aldermen, and in January 1836 another election was held to fill the vacancies thus created.[1]

In these elections the candidate with most votes was John Chambers, a popular non-partisan member of the old Corporation who had been mayor since September 1834. Second, with 178 votes, was the embodiment of the Thetford establishment, Leonard Shelford Bidwell: he had already been mayor eight times, would serve on four more occasions between 1836 and 1848, and was able to command a great deal of popular support by the exercise of patronage and distribution of favours; and, no doubt, because he owned more than half of the public houses in Thetford. But among the other 10 elected candidates were James Fison, Cornell Fison and Henry Bailey, the leaders of the anti-Bidwell faction which had been excluded from the old Corporation. There were sufficient of their supporters to ensure that on the new Council the Radical Party, the name by which this group quickly became known, had the largest number of seats, although not an overall majority. The monopoly of power previously exercised by the Anglican Tories had been broken, and this was emphasised by the election as mayor of the Radicals, Thomas Withers Gill (1837), Henry Bailey (1838), and James Fison (1840). They had sought power and, once available, every use was made of it.[2]

In Thetford, as in many boroughs where democracy was introduced in 1835, there followed a period of great political upheaval. The old guard, although badly bruised in the 1835 elections, was by no means defeated — there were, for example, eight members of the old Corporation on its democratic successor — and gradually recovered strength. In 1839 three of the four Radical candidates, all seeking re-election, were defeated by Tories, and in 1841 the Tories became the largest single party. The year 1843 was the most dramatic of all, with the Radicals winning all four seats, sweeping their party back into power and, taking into account gains in the previous year, obtaining an overall majority on the Corporation. Between 1843 and 1845 the Tories had fewer seats than at any other time in the history of the Corporation.

The Radicals, led by Henry Bartlett (mayor in 1844 and 1846) and Cornell Fison, made every effort to retain popularity, by making heavy reductions in the rates and, in 1846, by promising not to levy any rate. The Tories countered by accusing them of corruption and financial impropriety, and claimed that money had been illegally transferred from the Navigation Account to the General Borough Fund to permit the rate reductions. As a result, in an extraordinary reversal of fortune, the Radicals were crushingly defeated in the 1846 elections: Cornell Fison himself, having gained

245 votes in 1843, polled only two votes in 1846. In 1848 the Tories gained an overall majority and the Radicals had fewer seats than in any year since 1835.[3]

The 20 years from 1835 were marked by colourful, scurrilous and often savage political 'propaganda'. The two parties did not attempt to put forward policies in any modern sense: instead they both emphasised their own financial restraint and rectitude while highlighting the alleged recklessness or irregularities of the other party. Accompanying this was the intense personal dislike between the leaders of the two parties. Both sides used satirical poems, songs, parodies and drawings. An 1842 poem, referring to the elections, claimed that the Tories wanted

> 'To get up a FARCE for the Townsfolks to see;
> And whilst blinding their eyes with a glib and a hardgo
> They'd take what they wanted, the office and Fee'[4]

A vulgar poem of 1836 had listed all the new councillors and destroyed the character of each. The Corporation had only a small amount of revenue and it was suggested that the brewing Bidwells were rather dismayed by the limited opportunity for corruption:

> 'And Councillor B[idwell]
> Who makes the folkes p[iddle]
> With XX ale and small beer O!
> Sits still and speaks not —
> Being grieved to the bot-
> -tom that there's but a hundred a year O!'[5]

There were cynics who felt the whole of the Corporation and its party battles were undesirable. A poster printed in 1847 in the form of a mock circus handbill poked fun at the Radicals and Tories, then led by Henry Bartlett and Leonard Bidwell respectively.

TOWN HALL: BY PERMISSION

> 'Messrs. Alberti & Leonardo, will have the honor of exhibiting
> to the Public their unrivalled Collection of Train'd Animals,
> on Tuesday next, November 9th, In a Grand day performance,
> called Making a Mayor . . .'[6]

After 1847 public interest in Corporation affairs waned rapidly and the enthusiastic democracy of the previous 15 years was replaced by disdain and indifference. In 1847 a commentator claimed 'it was hoped that a contest might take place, but such is the low state which the Council is held in that respectable Inhabitants would not come forward'.[7] The results of the 1848 election were said to have been 'concocted' by the mayor, his predecessor and the town clerk 'over their Glasses in the *Bell* on the Monday evening, at a Meeting respecting the Fishing in the River'.[8] In 1851 it was alleged that 'so little interest did the Town take in the election that with the exception of the Mayor, assessors [auditors] & Town Clerk, only one vote was given'.[9] Lamenting this decline in public interest, and in the perceived quality of the Corporation, 'A Lover of the Borough' wrote in 1861 that he grieved 'to see the indifference of the *respectable* portion of the inhabitants concerning our Municipal Elections. It was formerly considered an *honour* to be a member of the Corporation, but alas! such is far from the case now'.[10]

Divisions between the two parties also became less pronounced, and by the mid-1860s the old Tory and Radical labels were falling into disuse. There were still important differences of opinion, gradually clarifying into one group which favoured modest municipal activity in such areas as sanitary improvement, and another which preferred to leave everything to the private sector or to individuals. Neither, however, advocated any extensive Corporation involvement in service provision, preferring to see intervention as a 'last resort'. Strong differences were usually over specific issues, such as the question of whether to provide Thetford with a sewerage system. Allegations of corruption and the misuse of power did not vanish entirely. When Cornell Fison conducted a lengthy and forceful argument with the Corporation over the nauseating smells emitted by the tanneries, during the 1860s and 1870s, he claimed that his case not being fairly considered because the tanneries were owned by Edward Frost, who happened to be the senior alderman of the Borough and Chairman of the Thetford Local Board of Health.[11] In general, however, the Corporation had settled down to a more harmonious and tolerant existence.

The Corporation continued to be very much a family concern until well into the present century, with the names Bidwell, Fison and Burrell most prominent. These families were the largest employers in the town, included its most prosperous and respected inhabitants, and were its greatest benefactors, so their dominance in town government was entirely to be expected. Other members of the Corporation were normally professional men, farmers and shopkeepers. The Bidwells remained influential until the Second World War. For example, Shelford Clarke Bidwell was mayor five times between 1857 and 1873. It was Lucy Emma Bidwell who, in 1921, became the first woman member of Thetford Corporation and who, in 1928, was the first woman mayor of the Borough. This was also the last occasion when a Bidwell served in that office, coincidentally exactly two centuries after Thomas Bidwell was the earliest member of the family to fill the mayoralty. Other political dynasties were equally powerful in the late 19th century. Charles Burrell (1817-1900), himself a councillor, had three sons who each served. Charles junior, elected in 1875, was mayor only two years later at the age of 30, and was a councillor or alderman continuously for 54 years until his death in 1929.

The Corporation which took office in 1836 had remarkably few duties. It ran the market and the Navigation, and was obliged to watch, or police, the Borough. Only gradually did it take other powers and rôles, and even then often reluctantly or under great pressure from central government. Street-lighting was begun in 1848, nuisance removal and sanitary inspections in 1856, refuse disposal in 1873, a public water supply was provided in 1877 and a fire brigade organised in 1880. In the early years of the 20th century a further series of functions was added: housing (1911), traffic regulation (1920s), parks and recreation (from 1904), while the Corporation was forced to consider the rudiments of town planning. In the 1920s a scheme to relieve unemployment became a very necessary task, and efforts were made to attract industry. By these gradual steps the Corporation became a local authority in the modern sense, involved in the management of the town and the regulation of its life.

Such a task had been attempted by its 16th-century predecessor, but studiously avoided during the intervening three centuries.

In 1837 the Municipal Boundary Commissioners reported to the Government that the area of the Borough should be reduced by 90 per cent., so that the boundary conformed closely to the built-up area.[12] The scheme, which caused great opposition locally, was rejected, and the Borough continued to comprise the three ancient parishes. In 1889, on the creation of Norfolk County Council, the parish of Thetford St Mary was formally transferred from Suffolk. For practical purposes it had been regarded as part of Norfolk for centuries, but not until this date was the legal change made. From 1889, too, Thetford was definitely considered as a municipal borough within the County of Norfolk: previously it had not paid the county rate, except for certain purposes such as police (from 1857), and had been in most senses quite independent.

In March 1924 the County Council made an Order uniting the three Thetford parishes for civil purposes: such a union would have been of great benefit prior to 1835, for the administration of the poor laws, but by 1924 it had little effect. Finally, in July 1931, Thetford Corporation attempted a modest expansion of the Borough boundaries. Thetford Rural District, a small and weak authority, was being dissolved by the County Council, and the Corporation requested permission to annex the parishes of Croxton, Kilverstone and Snareshill. These areas were, however, purely rural, and the County Council eventually assigned them to Wayland Rural District. The Borough boundary is therefore, in 1985, precisely the same as it has been for perhaps a thousand years.[13]

Parliamentary

During the 36 years after the 1832 Reform Act the elections in Thetford, the smallest British constituency, were probably the most scandalous. The two patrons, the Duke of Grafton and Lord Ashburton, exerted total control over the constituency, and eight of the 10 men who sat for Thetford during that period were members of one or other family. Most elections were uncontested: in 1852 it was said that 'under the present system the members may be said to elect themselves, for they certainly do not represent the sentiments of the town, but only of certain constituents with whom they are on terms of intimacy'.[14]

Of the 1865 election a local newspaper said: 'Mr. Dakin was the favourite by the show of hands & comparatively few were for Mr. Baring . . . & most of them were paid 2/6 pr. hour for Baring & [given] as much wine & Beer as they could drink'. That election was the first to be contested since the early 1820s, and the same report claimed it to be 'generally & even allowed by the triumphant party to be the most corrupt ever known in this Borough'. The *Norwich Mercury* reported that the town had become 'a bye-word for rottenness' and was in an 'abject soulless state'. It considered that the contesting of the election was a sign that 'mummified Thetford was waking from the sleep of ages'.[15]

Two members were sent to Parliament from Thetford until 1867. In that year complicated political manoeuvrings led to the abolition of one of the seats, in order to give an additional seat to Scotland. This placed Thetford in a position comparable with that of most other small boroughs, which had had only one M.P. since 1832. In common with these the Borough of Thetford was completely disfranchised, because of its tiny electorate — and no doubt because of its extreme corruptness — in a general reform passed in 1868. The Borough was merged, for parliamentary purposes, with the Western Division of Norfolk, losing the separate representation which it, or rather a small number of its inhabitants, had enjoyed since 1529.

Police, prison and fire brigade

The 1835 Act made little reference to the duties of the new municipal authorities, with the important exception of the obligation to make provision for the policing of the boroughs. At its first meeting, in January 1836, Thetford Corporation established a separate Watch Committee, and this considered several schemes before deciding in favour of the formation of a Thetford Borough Police Force. The new force was constituted in February 1836. It had six unpaid volunteer constables, but the chief constable, or superintendent, was a full-time official who also performed the duties of borough gaoler, for a salary of £50 a year.[16]

On the dissolution of the old Corporation the Borough Sessions, which had existed since the 16th century, were also abolished. No provision was made for their replacement, so by default Thetford became subject to the county sessions. An appeal for a grant of Quarter Sessions was rejected in 1836 on the grounds that Thetford was too small to warrant a separate court, but in December 1838 a second request was conceded when the Lord Chancellor agreed that Swaffham and Bury, the nearest county sessions, were too far distant. In January 1839, therefore, Thetford again became a Quarter Sessions borough, with a part-time paid Recorder.[17]

The Lord Chancellor had made improvements to the Borough Gaol a condition of the grant of Quarter Sessions, after receiving a critical report by the Inspector of Prisons. In 1839-40 three new cells were constructed, the south wall was reinforced, and a separate treadmill house was built. Accommodation for the chief constable was also provided, and the gaol served additionally as the police station. The Borough Police had little work to do, and the regular reports submitted to the Watch Committee almost suggest that the chief constable was bored! A typical report, in August 1844, stated simply that 'the town has been in an extraordinarily quiet state for the last Quarter'.[18] Nevertheless in November 1845 a second paid officer was appointed, and the governorship of the gaol was separated from the post of chief of police. Perhaps boredom was a contributory factor in the breakdown of discipline which led, in June 1846, to the dismissal of both policemen: 'the sub Police Officer made several charges against the Superintendent regarding his direlection [sic] of duties', and vice versa.[19]

In April 1840 the Corporation had opposed the creation of the Norfolk Constabulary, because it feared that the result might be the loss of its own police powers, one of its few significant functions. However the problems of maintaining a completely autonomous force of only two paid men, one of the smallest in Britain, were clearly very great. Efficiency was low and costs were high. The Watch Committee was told in October 1852 that the combined police force and gaol budget was £400 a year, whereas if the Borough paid the county rate for those services it would cost only £166. The Committee then voted in favour of amalgamation.

Opponents of the scheme saw the separate police force as a tangible demonstration of borough independence. In January 1853 they were able to reverse the earlier vote and promptly ordered new uniforms: 'a uniform coat with embroidered collar, one pair of Trowsers, one pair of Undress Trowsers, one hat, one pair of Police Boots, one pair of Ancle boots and one great coat'.[20] But the appeal of financial economy and administrative logic eventually outweighed the emotional argument of separateness. In August 1856 a formal request for union with the Norfolk Constabulary was submitted, and on 22 July 1857 the Thetford Borough Police Force ceased to exist. On the same day the county justices took over the gaol at a rent of one shilling a year. It was used as Thetford police station, and occasionally as a gaol, until its final closure in 1891.[21]

The Watch Committee also took responsibility for the fire service. As long ago as 1593 the Corporation had ordered that every burgess should have two buckets, every commoner one bucket, and every other householder a 'manikin, for the quencheinge of fyre which casuallie shall happen within the towne'.[22] But thereafter little concern was shown, although from the late 18th century a manual engine had been kept in a shed next to the Guildhall. Thatched roofs and wooden buildings meant that fires spread very rapidly: in September 1796 a house in Heathenman Street (Guildhall Street) caught fire and the ensuing blaze destroyed three other houses and five shops, killing a cow and two sheep and causing £583-worth of damage.[23]

Not until 1880 did the Corporation establish the Thetford Fire Brigade, manned by 20 volunteers and using the old manual engine as well as a new manual engine bought in 1879. It could also call in emergencies upon the private fire-engines kept at Elveden and Shadwell. The Brigade only attended 10 fires in the first 21 years of its existence, but in July 1903 the premises of A. & C. Catchpole, watchmakers, in White Hart Street were gutted in a spectacular blaze while the firemen stood helpless and watched.[24] In its subsequent report the Fire Brigade Committee urged that a steam engine should be bought to replace the ancient, decrepit and inefficient manual machines. A Merryweather steam engine was delivered in March 1905. Large crowds celebrated its arrival, with a concert, a tea, musical events and demonstrations of its power to shoot jets of water, being held in Castle Meadow. This engine stayed in use until the Second World War, although in 1930 the Corporation had to buy a small motor-tender to pull it, because it was so slow in getting to fires.[25]

Gas, water and electricity

The new Corporation took an early interest in street-lighting, on safety and security grounds. In January 1838 the Thetford Gas Company was formed, and in the following month a special meeting of the Corporation agreed that it was 'requisite to light the town with gas'.[26] Unfortunately in 1840 the Company collapsed, having achieved nothing. The Corporation was forced to reconsider the situation, but a motion that it should start its own gas operation – which it was permitted to do – was defeated in September as the cost was thought to be excessive. It was decided instead that the existing street-lighting should continue: this comprised four oil-lamps, one in the Market Place, one in King Street and two on the Town Bridge.

A new Gas Company was formed in the autumn of 1844, and quickly reached agreement with the Corporation on the supply of gas for street-lighting. As six members of the Corporation were also major shareholders in the Company that was not unexpected, but it did produce allegations of corruption.[27] In October 1845 the draft contract was put to the Corporation, and some members then objected to the levying of a lighting rate upon the whole town, since the unlit parts of the Borough would also have to pay. Almost three years of tedious argument followed and it was not until September 1848 that a contract could be signed. The rating of the whole town was found to be unavoidable: otherwise, any extension of the lighting, however small, would have required a completely new contract and rate. Thetford Gasworks had opened in the autumn of 1845. It was situated on the southern edge of the town, close to the Union Workhouse in Bury Road. The location was most inconvenient, remote from both the Navigation and the newly-opened railway line, so that the delivery of coal was always a difficult matter. In the late 1920s the Gas Company was taken over by the British Gas Light Co., and the street-lighting continued to be by gas until the Second World War.

Public water supplies were deplorably inadequate until 1877. The pollution of drinking water by raw sewage in both the river and in wells was the main cause of the serious epidemics which raged almost continuously in the town in the 1850s and 1860s. After great pressure from the Medical Department of the Privy Council, the Thetford Local Board of Health agreed, in 1870, to provide a proper supply as soon as possible.[28] It then did nothing. In April 1871 the Medical Department wrote to tell the Local Board that it had 'an imperative duty . . . to have an improved and wholesome' piped supply.[29] But not until 1874 was a contract signed, and only in July 1877 was pure piped water finally made available. It came from a 250,000-gallon covered reservoir on Gallows Hill, supplied by a steam engine which pumped water from the chalk aquifer up a 160-foot shaft.[30] The water was of exceptional purity and available in abundance, so that there was an immediate and considerable improvement in the health of the town. Polluted wells were closed, and by the mid-1880s most properties had access to a private or shared tap. It also became possible to wash the streets regularly, to water them in summer to keep down the dust, and to flush out such drains as did exist.

There was no electricity in Thetford until 1916, when Burrells began to produce power from a generator situated between Minstergate and the river. There was a sufficient surplus to provide a limited private supply to some properties in the town. In 1927 two public electricity suppliers sought to extend their areas to include Thetford. The Corporation favoured the Norwich Corporation undertaking, but after a public enquiry the government approved the application of the rival East Anglian Electricity Supply Company in July 1929. In the same year the Burrells generator ceased to operate with the closure of the works. The E.A.E.S.Co. proposed to install mains in most town-centre streets, but wanted to use overhead cables except in White Hart Street, London Road and King Street. The Corporation strongly opposed this on safety and amenity grounds, and two public enquiries and lengthy negotiations were needed before the inauguration of public electricity supplies in Thetford in the autumn of 1933.[31]

Health, sanitation and housing

Thetford Corporation had a poor record in the fields of health and sanitation, its characteristic attitude being a mixture of complacency and great frugality. It was only jolted from this by occasional scandals or the pressure of national legislation. In 1835 the town had no public water supply, no hospital, no paving in its streets, no drains, no sewers, no collection or disposal of refuse. Its muddy streets, the roaming ground of pigs, were full of household garbage, sink slops, and animal and human excrement. The main sources of drinking water were the river, into which the noxious and stinking effluent from the tanneries drained, and wells, which were frequently adjacent to leaking and unlined cesspools and privies. It is not remarkable that there was disease: it is more surprising that there was not more.

In 1832 Thetford was affected by the first of a long series of severe cholera epidemics which swept English towns at intervals during the 19th century. In the second outbreak, in the summer of 1848, the Thetford Local Board of Health was established, under the auspices of the Corporation, to take remedial action. It proved largely ineffectual, and although it was not abolished until 1872 it had little real impact upon the problem. The Corporation was extremely reluctant to take any steps which would involve the outlay of public money, and regarded official outside intervention as unwarranted interference.

It was not always able to avoid action, because certain duties were imposed by statute. Thus it was compelled in 1851 to adopt powers to regulate and license common lodging houses, of which there were two in the Borough. In 1847 a local surgeon, Henry Best, had written to protest at the nauseating state of the three church-yards in the town. These were desperately overcrowded and, according to Best, places where 'large accumulations of putrifying animal matter are calculated to be most prejudicial to the living'.[32] Seven years later, having done absolutely nothing, the Corporation was obliged to adopt the 1852 Burials Act, and to set up the Thetford Burial Board. This laid out and administered the St Margaret's Cemetery which was opened in 1855, allowing the closure for further burials of the three churchyard grounds.[33]

In February 1856 the Corporation formed a Sanitary Committee. This appointed the chief constable, John Tyler, to be the first Sanitary Inspector for Thetford, while Henry Best was asked to be medical adviser to the Corporation. But the effect of these measures was limited: a small amount of house inspection, some facilities for the removal of household waste to pits on Melford Common, and investigation of the worst cases of insanitary privies. In 1866 the Corporation reorganised the Thetford Local Board of Health. Theoretically it was a completely separate body which exercised all the sanitary and health powers of the Corporation, but in fact its creation was merely an administrative device. Its membership was automatically identical to that of the Corporation, and in official documents it is always described as 'the Corporation acting as the Local Board'. There was no serious intention to improve either the scope or the quality of public health and sanitation policies. The disgraceful inadequacies of public health in Thetford, and the failings of the Corporation, were only fully revealed in 1868. In July, Cornell Fison sent a letter to the Medical Department of the Privy Council saying that 'for the last 7 or 8 months Fevers of various kinds have been prevalent in this place. Since the hot weather Scarlet Fever has been epidemic to a fearful extent and the number of deaths among children very large ... the Authorities take no steps in the matter'. When asked for an explanation the Local Board replied that it had 'done all considered requisite for the prevention of disease, epidemic or otherwise'.[34] The Medical Department was not satisfied, and sent Henry Stevens, its Chief Medical Officer, to investigate. His report, published in October 1868, began with the damning sentence: 'I have carefully inspected every part of the Town, and I found scarcely any of the conditions necessary to the health and well-being of an urban population'. In the rest of the short report he catalogued the conditions which he did find.[35]

The town was crowded with cesspools which were unlined, so that 'the soil is saturated with sewage and excrementitious matter. I found this contaminated soil pierced in every direction by wells ... from which alone the inhabitants could obtain a supply of water ... Many of the wells I examined contained water that was filthily dirty to the eye, nauseous to the smell, or full of living things'. He described the absence of any drainage system, the open gullies of sewage, the piles of refuse and garbage 'against the poorer and some of the better dwelling houses', the house in Star Lane where nine children slept in one bed in a room 13 feet by 10 feet, the 'pestilential stench that emanates from the tan pits', the yard behind the *Rose and Crown* in which were 18 or 20 pigs and heaps of pig-manure, and in which was 'a well which must be contaminated in wet weather by soakage from such an assemblage of nastiness'.

But the most devastating part was the clear refutation of the claim by the local authority that all reasonable steps had been taken to prevent epidemic disease. Stevens simply listed the 'worst destroyers', the epidemics which had raged in Thetford in the previous ten years: measles in 1860 and 1865; diarrhoea (dysentery) in 1861, 1863, 1864 and 1867; smallpox in 1865; diphtheria in 1862; cholera in 1866 and typhoid in 1859, 1863, 1864, 1867 and 1868. There had been 14 major epidemics in 10 years, as well as a continuously high incidence of scrofula, or tuberculosis. The death rate for a decade had been at or above 30 per 1,000, which may be compared with 26 per 1,000 in the desperately poor Whitechapel district of London for the decade 1865-75. Ten recommendations were made: a public water supply, a sewerage system, a drainage system, proper refuse disposal, housing inspections, the removal of obnoxious trades, attempts to reduce overcrowding, the prohibition of pigs in residential properties, the paving of streets, and the appointment of a proper Medical Officer of Health.

The Local Board accepted the report, and very slowly began to consider the recommendations. In November 1870, after much deliberation, a survey and design for a drainage and sewerage system was commissioned. In March 1871 the submitted proposals, to cost £5,000, were rejected as being 'too elaborate and too expensive'.[36] Forty years were to pass before the idea was revived. Smallpox was prevalent in 1872, and the fifth typhoid epidemic in 10 years cost more lives in 1873. Also in 1872 the Local Board was replaced by the Thetford Urban Sanitary Authority, another pseudonym — or misnomer — for the Corporation, and in 1873 a Medical Officer of Health was appointed. He lived at Northwold. The T.U.S.A. did implement plans for a pure water supply, and nine years after Stevens' sensational report his most important recommendation was finally implemented.

The pure water supply had the desired effect, producing a steady reduction in the death rate, to 22 per 1,000 in 1878 and as low as 11.7 per 1,000 in 1888. The new Medical Officer did useful work in abolishing privy middens and introducing modern cesspools, while the frequency of street cleaning and the removal of refuse were increased. But he was too anxious to imply that no more action was needed: as early as 1876 he extravagantly claimed that 'we have every right to consider your Town a comparabal [sic] Hygeia'.[37] The Corporation became lethargic once more, and in the early 1890s the death rate began to increase rapidly. There were epidemics of smallpox and typhoid in 1891, and several dozen fatalities during an outbreak of diphtheria in 1892. Cornell Fison, a persistent critic of Corporation policies, described it as 'a sad and rude awakening'.[38] The death rate rose to 28 per 1,000 in 1892 and did not fall below 14 until 1906. In 1901 it was reported that the death rate in Thetford was worse than that in 22 of the 33 largest towns in England.[39]

The Medical Officer during this period was a great deal more critical than his predecessor. He repeatedly urged 'a thorough overhaul . . . to eliminate the old-fashioned, evil-smelling and offensive privy system', and made vigorous efforts to remedy housing defects. In November 1908 he carefully inspected every house in the Borough, and found innumerable examples of shocking sanitary defects: 731 privy vaults, 'practically none of them watertight, most of them merely holes in the ground'; 44 pail-closets still in use; 82 houses with shared privies, in several cases used by four families; and 76 houses with no back entrance, and 'hence when the privies are emptied all the contents have to be carried through the house in pails'. He concluded that 'no real or permanent improvement in the sanitation of the town can be made without a thorough system of sewerage'.[40]

The Sanitary Authority commissioned a report and plans for such a system. In February 1909 the proposals were published, involving a sewage farm a mile below Town Bridge and the sewering of the whole urban area at a cost of between £22,000 and £30,000.[41] The Corporation immediately rejected the scheme, 'the advantages to be obtained being not commensurate with the enormous cost in proportion to the resources of the town'. A public meeting convened by the Corporation some weeks later ratified that decision by 478 to 26 votes. It is hard to imagine that the case was objectively presented.[42]

In contrast housing action was more vigorous. After 1895 the worst cases were dealt with by compulsory closure, and properties in Pike Lane, Star Lane and St Mary's Row were either demolished or repaired. There was a growing need for alternative accommodation to rehouse the displaced families, as well as a general shortage of cheap, good houses for 'the working classes'. In May 1911, therefore, the Corporation bought 2.83 acres of land in Bury Road, and in 1912–14 built 50 council dwellings on the site. This allowed an accelerated programme of slum clearance, nine unfit houses being demolished in 1913.[43]

After the First World War advantage was taken of the generous government subsidies for new council housing. In 1919 a nine-acre site off London Road was bought, and 72 houses, the Newtown estate, were constructed in 1920–23. This and the Bury Road scheme were the first significant extension to the built-up area of Thetford for hundreds of years, and their construction also marked the first stage in the destruction of the archaeological evidence for the south bank Saxon town. Although no more municipal housing was built in Thetford until the late 1930s the two schemes were extremely important. Because of economic depression almost no new private houses were built between the wars: in no year more than two houses, in most none. The public sector thus accounted for no less than 85 per cent. of all house-building during the inter-war period.[44]

The Medical Officer continued to plead for the provision of a modern sewerage system, but in July 1924 even a proposal merely to appoint a committee of the Corporation to consider the issue was defeated.[45] The death rate, which was as low as eight per 1,000 in the early 1920s, crept up to 16 per 1,000 in 1929, well above the national average. Some limited slum clearance continued, and in 1930 a report listed 20 properties which required demolition or closure: there were small clearance projects in Nether Row and in Bentons Yard, St Nicholas Street. So in the mid-1930s, almost 70 years after Dr. Stevens had pointed to the urgency of the need for a sewerage system, Thetford still did not have one. Privy vaults, inadequate cesspools and surface drains were the rule. The standard of health was very much lower than it should have been. The only reason was the Corporation's refusal to incur the costs involved. It had ignored the 1908 advice of its Medical Officer: 'for my part I do not think that the cost would be prohibitive, but whatever it is I think we ought to face it'.

Education

The town remained without adequate education facilities well into the 19th century. The Grammar School provided 60 paying places for boarders and 30 free places for local boys, up to the age of 14 years; the latter were 'taught reading, writing and arithmetic; and eight of them may also be instructed in the classics'. In 1833 the Charity Commissioners enquired into the running of the school and the legal status of its trustees. They found serious irregularities, including inefficient management, great hostility between the two masters and misappropriation of certain revenues, and recommended that the Corporation should govern the school directly, but with the revenues from the endowed estates being separately administered. Thereafter the quality of the school began to improve, and the charitable funds were employed in the provision of better facilities and in increasing the number of places. The Girls Grammar School was opened in 1887, the costs of its construction being met from the charity reserves.

The education of children other than the favoured few who were chosen for Grammar School places was not organised efficiently until the late 1870s. Apart from the usual dame schools and unregulated informal establishments the first school in Thetford was the National School in Croxton Road, opened in 1825 and accommodating 140 pupils. There was also a Spinning, Knitting and Reading School for 30 poor girls, but the emphasis of its curriculum was very much upon the first two skills. The British & Foreign School Society also ran a small school during the 1840s. In 1835 the Corporation gave land in Norwich Road for the construction of a new Infants School.[46]

It was apparent by the middle of the century that these various schools were quite inadequate to cater for the number of children of school age, especially as the population was growing rapidly to 1861. The 1870 Education Act made infant schooling compulsory, but many Thetford children — perhaps seven or eight hundred — did not have school places and were educated solely at Sunday schools. The Act allowed this by entitling local authorities to provide new schools where existing provision by voluntary or charitable bodies was inadequate. In 1876, using this power, the rate-payers of Thetford agreed to the creation of the Thetford United School Board. This was a directly-elected authority covering the Borough of Thetford and the parishes of Snareshill and Kilverstone: it had no connection with the Corporation, although several of its Board members were also councillors, and the two bodies worked closely together. The Thetford School Board built new infant and junior schools on Norwich Road, to provide places for 750 children. These were opened in 1879, and in the same year the Roman Catholic Church School was opened in London Road, for 80 children: it replaced an earlier small Catholic school dating from 1829, when the first resident priest had come to the town. In 1902, as part of the national reform of education, the School Board was abolished, and Norfolk County Council took over responsibility for public education in Thetford.[47]

Geography and planning

A report published in 1837 was dismissive of Thetford as a town 'irregularly built, neither paved nor lighted', and noted that the built-up area had 'increased very little of late beyond its former limits'.[48] A comparison of Burrell's map (1807) and Browne's map (1837) shows this to be substantially true. The population had grown by more than 50 per cent. during that 30-year period, but the increase had largely been accommodated by building within the existing limits of the town, or by the subdivision of larger properties, a process noted as late as 1900 when W. G. Clarke reported that 'the old Temperance Hall has been converted into three cottages & there is one w.c. for 15 persons'.[49] New building beyond the existing urban area was confined to small terraced cottages such as those in Bury Road beyond St Mary's church; in Castle Row, where fine examples of both the older flint construction and the Victorian brick terraces can be seen; and in the neighbourhood of Abbey Green and Painter Street.

The expansion of Burrell's between 1845 and 1860, together with the continued development of maltings and other local industries, produced a continued growth in population, with a 21.5 per cent. increase in the 30 years to 1861. The high death rates, a consequence of the overcrowded and insanitary conditions prevailing in the town centre, meant that the increase was lower than might have been expected. There was a small decline in population in the 20 years after 1861, before renewed industrial activity and the improvements in sanitation and public health during the last quarter of the century brought about another large increase. The population reached 4,778 in 1911, the highest figure since the 11th century.[50]

During these years of growth there was a limited amount of building beyond the existing built-up area. Ribbon development extended fingers of housing along the Norwich, Bury and London roads. More significantly, a small new suburb began to grow northwards from the old town across the land between the present A11 and the railway station, which opened in 1845. Here, along the Croxton and Station Roads, and over some of the fields between them, was the first appreciable expansion of the town of Thetford for almost a thousand years. The development was piecemeal and fragmented, with no attempt to plan or to provide such facilities as sewers or drains, and this is reflected today in the wide variety of housing types and architectural styles. Elsewhere the building in the town centre produced rows of tiny cottages with few or no amenities, such as those in Thompsons Row off Castle Street, and in Pike Lane, which quickly became sub-standard.

After 1911 industrial stagnation was reflected in a marginal decline in population. During the 1920s, as Burrell's works were run down prior to complete closure in 1928, the population fell sharply. Almost 800 people left the town between 1921 and 1931, and there was a 12.9 per cent. decrease in population in that decade. The decline slackened pace in the early 1930s, but by 1939 the town once again had under 4,000 inhabitants, the lowest figure for over a century. As a result of the demographic and economic depression in inter-war Thetford there was minimal new building, with the exception of the Newtown council estate. The density of population in the town centre, disturbingly high in the late 19th century, fell due to out-migration and the rehousing of slum occupants in the new council houses (map 17).

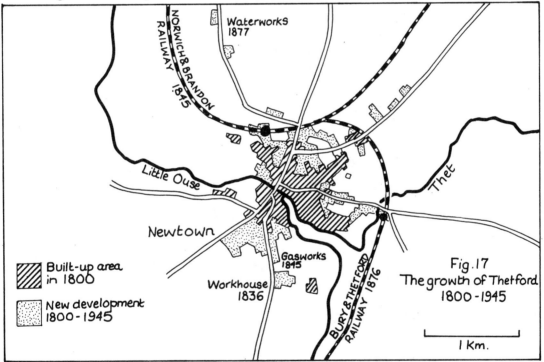

Fig. 17
The growth of Thetford
1800 - 1945

Built-up area in 1800

New development 1800 - 1945

1 Km.

Until the Second World War, with the small changes of the later 19th century and the more substantial Newtown scheme as the only exceptions, Thetford was in shape, plan and extent largely a medieval town. In appearance it was mainly 18th- and 19th-century, as a result of the superficial changes described in the previous chapter. Most of the remaining thatched and timbered buildings were re-built or re-fronted in the course of the 19th century, although by way of compensation the superb Ancient House, dating from about 1500, was discovered in 1867 hidden behind later frontages. Its discovery caused immense public interest and a growth in local awareness of the historical heritage of Thetford. The Corporation received the house as a gift from

Prince Duleep Singh in 1921, and in 1924 it was opened as a museum and art gallery for the town. In 1904 the Castle Meadows were purchased by the Corporation as a public open space, and in 1922-25 the Castle Hill and its ramparts were added to this, and given proper protection as ancient monuments.

Turnpikes, railways and the Navigation

Improvements in communications in the Thetford region began with the construction of the Navigation in the late 17th century, and continued a hundred years later with the development of a network of turnpikes — roads, usually already in existence, which were upgraded by private or semi-private trusts, and on which tolls were charged. The length of the Norwich road between Wymondham and Attleborough had been the subject of the third turnpike Act to be passed in this country (1693), but it was not until 1767 that another Act was obtained, to turnpike the Attleborough to Thetford section.[51] The Norwich & Thetford Turnpike Trust, with a number of county justices as its trustees, then managed the entire 27-mile road between the two towns. In 1768 a further Trust was created to be responsible for the road between the Christopher Bridge, Thetford, and Newmarket. By 1785 these and other trusts had improved — by surfacing, fencing, draining and marking with milestones — the whole of the London to Norwich road.[52]

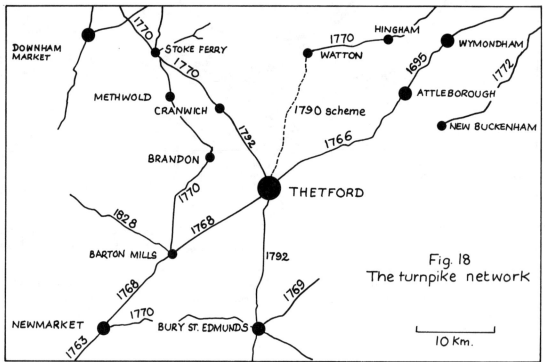

Fig. 18
The turnpike network

Branch roads were also affected. An Act of 1770 authorised the turnpiking of several roads radiating from Stoke Ferry, including the Thetford road as far south as Cranwich. In 1792 the Cranwich-Thetford–Bury St Edmunds road was put under the control of yet another trust. The unco-ordinated and fragmentary nature of the process is evident, and there was never any attempt to produce a coherent network on a regional or national basis. Most trusts operated for fixed terms with powers which had to be renewed, but in the case of the 1792 Cranwich-Thetford-Bury road the powers were never extended, and the turnpike lapsed in the early 19th century. Other local schemes were projected but did not come to fruition. Notable among these was the Thetford and Watton project of 1790-1800, for which detailed plans were prepared. Although a Bill was placed before Parliament in 1799 the opposition of Lord Walsingham of Merton, whose lands were affected, meant that the scheme was eventually abandoned (map 18).[53]

Turnpikes brought considerable benefits to towns such as Thetford, allowing the development of regular and fast passenger, mail and freight services. Coaching inns — in Thetford these were the *Bell*, the *Anchor* and the *White Hart* — flourished, and generated a good deal of trade and employment. They suffered acutely after 1845, when the opening of the railway resulted in the immediate withdrawal of almost all the coach and mail services. Of the three inns only the *Bell* retained its 'quality' status, the others being reduced to mere public houses.

The railway history of East Anglia is marked by a series of highly complicated, bitter, expensive and futile battles between rival companies in 1835-65, followed by the establishment of a virtual monopoly by the Great Eastern Railway, after it had squeezed out possible competitors.[54] In 1844 the Norwich & Brandon Railway, one of the products of the inter-company battles, was incorporated. It was to join at Norwich with the Yarmouth & Norwich Railway, opened in that year, and at Brandon with a projected line from Bishops Stortford to give access to London. At Ely there would be a connection with a proposed east-west route to Peterborough. On 30 July 1845, after a remarkably short period of construction (reflected in the deplorable standard of the track) the line, by now taken over by the Eastern Counties Railway, was opened throughout from Bishops Stortford to Norwich via Thetford, completing the first rail link from London to Norwich. In January 1846 the last road coach between the two cities was withdrawn, and the fortunes of the Turnpike Trust began the rapid decline which led to its winding up in 1870.

The original intention had been that the railway would run direct from Santon to Roudham Heath with an intermediate station at Croxton, where a branch 2½-miles long would link with Thetford, running along the valley to a terminus located, with quite remarkable philistinism on the part of the promoters, in the middle of the priory ruins. The prospect of being left at the end of a branch line caused dismay in Thetford: the loss of the priory was not the cause of much alarm. Work on the main line had already begun when the company was persuaded to alter the route so that the railway followed its present course along the valley to serve Thetford directly (map 19).

Thetford later became a minor junction. In 1865 the Bury & Thetford Railway was incorporated, closely followed by the Thetford & Watton (1866) and the Watton & Swaffham (1869). Of these three small companies only the T. & W.R. could raise sufficient funds to built its line quickly: it opened in 1869. The company then contributed to the W. & S.R. and the B. & T.R., and this enabled those lines to open, in 1875 and 1876 respectively. T. & W.R. trains worked all three lines, and in 1875 that company opened a spur at Thetford which allowed direct Bury-Thetford-Swaffham services,

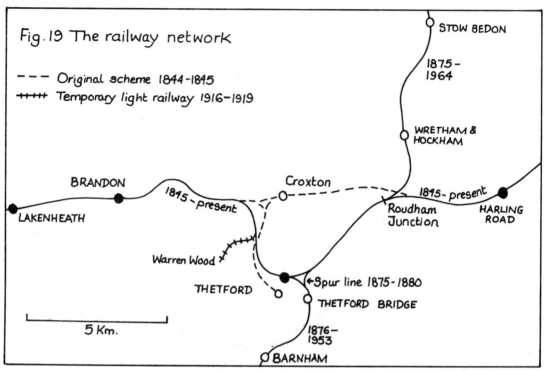

Fig. 19 The railway network

– – – Original scheme 1844-1845
++++ Temporary light railway 1916-1919

STOW BEDON

1875–1964

WRETHAM & HOCKHAM

BRANDON   Croxton
LAKENHEATH   1845-present   1845-present
                              Roudham   HARLING
                              Junction   ROAD

Warren Wood

THETFORD   ←Spur line 1875-1880
                    THETFORD BRIDGE

5 Km.

1876–1953

BARNHAM

calling at its own independent station, Thetford Bridge. An attempted amalgamation in 1878 was defeated by the Great Eastern Railway, which saw it as a major threat to its monopoly of railways in East Anglia. In 1879-80 the G.E.R. bought out the minor companies, ended through services, closed the spur and operated the Bury and Swaffham lines as separate branches.

The railway did not destroy the Navigation as quickly as it did the turnpikes. The year 1845 was the most successful in the history of the river, with the highest toll income and the largest tonnage carried. Coal traffic alone amounted to 15,000 tons in that year, although a high proportion of the remainder consisted of construction materials for the adjacent railway line. Tolls in 1845 were £1,728. The effect of the railway can be seen by the dramatic fall, to £439 in 1849. But thereafter trade stabilised, and for 30 years there was a steady traffic in coal, timber, flour and fertilizers and chemicals. In the 1880s Burrells even built small steam vessels at Thetford, and there was some pleasure traffic in the form of trips to and from Cambridge. These varied sources of business allowed the river to survive as a working navigation into the late 19th century, but there was by then a pressing need for very expensive renovation work.[55]

Thetford Corporation was now bound by law to run the Navigation as a separate business, and could not subsidise it from the rates: equally, money could not be transferred from this account to the Borough Fund, and in 1859-62 an attempt to combine the two accounts had been defeated after a protracted legal case. As a result no money could be found to pay for the renovation. Trade fell away, and was diverted to rail, and in 1904 the Navigation Account was declared to be insolvent: the business was bankrupt. This meant the end of the Navigation as a commercial waterway; the staunches fell into decay and in 1929 navigation rights were formally extinguished. Parts of the river are still usable by very small craft, and restoration to Thetford for leisure use might yet be possible, and would certainly be desirable, even though expensive and time-consuming.

Industry and employment

Despite the existing diversity of trade and the wide range of small industries the economy of Thetford in the century after 1835 showed an increasing dependence upon one basic industry. The collapse of this industry in the 1920s produced extreme economic hardship and social distress, providing a textbook example of the dangers inherent in over-reliance upon a single trade. The industry was of course Burrell's agricultural engineering works, which was already well established by the 1830s.

Under Charles Burrell (1817-1900) the Company embarked upon a large-scale expansion, which involved the almost total reconstruction of its St Nicholas works in 1846-7. Its success was based upon the early and effective adaptation of industrial steam engines for a wide variety of agricultural uses, and in particular the development of locomotives which could also be used as stationary engines to drive ploughing, threshing, baling and drilling machines. In 1848 a simple lightweight (a relative term!) engine was produced and from this developed the earliest traction engines: Burrell's co-operated with the engineer James Boydell to design the so-called 'elephants foot engine' of 1856, depicted on a wall plaque at the St Nicholas works. Engines such as these could pull enormous loads, but were expensive to operate and unfortunately ruined the road surfaces. By 1875 more refined versions had been devised, and the traction engine in its modern form was in production: Burrell's were the largest manufacturers of traction engines in the world. Later in the century they diversified into the production of sawmill engines, marine engines, trams and small steamboats, and after 1890 made a speciality of fairground engines and steam roundabouts, of which they produced far more than any other firm.

Burrell's soon became the largest employer in Thetford. By 1879 they had 220 men working in the assembly shops as well as clerks, apprentices and those working in the associated foundries. The St Nicholas works continued to expand during the century, eventually occupying the entire area between St Nicholas Street and the Little Ouse river. The magnificent red-brick buildings, now listed as being of architectural and historical importance, survive although they have been vacant for many years, and it is hoped that alternative and appropriate uses may be found for them.

During the First World War the Company also produced shells and gun-mountings, and enjoyed a last period of prosperity, but despite ambitious development plans in 1919-20 it became clear that the steam engine had no future. In 1920 Burrell's amalgamated with several other firms in an attempt to rationalise production, but during the next few years the workforce was gradually reduced, and in 1928 the Thetford works was closed.[56] The loss of so many jobs, almost one-quarter of the male work-force in the town, was a grievous blow to the economy of Thetford. In 1927 the Medical Officer of Health had expressed concern at the 'severe unemployment . . . which is due to the continued depression in the main industry', and this was made much worse by the complete shutdown in the following year. His 1930 report said that 'a good number of families have left the town as the breadwinner found work in other places and the young people also go away in search of employment, there being now no industry in which they may serve an apprenticeship'.[57]

The town had come to rely on Burrell's; in 1865 its diverse economy had been described as including brewing, tanning and leather, brickmaking, lime-burning, paper-making, flour milling, malting, bone-crushing, manure and chemicals, coach-building and rope-making, as well as heavy engineering. In the later 19th century, however, many of these trades had disappeared, and Burrell's achieved pre-eminence. The growth of a successful heavy engineering industry in Thetford was due to the chance circumstance whereby a family with a talent for invention and salesmanship was living in the town. There were no other 'natural' advantages, since Thetford was remote from sources of raw materials — iron, steel and coal — needed to sustain the industry, had rather poor communications and was distant from the major industrial regions of England. No other heavy industries developed and, once Burrell's failed to adapt to the changing market and did not diversify into other types of engineering, the fate of the business and of the Thetford economy was sealed.

None of the other industries — several very successful in their own fields — could compensate for the loss of Burrell's. Fisons had expanded very rapidly after 1846, when the firm had adopted newly-invented processes for the manufacture of chemical manures, using as raw materials: crushed bones, chalk and coprolite (phosphate-rich concretions found in chalk). Chemical fertilizers, with which the name of the firm became synonymous, were its main product, with vitriol (sulphuric acid) and other chemicals as by-products. The Fisons chemical works was at Two Mile Bottom, below the town between the river and the railway. Materials and the output of the factory were carried by water until the 1890s, this being one of the main sources of business for the Navigation.[58]

In 1879 the Thetford Moulded Products Co. took over the disused paper-mill and fitted it out with second-hand machinery bought from the charmingly-named Sultana Hat Company. The firm carried on a patent process whereby jute bags and sacking were pulped and then the resultant sludge was moulded and baked to make a papier-mâché-like substance. The moulded material was extremely hard and tough, but very light, and could be painted, embossed or enamelled. A very wide range of items could thus be manufactured, ranging from bowls, vases, trays and jugs to safety equipment and helmets for the mining industry. During the two World Wars the Company produced fuel tanks for aircraft, fire-fighting equipment, components for tanks and ships, as well as portable baths and household wares for temporary accommodation. The works was also used for the pulping of top secret documents! During the mid-1950s the supply of jute became increasingly expensive and unreliable, and with commendable enterprise the Company converted to the production of moulded plastic goods, many of them identical to the articles formerly produced. The pulp-mill, as it has invariably been known for over a century, still flourishes, and so the site has been in almost continuous industrial use for a thousand years.[59]

Other industries, of a more traditional character, underwent change during the 19th century, and some disappeared. The brewing and malting trade prospered until the First World War, and new maltings were being built as late as the 1860s. Most of the business was still conducted by water, but several maltings were constructed south of the railway between 1845 and 1870, served by sidings. Shunting operations associated with these regularly blocked the main Stoke Ferry road, which crossed the railway by a level-crossing immediately west of the station, and after prolonged disputes between the Corporation and the Great Eastern Railway an under-bridge was eventually constructed to eliminate the problem.[60] The tannery also survived until after the First World War, and was for many years the only active one left in Norfolk. Edward Frost, who bought the business in 1837, 'made a fortune out of fellmongering', treating sheepskins and rabbit skins which he obtained locally, and growing his own oak bark in groves at Merton, Sapiston and Culford. The tanneries, in the very centre of the town, were a notorious source of pollution, with noxious effluent being released into the river and the constant stench of rotting skins pervading the air. The tan-pits were located on the flat land between the river and Tanner Street, where the car-park has now been built.[61]

Forestry developed after the Great War, although exploitation of local timber to provide pit-props had started during the war itself, when a temporary railway ran from the main line at Two Mile Bottom into the Warren Woods.[62] After the war, the Forestry Commission bought up huge tracts of uncultivated heathlands and warrens, and most of the sheepwalks in the area, and by the late 1950s had created a forest of 80 square miles, the largest in England. The employment offered by Thetford Forest was limited in relation to the area involved, and did not reach its potential until commercial exploitation began in the 1940s.[63]

In 1921 the Corporation started to allocate funds for small public works projects, to provide jobs for the unemployed. During that year, for example, unemployment relief projects included removing debris from the river, laying kerbs and pavements, renovating the Nuns Bridges bathing-place and tidying up Castle Meadow. Although intended as a short-term measure these and similar projects were continued until the late 1930s, as the unemployment position deteriorated and the town became a severely depressed area. From time to time there were attempts to attract new industries to Thetford.[64] In September 1924, for example, Messrs. R. W. Myhill & Co. of Leicester were offered the use of the disused Bidwells Brewery in Old Market Street as a hosiery factory,[65] and in 1929 the Town Clerk wrote to the Ministry of Agriculture & Fisheries to point out that Thetford was a very suitable location for a sugar-beet factory.[66] There was great optimism in 1932 when a small canning factory for fruit and vegetables opened in the derelict Minstergate works of Charles Burrell & Co., but it had to be conceded that the plant only employed 'a few hands in the season'.[67]

All these attempts were, at best, but minor improvements in an acute and worsening economic decline. The town was so seriously depressed as a result of the closure of Burrell's that drastic action was needed to overcome the loss of the staple industry, the problems posed by the outdated infrastructure — poor roads, no sewerage — and the disadvantages of a remote location. Not until the 1950s was such a remedy found: and this, in its turn brought another set of difficulties.

Chapter Seven

THETFORD IN THE PAST FIFTY YEARS

MANY PEOPLE in the 1930s saw Thetford as a town without a future, a community which was slowly dying. Its 19th-century development as an industrial centre had come to a sudden and traumatic end, unemployment was at a very high level, trade and economy were in deep depression, and all efforts to find solutions to these problems had been to no avail. The population, which had increased with few interruptions in the 150 years to 1920, was in sharp decline, and the physical growth of the town had ceased. It appeared as if the long stagnation of the medieval and early modern period was to be repeated, since the chances of reversing these trends were negligible in a small, isolated town with outdated amenities and no obvious geographical advantages.

Yet 50 years later Thetford had been totally transformed. In 1985 it was more than four times larger, in both size and population, than in 1935. Its economy had been radically altered, its physical appearance was almost unrecognisable from the town of the 1930s. It had recovered its economic dynamism with conspicuous success, and only the general national depression of the 1980s has tarnished that achievement. These changes, by far the most rapid, dramatic and far-reaching the town has ever known, were a direct result of deliberate decisions and policies of Thetford Borough Council. For the first time in its history the Corporation took the lead in promoting and implementing radical and — at least by the standards of the time — progressive policies. Whether these policies were truly justified or desirable, whether their implementation was properly accomplished, and whether and by which criteria they may be judged successes or failures, are questions which although important cannot be answered in this book.

Prelude to expansion

The recovery in the national economy brought about by the preparations for the Second World War had some effect in Thetford. Unemployment in 1937–9 was markedly lower than in the early 1930s because, although no new industries had been established, jobs had been created by 'the erection of Aerodromes and other public works in the neighbourhood'.[1] In 1939 the population had fallen to 3,987, but as this was only a minimal reduction upon the 1938 figure there was reason to suppose that the period of severe decline had at last come to an end. Nevertheless, grave doubts about the long-term future remained. Much of the employment which did exist was seasonal or unreliable: forestry, sugar-beet cultivation and sugar-refining, as well as temporary public works for which labourers were needed. Furthermore, many of these jobs were not in Thetford itself, and the town attracted very little new employment. Workers regularly travelled long distances into the rural areas to reach agricultural or public works projects. In the town no new heavy industry came to take the place of Burrell's, and unemployment among skilled men continued to be disturbingly high.

The Corporation was now belatedly aware of the need to improve the facilities and amenities of the town, as a means of attracting new industry, but it was faced with acute difficulties in raising revenue for such projects. In 1938 the rateable value of Thetford was only £16,196, and a penny rate amounted to just £62 8s. 8d. These figures represented a reduction of over 10 per cent. since 1927, since the closure of Burrell's in 1928 had greatly reduced the rateable value of the town.[2] Small, and indeed declining, income meant that the Corporation could not easily contemplate any significant public works schemes, unless it was prepared to borrow extensively or to overburden the ratepayers. Yet until such works were undertaken industry was unlikely to be tempted to the town, and the rate income would remain low.

The problem of sanitation (or the lack of it) continued to be a serious disadvantage for the town. The death rate was still appreciably worse than the national average, reaching 12.6/1,000 in 1939, 14.0/1,000 in 1940 and 14.5/1,000 in 1945. The town was still completely without any form of modern sanitation, with no sewerage system and only a partial network of surface drains. In 1938 the Medical Officer of Health recorded that of the 1,271 houses in Thetford only 23 per cent. had a flush toilet, and that every one of these drained into a cesspool or the river. Another 45 per cent. had pail-closets, more or less regularly emptied by hand, and no less than 32 per cent., or 414 homes, still had privy middens which were in normal circumstances undrained and unempted, relying simply on absorption into the earth. Minor remedial action could be taken, but the lack of sewers meant that real progress was quite impossible.[3]

The disposal of household refuse was equally troublesome. The Corporation could not afford to build a modern incinerator, or to pay for the use of facilities operated by other local authorities, and so dumping in open pits remained the only means of disposal. In 1937 it was agreed that the use of the Melford Common pits, a dumping ground for centuries, should be terminated because of the proximity of housing, and the old Mundford Road gravel pits were taken over instead. In the following year a motor dust-cart and a night-soil cart were bought to replace the inefficient horse-drawn vehicles in use hitherto. But even after the war it was noted that the scavenging service was understaffed and less than satisfactory.[4]

The outbreak of war put an end to immediate hopes for sanitary improvements, but in 1943 the Corporation, as part of its planning for peacetime, accepted in principle the construction of a full sewerage network. A formal application was made to the Ministry of Health in 1946, in which year the Medical Officer for the Borough condemned the 'sanitary state of the town (which) remains in its extremely antiquated and precarious position'.[5] The Ministry Inspector, in his report on the public enquiry into the proposals, 'averred that he had never heard of a case of greater necessity'. The sewerage scheme was undertaken by the Corporation in 1949–52, a sewage farm being built on the north bank of the Little Ouse some distance below the priory ruins. It proved possible, within five years, to connect all the properties in the urban part of the Borough, and finally to put an end to the disgraceful conditions which had prevailed for so long. Thus, a mere 80 years after he had written his devastating report, Thetford Borough Council at last implemented the most urgent and important of Dr. Stevens' recommendations.

Housing activity was also limited until after the Second World War. Only 36 new dwellings were built between 1925 and 1939, and of these 22 were in a council scheme at Newtown, an extension of the original estate, developed in 1938-9. This was the third housing project undertaken by the Corporation and brought the total number of council houses to 144, or 11 per cent. of the housing stock.[6] There was some small-scale slum clearance in the town centre, but most of the new houses were intended to relieve overcrowding, there being 18 families listed as needing rehousing on that criterion in 1938. After the war the Medical Officer of Health referred to the numerous houses in poor condition, 'mainly in Pike Lane, Castle Row, St Mary's Row, Abbey Green, Painter Street and St Nicholas St.', but except in a few instances these could not be categorised as slums. The Council built 40 more houses on the St Mary's Estate, in 1946-8, to reduce the long waiting list, which had been greatly increased by the addition of newly-married couples.[7]

As a background to all this the economy of the town remained troubled and depressed. The pre-war industries were, with the exception of the moulded products factory, either small in scale or of doubtful viability: motor-engineering, malting, chemical manure manufacture, fruit-canning, forestry products and the preparation of instant coffee at the former Pitt Mill. During the war an R.A.O.C. repair centre had been established, taking mainly female labour, and this, together with other war work and of course conscription, had largely removed the unemployment problem. But in the autumn of 1946 the R.A.O.C. centre was closed, and the servicemen had returned home; unemployment once again became severe, and it was apparent that little real progress had been made since the mid-1930s. As the influx of war-workers, evacuees and military personnel during the war had resulted in a significant increase (1939, 3,987 people; 1946, 4,344 people) the problem was perhaps even greater. Now, however, the Corporation was prepared to play an active rôle in the efforts to find a lasting solution.

The great expansion 1958-80

Initially these efforts did not meet with a great deal of success, for Thetford was not an attractive location for industry. The great expansion which took place between 1958 and the late 1970s was instead made possible by rather more 'artificial' means: the Town Development Act of 1952.[8] This legislation was intended to continue the work of the earlier new towns programme by allowing the reception in existing towns of planned overspill from the great conurbations. Industrial development and the improvement of amenities and communications were to accompany the movement of population. The Act thus represented a chance to revive stagnant and depressed country towns, as well as to remedy the problems of the conurbations, although it is now realised that many of the acute problems of the inner cities stem at least in part from the policies which underlay the Act. Several East Anglian towns expressed interest, and Thetford Borough Council was the most optimistic of all. In the autumn of 1952 it established a Town Development Committee to formulate a scheme under the Act, and in February 1953 made a formal approach, said to be the first from any town, to the London County Council.

The L.C.C. gave an encouraging response, and agreed to include Thetford in the list of towns with which overspill agreements might be negotiated. The Borough Council then worked on outline plans to show the scale and location of possible expansion. These proposals were published in autumn 1953, and involved the reception in Thetford of 10,000 Londoners, but in January 1954 the Ministry of Housing and Local Government rejected a scheme of this magnitude. Negotiations with the L.C.C. therefore proceeded on the assumption that 5,000 overspill inhabitants would be accommodated. These discussions were protracted, not least because by this time numerous towns were pleading for agreements, several on a very large scale, and Thetford was by no means the most attractive of these. Only in February 1957 were detailed proposals announced, as a prelude to a formal undertaking.[9]

The Mayor explained the rationale behind the scheme from the viewpoint of the Borough Council. He said that 'the Council has been considering for a good many years how best it could attract more and varied industrial employment . . . there has also been for 30 years the constant problem of the failure of the existing places of employment to provide sufficient opportunities for the more enterprising youth . . . The Council has also realised that many of the town services could be much more economically run with a larger population to help pay for such services'.[10] In 1955 Thetford had the highest rates of any urban authority in Norfolk: in 1968 it had the lowest. To that extent, at least, the aims of the Borough Council were fully realised. But the corollary of expansion was that in 1968 the Council's loan debt, at £6 million, was one of the highest per head in Britain.[11]

In May 1957 the Thetford Borough Council and the L.C.C. signed the formal agreement whereby the town expansion scheme was implemented. It provided for the construction of 1,500 houses on 283 acres of land, to accommodate 5,000 Londoners. The shops, schools, roads and other essential services would be provided under the agreement, and a 40-acre industrial estate was to be built. The sewage farm, only 10 years old, was to be doubled in size, and the waterworks greatly increased in capacity by the building of a second reservoir and a pumping station bringing water from deep boreholes on Barnham Cross Common. The L.C.C. would carry out all the construction work, handing over each project to the Borough Council upon completion. The success of the negotiations was due to continuous pressure and persistence on the part of the Borough Council, since in several important respects – notably the provision of amenities and the ease of access – Thetford was not the choice of the L.C.C. One researcher has stated that 'legend has it that what finally won the hearts of the London councillors was a plea by a Thetford woman councillor that "even taking on another dustman meant putting sixpence on the rates"'.[12]

Work began in October 1958, and the first overspill tenants moved in during April 1959. The development during this phase was concentrated in two large residential units, south-west of the old town and extending across the land between the Brandon and Bury roads. The first, south of London Road, was designed on conventional planning principles but the second, Redcastle Furze, involved the adoption of the so-called 'Radburn principle' of pedestrian and traffic segregation. There was a more complex system of footpaths with a direct pedestrian route to the town centre, and houses were grouped around communal landscaped areas. The industrial estates lay on either side of the main A11 for ease of access, so that the heavy traffic did not have to pass through the town centre.[13]

The implementation of the scheme was barely under way before major extensions were being mooted. In October 1959 the County Council accepted the principle of growth to give a population of 17,000 by 1980, about 60 per cent. of which would be overspill inhabitants. The L.C.C. was then approached by the Borough Council, and in March 1960 a second agreement was signed, involving the reception of another 5,000 people.[14] This time a more formal planning policy was followed. In 1962 the Thetford Town Map, part of the Norfolk County Development Plan, was published, zoning the land within the Borough according to future use, and laying down guidelines for development to 17,000 people, with potential for further growth.[15] By 1965 almost 1,500 new houses had been built for the Borough Council by the L.C.C. and in addition there had been substantial private development in Norwich Road, Vicarage Road, the Redgate estate and the Weavers Close area south of Nuns Bridges. With the rapid industrial development in 1958–65, and the expansion of its educational, social and commercial facilities, Thetford for the first time in its history had a significant middle-class professional and managerial sector. The construction of private housing on a hitherto unprecedented scale was a major consequence of this.

The second phase of expansion was concentrated in one huge estate at Abbey Farm, with more than 1,000 houses and covering over 100 acres. The ambitious plans involved a self-contained unit enclosed within a peripheral ring-road, and with a sophisticated internal footpath network. Building began in 1967, by which time cost constraints had forced the scaling-down of these proposals, and a rather more traditional plan was eventually adopted. The estate spread across the area between the railway and the Little Ouse, westwards from the priory ruins. A new bridge across the river gave access to the Brandon road, and public open space and footpaths were laid out along both banks to link with the town centre (map 20).

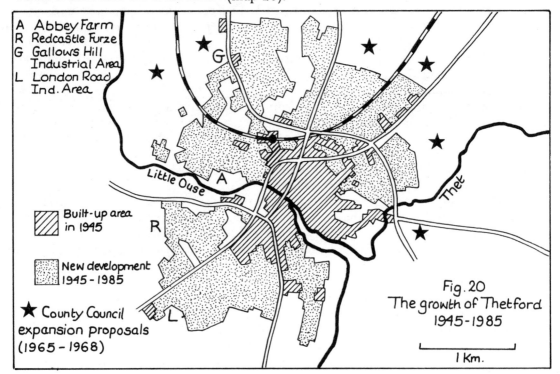

A   Abbey Farm
R   Redcastle Furze
G   Gallows Hill
     Industrial Area
L   London Road
     Ind. Area

Built-up area in 1945

New development 1945–1985

★ County Council expansion proposals (1965–1968)

Fig. 20
The growth of Thetford
1945–1985

1 Km.

During 1966 the County Council undertook analysis of the long-term population and planning trends within Norfolk, and suggested that Thetford had the potential for even greater expansion. Proposals for town-centre redevelopment had assumed that, with natural increase, the population might reach 23,000 by the early 1980s, but in November 1966 Norfolk County Council announced proposals for a doubling of this, to about 50,000 people, with the long-term possibility of 75,000. Such tremendous increases would have swamped the old country town, and the effect would thus have been that of a new town rather than a town expansion. It was inevitably the cause of growing controversy within Thetford, with old and new residents alike opposing the plans, although many others were in favour, seeing continued growth as the only means of ensuring economic dynamism.[17]

In October 1967 the Borough Council approved an outline plan for several new housing areas in an arc stretching from Croxton Road around the eastern side of the town as far as Bury Road, across the Green Lane and Snarehill districts. By one vote, the narrowest of margins, it supported expansion to 40,000 people with the construction of another 3,000 homes. The County Council at the same time produced a document showing an eventual intention to develop along the Ouse valley as far as Two Mile Bottom. The Thetford Borough Council elections of 1968 resulted in the unseating of several councillors who had favoured the large expansion schemes, and it appeared inevitable that the proposals would be bitterly contested when they reached the public enquiry stage.[18]

In the end, however, the ambitious projects of the late 1960s were defeated not by public opinion but by changes in economic and social circumstances. By the early 1970s town expansion and overspill schemes had begun to lose their attraction, but more significantly the period of economic growth, which had permitted the easy movement of industry, was coming to an end. In 1970 the Borough Council was anticipating a population of 28,000 by the end of the decade, but only six years later the County Council, in the Norfolk Structure Plan, predicted that growth beyond 22,000 by 1990 was unlikely. The present (1986) population is about 21,000, so that projection seems to be accurate. Between 1961 and 1971 Thetford grew faster than any other town in England and Wales, with an increase in population of no less than 154 per cent., and during the period 1951 to 1981 the population grew by an astonishing 441 per cent. In 1951 Thetford was smaller than East Dereham, North Walsham, Sheringham and Wymondham: it has now outstripped all of these to become, once again, after an interval of several centuries, the fourth town of Norfolk. Large-scale expansion is now abandoned, and in future growth will be confined to natural increase and, perhaps, a limited amount of voluntary in-migration.[19]

The economy of Thetford was transformed by the town development scheme. The unemployment rate fell steadily, until in 1964 it was only 0.9 per cent., and as late as 1975 it was still below 3 per cent. Thus the industrialisation provided jobs not only for the newcomers but also for the existing unemployed inhabitants of the town, amply fulfilling the hopes of the Borough Council. By 1968 more than 200 acres of land had been developed for industry, with a mixture of purpose-built factories for specific firms, standard units built by the Council for sale or lease, and nursery units intended as a basis for new enterprises which could be expanded as business increased. In the first 10 years some 50 companies moved to Thetford, almost all of them from Greater London, and some 9,000 new jobs were created.[20]

With few exceptions the industries were of the 'light industry' type, for which Thetford was particularly suitable. Plastics, electrical and electronic goods, furniture and furnishings and light engineering products were the most common categories of output, and the firms coming to Thetford included such household names as Jeyes, Thermos and Danepak. The attractions of the town were clear: the rates were low, factories were either ready-built or cheaply available, there was ample land and a pleasing environment. Rather less admirable was the great attraction of cheap labour, since East Anglian wages were, and still are, among the lowest in the country: many Londoners found that their incomes fell after the move to Thetford. A serious deficiency was that most of the firms employed high proportions of female labour, so that the industrial structure of the town still offered too few opportunities for skilled male employment. During the 1980s the national economic depression and the 'rationalisation' practised within many industries have combined to create very considerable economic problems for Thetford. Unemployment has risen sharply as anticipated industrial grown has not materialised, and as existing large employers such as Jeyes have enforced substantial redundancy programmes.[21]

Similar difficulties have affected the plans for the redevelopment of the central area. In the original overspill proposals it was stated that there would be few local shops, and that the commercial area of the town centre should be enlarged to cater for the increased population. In October 1959, when further growth was already anticipated, design work began, and the details of the project were released in June 1962. The new centre was to serve a population of 23,000: it would have a substantial amount of traffic and pedestrian segregation, a redeveloped and enlarged shopping area, a new relief road and a system of link roads and service areas, and a major improvement of the riverside. These principles have remained basic to the planning of the centre even though the designs have greatly altered in detail. At a press conference it was claimed that one of the aims was the retention of 'the most handsome features of the old town', but this was rather contradicted at the same meeting when the County Planning Officer was reported as saying that 'much of old Thetford would come down. Much of it was overdue to come down anyhow. But the essential character of the old town would be retained and it was hoped to incorporate on new buildings flints from demolished old buildings'.[22]

The potential devastation of old Thetford, with the suggestion of such alarming features as overhead roads crossing the town centre at roof level, produced strong opposition at the 1963 enquiry into the scheme. The plans were then scaled down, but nevertheless between 1965 and 1975 many unimpressive but attractive and historic buildings were lost as the town centre was redeveloped. The riverside maltings were cleared away to make room for extensions to the *Bell Hotel* and for the Riverside shopping precinct. A second shopping complex was built along two sides of the block between Tanner Street and King Street, with the remainder being cleared in anticipation of further development.[23] Between 1951 and 1961 the number of shops in the town had fallen from 133 to 74, as small businesses closed and specialist traders faced supermarket competition. The redevelopment of the town centre reversed that trend, so that by 1971 the number had risen to 92 shops. The turnover of shops, which in 1961 was about £1 million, showed a spectacular increase to £4 million in 1971, as the size of the town grew and the scope of its shopping centre drew custom from farther afield.[24]

Along the river bank the Borough Council laid out parks and gardens, while the river itself was cleaned and improved above the Town Bridge. The opening-out of this area was emphasised by the clearance of the south bank to provide space for a new 'bus station and car park, necessary facilities but not adding greatly to the visual quality of this key location in the town. Within the centre traffic circulation was made more confusing by the closure of several streets, and the introduction of one-way systems, but these — and the construction of the town centre relief road in 1968-9 — have dramatically improved environmental conditions in the shopping area. King Street, Tanner Street and several adjacent lanes have been pedestrianised, although a negative consequence has been the construction of ugly and crudely-designed service access areas at the rear of the main shopping streets.

In 1979 Breckland District Council reviewed the town centre plans. It considered that the traffic system, the redevelopment of the shopping facilities and the provision of such public amenities as parks, a new library and courthouse, and car parks, had been accomplished with varying degrees of success. It was suggested that the reduction in the projected population levels made continued large-scale schemes unnecessary, while changing views of conservation and environment made such plans undesirable. The 1979 report therefore signalled the end of comprehensive redevelopment within the town centre, and the formal abandonment of such disruptive schemes as the Nuns Bridges-Castle Lane link road, the Limekiln Lane-Nether Row link road, and the building of multi-storey shop blocks and car parks in Tanner Street.[25]

It is to be hoped that the historic character of the centre can be protected and augmented, with the improvement of the environment and architecture of such areas as Bell Corner, the Old Market Place, Magdalen Street and Castle Street. The town centre includes many listed buildings, ranging from medieval houses to the 19th-century premises of Burrell's, along Minstergate, and it is now recognised as a conservation area of national importance. It is vital that the erosion of this character, and the loss of historic buildings, should not continue, and that every effort is made to ensure that new development is fully in keeping with the scale and appearance of the older setting. Thetford has, in the past 40 years, lost too much of its historical and architectural heritage, and cannot afford to lose any more. As recently as 1979 the former Borough Surveyor was reported as saying that 'no more public money should be wasted on listed buildings'.[26] If Thetford is fortunate, that attitude will not longer have any influence.[27]

Government and administration

Since the Second World War local government in Thetford has undergone dramatic changes. The Borough Council, which until the war had many similarities in character to its *laissez-faire* predecessors, became notably more active after 1945. It began to borrow, and to increase the rates, in order to provide improved services for the town. It is perhaps unfortunate that this was not done much earlier, when these projects could have been carried out more easily and more cheaply and, in the case of the sewerage network, with some saving of human life. By the late 1950s the Council was vigorously and tenaciously pursuing the plans for town expansion, and for the first time became fundamentally involved with what was happening in Thetford, leading rather than following or ignoring. In 1970 the Borough Council owned no less than 65 per cent. of all houses in the town, as well as industrial land and premises. It had provided new water and sewerage facilities, was redeveloping the central area, and was extending the parks and footpath networks.

The Council had also become more politicised, as the influx of new residents from London strengthened the Labour party and challenged the authority of the ruling Conservative–Independent group. In 1972 there were five new Thetfordians on the council of 12, and in that year Leslie Broadhurst, who had arrived in 1965 as manager of Danepak, was the first newcomer to be elected mayor of the town. In that year the Labour party, with six members, for the first time equalled the strength of the Conservatives, and Thetford has continued to be one of the relatively few areas of regular Labour support in Norfolk.

The greatest change, however, was the abolition of Thetford Borough Council as a result of the 1972 Local Government Act. On 31 March 1974 the Council was dissolved, and for the first time in at least seven centuries Thetford ceased to be administered by its own separate borough authority. From 1 April 1974 it was amalgamated with the Urban Districts of East Dereham and Swaffham and the Rural Districts of Mitford & Launditch, Wayland and Swaffham, to form the new District of Breckland. Within this authority Thetford has approximately 20 per cent. of the population but only 16 per cent. of the elected councillors. The headquarters of Breckland Council is at Attleborough, although there are branch offices at the King's House in Thetford. To replace the Borough Council Thetford now has a Town Council, which meets in the old council chamber and, as before, has a mayor, but its powers are only slightly greater than an ordinary parish council, and in all significant matters the authority rests with Breckland.

The changes of 1972–74 were bitterly opposed in Thetford, as in many other towns. The loss of local self-government was deeply resented. Had Breckland been a 'logical' unit of administration the opposition would have been more muted, but it is not. Its five towns — Thetford, Watton, Swaffham, Dereham and Attleborough — are each peripheral to the area and have little in common, while the district stretches as far as Colkirk, only three miles from Fakenham and 30 miles north of Thetford, another world as far as local matters are concerned.

Since 1974 several attempts have been made to separate Thetford and its adjacent parishes from Breckland, and to re-establish a more local unit of government. So far these have failed, as have similar attempts elsewhere in the country. But there seems little chance of Breckland ever winning an affectionate place in the hearts of the people of Thetford, and maybe one day, at some future reorganisation of local government, Thetford will once more become a proud and independent authority, as it has been for most of recorded history.

NOTES AND REFERENCES

Chapter One: Beginnings

1. Chatwin, C. P., *British Regional Geology: East Anglia* (1961)
2. Darby, H. C., *The Medieval Fenland* (1974 ed.)
3. A 'breck' was an area of heathland which was ploughed for arable use for a few years and then abandoned to regenerate. The name was coined by W. G. Clarke
4. The ecological impact of early man in East Anglia is considered by Armstrong, P., *The Changing Landscape* (1975); Murphy, P., *Prehistoric environments and economies* (1984); Bradley, R., *The Prehistoric Settlement of Britain* (1978) gives a wider context
5. Clarke, R. R., *Grime's Graves, Norfolk* (1966)
6. Burrell, G. B., *Untitled rough draft of 1807 map of Thetford* (c. 1805) T/C1/17/43
7. Green, B. and Clarke, R. R., *Thetford Castle Excavations 1962* (1963)
8. Clarke, R. R., 'The Iron Age in Norfolk and Suffolk', *Archaeological Journal*, vol. XCVI (1939)
9. Gregory, A., 'Excavations at Gallows Hill, Thetford', *Norfolk Archaeological Rescue Group News*, 27 (1981), pp. 1-4
10. Another possible seat of government was at Woodcock Hall, Saham Toney, where a substantial settlement of the Icenian period, probably with its own mint, was succeeded by a sizeable Roman settlement including a possible fort
11. Blomefield, F., *History of Norfolk*, vol. II (1739); Martin, T., *The History of the Town of Thetford, in the counties of Norfolk and Suffolk, from the earliest accounts to the present time* (1779) (hereafter, *History*)
12. Potter, T. and Johns, C., 'The Thetford Treasure', *Illustrated London News* (April 1981), pp. 54-5
13. Green, B., 'Thetford Roman Coin Hoard', *Norfolk Archaeology*, vol. 37 Part II (1979) pp. 221-3
14. Dymond, D., *The Norfolk Landscape* (1985), pp. 37-59, gives a general account of the early history and landscape of the county

Chapter Two: The rise and fall of Saxon Thetford

1. Much of the material in this chapter is based on Dunmore, S. and Carr, R., *The Late Saxon Town of Thetford: an archaeological and historical survey* (1976) and Rogerson, A. and Dallas, C., *Excavations in Thetford 1948-59 and 1973-80* (1984), to both of which sources full acknowledgement is made
2. Knocker, G. M., 'Excavations at Red Castle, Thetford', *Norfolk Archaeology*, vol. 34 (1967), pp. 119-86
3. Martin, T., *History* (1779), p. 9
4. ibid.
5. Dunmore, S. and Carr, R., *The Late Saxon Town of Thetford* (1976), part v
6. Hurst, J. G., 'Saxo-Norman Pottery in East Anglia: Part II, Thetford Ware', *Proceedings of the Cambridge Antiquarian Society*, vol. 50 (1957), pp. 29-60
7. Dunmore, S. and Carr, R., *The Late Saxon Town of Thetford* (1976), p. 10
8. Knocker, G. M., 'Excavations at Red Castle, Thetford', *Norfolk Archaeology*, vol. 34 (1967).
9. Green, B. and Clarke, R. R., *Thetford Castle Excavations 1962* (1963)

10. The map may be seen at the Ancient House Museum, Thetford
11. I am most grateful to Alan Davison, who is undertaking extensive research into the topography and nomenclature of Saxon and medieval Thetford, for discussing these questions with me
12. Knocker, G. M., *Theodford: The Story of Anglo-Saxon Thetford* (n.d.)
13. Dunning, G. C., 'The Saxon Town of Thetford', *Archaeological Journal*, vol. 106 (1951), pp. 72-3; Davison, B. K., 'The Late Saxon Town of Thetford: An Interim Report on the 1964-66 Excavations', *Medieval Archaeology*, vol. 11 (1967), pp. 189-91 discuss the character and plan of the Saxon town
14. Alan Davison strongly questions the identification of the church of St Edmund with that found on the gas-works site beside the Bury Road
15. Hare, J. N., 'The Priory of the Holy Sepulchre, Thetford', *Norfolk Archaeology*, vol. 37 Part 2 (1979), pp. 190-200
16. Dunmore, S. and Carr, R., *The Late Saxon Town of Thetford* (1976), pp. 8-9
17. Rogerson, A. and Dallas, C., *Excavations at Thetford 1948-59 and 1973-80* (1984) describe in detail the finds relating to industrial and domestic sites from the Saxon town
18. The archaeology and interpretation of the Saxon town are placed in context in Wilson, D. M. (ed.), *The Archaeology of Anglo-Saxon England* (1976)
19. Whitelock, D. (ed.), *The Anglo-Saxon Chronicle* (1961), p. 46
20. Carson, R. A. G., 'The Mint of Thetford', *Numismatists Chronicle*, 6th series vol. IX (1949), pp. 189-236
21. Whitelock, D. (ed.), *The Anglo-Saxon Chronicle* (1961) p. 73: it has been argued that the abbot was not a local man (see e.g. Hart, C. R., *The Early Charters of Eastern England* (1966), p. 157 for discussion of this point)
22. Blake, E. O. (ed.), 'Liber Eliensis', *Camden Society*, Third Series vol. 152 (1962), p. 100
23. Whitelock, D. (ed.), *The Anglo-Saxon Chronicle* (1961), p. 87, 90
24. Hart, C. R., *The Early Charters of Eastern England* (1966), no. 126, p. 83
25. The history of the diocese is given by Martin, T., *History* (1779), chap. V; also Dodwell, B., 'The foundation of Norwich Cathedral', *Transactions of the Royal Historical Society*, 5th series vol. VII, pp. 1-18
26. Brown, P. (ed.), *Domesday Book: Norfolk* (1984), 1: 69 and 70
27. Knocker, G. M., 'Excavations at Red Castle, Thetford', *Norfolk Archaeology*, vol. 34 (1967), pp. 119-86
28. Killick, H. F., 'The Origin and History of Thetford Hill', *Norfolk Antiquarian Miscellany* (ed. W. Rye), Series II, part III (1908), pp. 1-28
29. Dymond, D., *The Norfolk Landscape* (1985), chaps. 7 and 12, considers Thetford and other Norfolk towns and markets in their context and comparatively
30. Darby, H. C., *Historical Geography of England before 1800* (1969), pp. 220-1

Chapter Three: Medieval Thetford

1. According to Burrell the records were held by Thomas Martin while he researched his *History of the Town of Thetford*, but after publication of the book posthumously they were sold as waste paper to Peter Sterne, grocer and a member of the Corporation. Much of the earlier material was then destroyed or dispersed: T/C1/17/13
2. *Thetford Town Book*, T/C1/6
3. Martin, T., *History* (1779), pp. 265-6
4. ibid., chap. XVIII, The Corporation
5. Le Strange, H., *Norfolk Official Lists* (1890), pp. 222-7
6. The petition to the Chancellor of the Duchy of Lancaster is printed in Martin, T., *History* (1779), Appendix XXXIII
7. T/C1/11, p. 9: the document also mentions 'Mathew de Bryggegate', showing that the Town Bridge existed well before 1290

8. The account roll of Mayor Ranulph de Foxle (1337-8) lists a variety of sources of income, including the various fairs and tolls: T/C1/11, p. 45

9. These are collected in T/C1/11

10. T/C1/11, p. 15

11. ibid., p. 13

12. ibid., p. 13

13. ibid., p. 15

14. Martin, T., *History* (1779), pp. 42-4

15. ibid., p. 45

16. ibid., Chaps. X to XVI are the basis of this section

17. Clarke, W. G., *Notes on the history of crime, justices and punishment in Thetford* (early 1900s) in MS125 (T131D) L7322(a)

18. Raby, F. J. E. and Baillie Reynolds, P. K., *Thetford Priory* (1979), is the best and most comprehensive account of the priory: its historical section derives much from Martin's description

19. Martin, T., *History* (1779), Appendix XVIII gives an account of the miraculous statue as supposedly told by John Bramis, a monk of the priory

20. ibid., Appendix VIII transcribes a very detailed contemporary account of the elaborate funeral ceremonies of the second Duke

21. Hare, J. N., 'The Priory of the Holy Sepulchre, Thetford', *Norfolk Archaeology*, vol. 37 part II (1979), pp. 190-200

22. Martin, T., *History* (1779), p. 209: the full will is transcribed in mf/NRO/reel 173/7

23. This note is made in an annotated copy of Martin's *History*: T/C1/17

24. Harvey, J. H., 'The Last Years of Thetford Cluniac Priory', *Norfolk Archaeology*, vol. 27 (1941), pp. 1-28

25. Martin, T., *History* (1779), Chap. IX, gives details — usually reliable — of individual Thetford churches

26. Beacon, T., *Reliques of Rome* (1563), fol. 191, no. 6 in folio

27. The details of the union of the two parishes are transcribed in an uncatalogued notebook compiled by G. B. Burrell

28. Burrell, G. B., *A plan of the ancient town of Thetford* (1807), Thetford Borough Records Map 9

29. *Evidence Book of Sir Richard Fulmerstone's Estates* (compiled *c.* 1616), mf/NRO/reel 173/7

30. Green, B. and Clarke, R. R., *Thetford Castle Excavations 1962* (1963)

31. T/C1/11, p. 9

32. College of Arms 326/142

33. This note is made in an annotated copy of Martin's *History*: T/C1/17

34. ibid., Burnt Lane ran south from Ford Street, about halfway along its length, to the bank of the river: it was closed in the early 1800s

35. It is also significant that the boundary of St Cuthbert's parish ran along the line of Cage Lane and Pike Lane, suggesting that the land to the south-east was regarded as a quite distinct block

36. This note is made in an annotated copy of Martin's *History*: T/C1/17

37. Firth, C. B., 'Village Gilds of Norfolk in the 15th Century', *Norfolk Archaeology*, vol. 18 (1941), pp. 161-203

38. Le Neve Collection, Frere MSS: Thetford folder

39. T/C1/11, p. 9

40. *Thetford Corporation Assembly Books* (hereafter *A.B.*), 19 September 1805: T/C2/8

41. Patten, J., *English Towns, 1500-1700: Studies in Historical Geography* (1978)

42. T/C1/11, p. 16

43. Reid, A. W., 'The Rising of 1381 in South West and Central Norfolk', in Cornford, B. (ed.), *Studies towards a History of the Rising of 1381 in Norfolk* (1984), pp. 11, 14-15

44. Hudson, W., 'The Assessment of the Townships of the County of Norfolk for the King's Tenths and Fifteenths . . .', *Norfolk Archaeology*, vol. 12 (1895), pp. 243-97

45. Maddock, A., *The Ancient House, Thetford* (1979)
46. T/C1/11, p. 102
47. ibid., p. 124
48. Le Neve Collection, Frere MSS: Thetford folder
49. College of Arms 326/140
50. ibid., 326/142
51. Williams, J. F., 'A Bailiff's Roll of Thetford, 1403-4', *Norfolk Archaeology*, vol. 24 (1932), pp. 7-12. The roll is now at the Norfolk Record Office: Basil Cozens Hardy 2/12/1963, no. 16
52. Bruce-Mitford, R. L. S., 'A Late Medieval Chalk Mine at Thetford', *Norfolk Archaeology*, vol. 30 (1952), pp. 220-2; Hewitt, H., 'Chalk Mines at Thetford', *Norfolk Archaeology*, vol. 31 (1957), pp. 231-2
53. *Orders relating to the Town and Common Lands 1598*: T/C1/8
54. *Thetford MSS 1809*: Thomas 4/1/1971 R154D: 13 July 1573
55. Court Leet proceedings September 1564: T/C1/11, p. 196
56. There were still strips at the time when the surveyors to the Enclosure Commissioners made their sketch plans of the field in 1804-5
57. Deed dated 12 July 1744: Petre (NCC) MSS box 4
58. *N.C.C. Wills* 1509, John Judy, burgess of Thetford: 159, 160 Spyltymber
59. Martin, T., *History* (1779), appendix XII, gives the full text of the order
60. *Evidence Book of Sir Richard Fulmerstone's Estates* (compiled *c.* 1616), mf/NRO/reel 173/7
61. *Papers of the Thetford Enclosure Commissioners* (1804-10), BR90/11: particularly /11 (Abbey Farm); /12 (Channons Farm); /13 (Croxton Park and Norwick Farm)
62. Court Leet proceedings September 1560: T/C1/6
63. *Orders relating to the Town and Common Lands 1598*: T/C1/8
64. Armstrong, P., *The Changing Landscape* (1975), chap. 5
65. Rigold, S. E., 'Thetford Warren Lodge', in Raby, F. J. E. and Baillie Reynolds, P. K., *Thetford Priory* (1979)
66. General accounts of the agriculture of the Thetford district may be found in Armstrong, P., *The Changing Landscape* (1975); Dymond, D., *The Norfolk Landscape* (1985); Young, A. *General View of the Agriculture of the County of Norfolk* (1804)

Chapter Four: Thetford 1540-1700

1. Martin, T., *History* (1779), appendix XXX
2. ibid., pp. 218-21
3. T/C1/11, p. 247
4. *Calender of State Papers Foreign and Domestic, Henry VII 1539*, vol. XIV Pt. II, 815 and 816
5. Martin, T., *History* (1779), pp. 45 and 53
6. *List of persons in the Bridgegate Ward (Mayoralty of William Lord)*: T/C1/11, p. 163; *List of persons in the Bailey End Ward*: T/C1/11, p. 186
7. *Thetford MSS 1809*, Thomas 4/1/1971 R154D 13 July 1573
8. *Laws, Statutes and Ordinances made ordained constituted decreed and agreed upon for the better government rule and mayntenance of the Borough of Thetford* (1668) (hereafter *Laws, Statutes and Ordinances*), no. 12: T/C1/19
9. *A.B.* 4 October 1578: T/C1/1
10. Court Leet proceedings 1558: T/C1/8
11. *N.C.C. Wills* 1602, John Snelling of Thetford, gentleman: 172 Candler
12. Court Leet proceedings 10 March 1558: T/C1/8

13. Lipman, V. D., *The Jews of Medieval Norwich* (1967), pp. 12-21. There is a possibility that, as in Bungay, the Jews of Thetford were under the protection of the Bigod family, and that after the defeat of Earl Bigod in the 1173 rebellion the community was dispersed.
14. *Poll Tax on Aliens 1586: Thetford returns*: T/C1/11, p. 267
15. *A.B.* 25 February 1580: T/C1/1
16. ibid., 27 December 1578
17. *Laws, Statutes and Ordinances* (1668), no. 10: T/C1/19
18. T/C1/11, p. 94
19. ibid., p. 54
20. ibid., p. 247
21. They are marked on sketch maps BR90/11/22
22. Summons to the Mayor and Burgesses of Thetford, *Thetford MSS 1809* Thomas 4/1/1971 R154D
23. *A.B.* October 1577: T/C1/1
24. ibid., 28 February 1591: T/C1/2; 5 October 1582: T/C1/2; 27 October 1625: T/C1/4
25. ibid., 26 February 1597: T/C1/2
26. ibid., 17 January 1579: T/C1/1
27. ibid., 20 June 1579: T/C1/1
28. Martin, T., *History* (1779), Appendix XXXI. The provisions were reiterated under Edward VI (1548) and Elizabeth I (1566)
29. ibid., p. 214-22
30. T/C1/11, p. 179
31. ibid., pp. 280-1 and 234; also p. 179
32. Historic Manuscripts Commission *Various Collections VII*
33. There is a single parish register for the whole Borough 1653-66, PD169/1; St Mary's, Thetford parish records: see also *CSPD 1656-7 Commonwealth*, 123
34. *Thetford MSS 1809* Thomas 4/1/1971 R154D contains transcripts of the correspondence between Lord Towsend and the Corporation, and Townsend's report on the affair.
35. *Calendar of State Papers Domestic Charles II, 1681*, nos. 40 and 80
36. ibid., *1682*, no. 15
37. *A.B.* 30 April 1688: T/C2/6
38. ibid., 26 September 1688
39. T/C1/12 has a transcript of the re-issued Charter of William and Mary 1692
40. *Carr Collection* MC 98/1/1,543 x 2 (MS 21780)
41. Details of parliamentary history 1670-1700 are contained in notes by Clarke, W. G., *Parliamentary History of Thetford* (early 1900s) in MS121 (T131D) L7322(a)
42. T/C1/11, p. 165
43. Court Leet proceedings September 1564: T/C1/11, p. 196
44. *Laws, Statutes and Ordinances* (1668), no. 8: T/C1/19
45. T/C1/11, p. 165
46. *A.B.* 22 April 1579: T/C1/1; 7 December 1610: T/C1/3; 19 October 1696: T/C2/6
47. Martin, T., *History* (1779), Appendix XII
48. *A.B.* 7 November 1578: T/C1/1
49. ibid., 5 June 1626: T/C1/4
50. *Privy Council Acts 1552-4*, p. 293
51. T/C1/11, p. 240
52. *A.B.* 28 December 1586: T/C1/2
53. *N.C.C. Wills* 1572, John Gooch of Thetford, burgess: 502 Brygge
54. *A.B.* 7 December 1578: T/C1/1
55. ibid., 19 December 1578
56. ibid., 5 October 1582
57. ibid., 23 May 1621: T/C1/3
58. ibid., 16 April 1630: T/C1/4; ibid., 14 March 1633; ibid., 25 March 1633
59. ibid., 24 July 1635
60. ibid., 8 October 1649: T/C1/5

61.   *A.B.* 25 October 1632: T/C1/4
62.   *Laws, Statutes and Ordinances* (1668), no. 21: T/C1/19
63.   T/C1/11
64.   *A.B.* June 1579 (no day given): T/C1/1
65.   ibid., 30 November 1582: T/C1/2; also see *A.B.* 17 October 1577: T/C1/1
66.   ibid., 27 December 1578: T/C1/1; also ibid., 16 August 1578
67.   Clarke, W. G., *Notes on the history of crime, justice and punishment in Thetford* (early 1900s) in MS125 (T131D) L7322(a)
68.   *Beeston next Mileham first register* PD377/1 (a long note in Latin records the burial of the infant son of the murdered vicar and his executed wife 8 November 1609)
69.   *A.B.* 17 October 1577: T/C1/1
70.   *Calendar of State Papers Domestic Elizabeth, 1598-1601*, p. 186
71.   *A.B.* 12 October 1585; T/C1/2
72.   ibid., 18 December 1583: T/C1/1
73.   Jennett, S., *The Travellers Guides: Norfolk* (1966)
74.   Martin, T., *History* (1779), chap. XVII
75.   ibid., p. 230
76.   *A.B.* 25 May 1578: T/C1/1
77.   ibid., 21 June 1578
78.   ibid.
79.   ibid., 17 August 1578
80.   ibid.
81.   ibid., 16 August 1578
82.   *Privy Council Acts* 1578, p. 316

Chapter Five: Thetford 1600-1835

1.   A good introduction to the life of Thomas Paine is provided by Maddock, A., *Thomas Paine 1737-1809* (1983)
2.   *A.B.* 26 February 1700: T/C2/6
3.   ibid., 1707-12, especially 9 June 1707; 26 July 1707; 12 August 1707; 14 August 1707; 5 May 1712
4.   Le Strange, H., *Norfolk Official Lists* (1890), pp. 231-3
5.   A very thorough eye-witness account of the events of 26 September 1792 and the subsequent court case is entered in *Thetford MSS 1809* Thomas 4/1/1971 R154D by George Bird Burrell, who was a member of the Corporation
6.   *A.B.* 13 March 1809: T/C2/8
7.   Thompson, Sir E. M. (ed.), *Letters of Dean Prideaux to John Ellis* (1875), pp. 199-200
8.   Le Strange, H., *Norfolk Official Lists* (1890), pp. 241-4
9.   Petre (NCC) MSS, box 4
10. *A.B.* 2 May 1831: T/C2/11
11. Parliamentary Representation Commissioners, *Report on the Borough of Thetford* (1832)
12. Municipal Corporations Commissioners, *Report on the Borough of Thetford* (1835)
13. Thetford Borough Council, *Reports and Minutes of the Quarterly Meetings* (hereafter *T.B.C.Q.R.*), December 1835-January 1836: T/TC1/1
14. The account of the Navigation in this section is based mainly upon Boyes, J. and Russell, R., *The Canals of Eastern England* (1977), pp. 183-9
15. Martin, T., *History* (1779), Appendix XXXIV
16. ibid., Appendix XXX
17. *Calendar of State Papers Domestic Charles I, 1635-6*, 27 April 1636
18. *A.B.* 5 April 1729: T/C2/7
19. Municipal Corporations Commissioners, *Report on the Borough of Thetford* (1835), section 34

20. *Universal British Directory* (1790), pp. 602–5
21. *A.B.* 5 April 1729: T/C2/7
22. Petre (NCC) MSS, box 4
23. T/C1/17/5
24. Shorten, D., 'Paper Making in Norfolk', *Norfolk Archaeology*, vol. 36 Pt. III (1967), pp. 247–8
25. Clarke, W. G., *Notes on industry in Thetford* (early 1900s), in MS125 (T131D) L7322(a)
26. Maddock, A., *Burrells of Thetford* (1979)
27. Clarke, W. G., *Notes on industry in Thetford* (early 1900s), in MS125 (T131D) L7322(a)
28. *N.C.C. Wills* 1720, Theophilus Barber of Thetford, bookbinder; 108 Blomefield: 1785, John Colman of Thetford, barber and peruke maker; 34 Ives: 1794, Samuel Hudson of Thetford, peruke maker, 144 Coe
29. *A.B.* 31 March 1737: T/C2/7
30. *Universal British Directory* (1790), pp. 602–5
31. Pigot & Co., *London & Provincial New Commercial Directory* (1822), pp. 312–3
32. ibid. (1830), pp. 591–3
33. *A.B.* 12 July 1739: T/C2/7
34. Petition 30 April 1782; Letter 13 July 1782: Petre (NCC) MSS, box 17
35. The account for the sale of the lead to George Burrell and a note about the building: T/C1/17/12
36. White, W., *History, gazetteer and directory of Norfolk and the city and county of Norwich* (hereafter *Directory*) (1845), pp. 406–10
37. Pigot & Co., *London & Provincial New Commercial Directory* (1822), pp. 312–3
38. Order pasted on inside cover of T/C2/6: dated 15 January 1664
39. Martin, T., *History* (1779), pp. 301–20
40. Sketch on rough map of Thetford (*c.* 1760) in Ancient House Museum
41. T/C1/17/28 Notes by H. F. Killick on the history of the King's House
42. The plaque is in poor condition but still legible: it should be restored and protected
43. *A.B.* 15 April 1794; 18 August 1794: T/C2/8
44. ibid., 8 March 1828: T/C2/11. The contract for the bridge construction is T/MSC/11
45. Martin, T., *History* (1779), p. 53
46. White, W., *Directory* (1845), p. 404
47. *Tyrrell papers*: MC114/1/11,582 x 5 T. E. Rudling & Co. 6/8/1975
48. T/MSC/4
49. *The Enclosure Act* (1804), MC30 MS18623/112,365 x 6 (Watson, Digby and Pope): this copy of the Act includes draft minutes of the Enclosure Commissioners
50. *Papers of the Thetford Enclosure Commissioners* (1804–10), BR90/11/1–28: especially Reference Book (/4); particulars of estates and allotments (/5–/9); statements of common rights (/11–/14); sketch maps of property to be sold and allocated (/22–/28)
51. *A.B.* 20 August 1734: T/C2/7
52. Norfolk Quarter Sessions *Road Orders* (1805), Box 3, No. 6
53. *Thetford MSS 1809* 4/1/71 Thomas R154D
54. T/C1/17/5
55. *Thetford St Cuthbert parish records*: PD168/43 and PD168/44; *Thetford St Mary parish records*: PD169/93 and PD169/95; *Thetford St Peter parish records*: PD167/63 and PD167/64
56. *A.B.* 19 October 1750: T/C2/7
57. ibid., 28 January 1748
58. Martin, T., *History* (1779), p. 271
59. *Thetford St Cuthbert parish records*: PD168/36–42; *Thetford St Mary parish records*: PD169/75–80; *Thetford St Peter parish records*: PD167/58–62
60. *Thetford St Mary parish records*: PD169/85
61. Thetford Poor Law Union, *Minutes* (1835–37), C/GP/17/1
62. Martin, T., *History* (1779), pp. 267–74

63. Williamson, Sir Joseph, *Letters* (1681-5) pasted into uncatalogued notebook compiled by George Bird Burrell

64. Sir Joseph Williamson's Binding Out Charity Trustees, *Minutes and other papers* (1719-1818), T/MC/1

65. Municipal Corporations Commissioners, *Report on the Borough of Thetford* (1835), section 26

66. ibid., section 27

67. Clarke, W. G., *Notes on the history of crime, justice and punishment in Thetford* (early 1900s), in MS125 (T131D) L7332(a)

Chapter Six: Thetford 1835-1935

1. Mills, S., *An Abstract of the Votes for Councillors of the Borough of Thetford December 26th 1835* (1835) T/TC1/2

2. Le Strange, H., *Norfolk Official Lists* (1890), pp. 233-4

3. Details of the election results with commentaries are included in ms annotations to the Quarterly Reports of the Borough Council, 1835-60, T/TC1/2-5

4. Anonymous poem, *Oh! have ye not heard of a crafty young warrener* (c. 1842), bound into T/TC1/4

5. Anonymous poem, *The Corporate Electors to the New Town of Thetford* (1836) bound into T/TC1/3

6. Handbill, *Town Hall: By Permission* (1847), bound into T/TC1/4, with accompanying explanation by H. W. Bailey of the circumstances of the November 1847 election.

7. Annotation of *T.B.C.Q.R.* (November 1847) by H. W. Bailey: T/TC1/4

8. Bailey, H. W., *Notes on the election of 1 November 1848* (1848), bound into T/TC1/4

9. ibid., *Notes on the election of 1 November 1855* (1855), bound into T/TC1/4

10. Anonymous handbill, *A Lover of the Borough* (1861): T/TC1/6

11. Thetford Local Board and Urban Sanitary Authority, *Minutes* (1865-75): T/TC3/0 and T/TC3/1

12. Municipal Corporations Boundary Commissioners, *Report on the Proposed Municipal Boundary of Thetford* (1837)

13. *T.B.C.Q.R.*, 8 July 1931: T/TC1/17

14. *Norwich Mercury*, 3 April 1852

15. ibid., 14 July 1865

16. *T.B.C.Q.R.*, January 1836-March 1836: T/TC1/1

17. ibid., 29 April 1836; 20 August 1838; 8 October 1838: T/TC1/2

18. ibid., 3 August 1844: T/TC1/3

19. ibid., 8 June 1846: T/TC1/4

20. ibid., 3 February 1853: T/TC1/5

21. ibid., 26 August 1856-22 July 1857

22. *A.B.*, 24 December 1593: T/C1/2

23. Eye-witness account by George Bird Burrell bound into T/C1/17

24. *T.B.C.Q.R.*, 25 July 1903: T/TC1/12

25. Clarke, W. G., *Notes on miscellaneous aspects of the history of Thetford* (early 1900s), in MS121 (T131D) L7318(a)

26. *T.B.C.Q.R.*, 24 February 1838: T/TC1/3

27. Bailey, H. W., *Memorandum on negotiations with the Thetford Gas Company* (1848) T/TC1/4: also *T.B.C.Q.R.* 1840-8: T/TC1/3 and T/TC1/4

28. Thetford Borough Council and Messrs. Gotto & Beesley, *Report on the Drainage and Water Supply of Thetford* (1870)

29. Thetford Local Board, *Minutes*, 1 May 1871, quotes a letter from the Medical Dept. of the Privy Council following an unfavourable report from Dr. Frankland and Mr. Taylor: T/TC3/0

30. Thetford Borough Council, *Proposed sewerage and drainage scheme: miscellaneous papers* (1870-6): T/S1/2
31. *T.B.C.Q.R.*, 14 March 1933; 21 April 1933: T/TC1/17
32. ibid., 18 October 1847: T/TC1/4
33. Thetford Burial Board, *Minutes* (1854-5): T/BB/1
34. Thetford Local Board, *Minutes*, 27 July 1868: T/TC3/0
35. Stevens, Dr. J., *Report on the Sanitary Condition of the Borough of Thetford* (1868): T/TC5/35
36. Thetford Local Board, *Minutes*, 5 October 1870-13 March 1871: T/TC3/0
37. Thetford Urban Sanitary Authority (hereafter T.U.S.A.), *Annual Report of the Medical Officer of Health* (hereafter *M.O.H. Rept.*) *1876* (1877) T/MH/1
38. ibid., *Minutes*, 17 March 1892: T/TC3/2
39. Clarke, W. G., *Notes on sanitation in Thetford* (early 1900s) in MS125 (T131D) L7322(a); T.B.C., *Statistics of Health and Mortality in Thetford* (1905): T/TC5/51
40. T.B.C., *Medical Officer's Report on House-to-House Inspection of the Borough* (1908): printed in T/TC3/5. The inspection followed unfavourable comments on the situation contained in Spencer Low, Dr. J., *Report to the Local Government Board upon the sanitary circumstances and administration of the three Sanitary Districts comprised within the Thetford Registration District* (1907)
41. ibid., *Report of E. Bailey Denton on Proposed Sewage* [sic] *scheme for the Borough of Thetford* (1909), T/SS1/1
42. ibid., *Reports of the Sanitary Committee of July and October 1909 into the Sewerage Scheme of E. Bailey Denton* (1909) T/SS/1/1
43. *T.B.C.Q.R.*, 3 May 1911-19 November 1913: T/TC1/13 and T/TC1/14: a Housing Acts Committee was set up in May 1911
44. ibid., 15 May 1919-22 February 1922: T/TC1/15
45. ibid., July 1924: T/TC1/16
46. White, W., *Directory* (1845), pp. 400-5
47. Thetford United School Board, *Minutes* (1872-85), T/SB/1-4
48. Municipal Corporations Boundary Commission, *Report on the Proposed Municipal Boundary of Thetford* (1837)
49. Clarke, W. G., *Notes on sanitation in Thetford* (early 1900s), in MS125 (T131D) L7322(a)
50. All census figures in the book are from the published reports 1801-1981
51. Albert, W., *The Turnpike Road System in England 1663-1840* (1977), pp. 202-23 lists almost all known turnpike acts
52. Norwich and Thetford Turnpike Trust, *Minutes* (1786-1870), T/3/1-3
53. Walsingham (Merton) MSS: WLS XVII/7,410x; XVII/9,410 x 6; XLI/13,426 x 6
54. Gordon, D. I., *A Regional History of the Railways of Great Britain: The Eastern Counties* (1981 ed.); Allen, C. J., *The Great Eastern Railway* (1968)
55. Boyes, J. and Russell, R., *The Canals of Eastern England* (1977), pp. 183-9
56. Maddock, A., *Burrells of Thetford* (1979)
57. Thetford Borough Council, *M.O.H. Rept. 1927* (1928); *M.O.H. Rept. 1930* (1931)
58. Clarke, W. G., *Notes on industries in Thetford* (early 1900s) in MS125 (T131D) L7322(a)
59. Thetford Moulded Products Ltd., *100 Years of Thetford Moulded Products 1879-1979* (1979)
60. *T.B.C.Q.R.*, 1857-62, T/TC1/5 and T/TC1/6
61. Clarke, W. G., *Notes on industries in Thetford* (early 1900s) in MS125 (T131D) L7322(a)
62. *T.B.C.Q.R.*, 1916-8, T/TC1/14
63. Armstrong, P., *The Changing Landscape* (1975) and Forestry Commission, *East Anglian Forests* (1972) give useful introductions to the afforestation of the Thetford area
64. *T.B.C.Q.R.*, 1921-30: T/TC1/15; T/TC1/16; T/TC1/16
65. ibid., 24 September 1924: T/TC1/16
66. ibid., 2 December 1929: T/TC1/17
67. Thetford Borough Council, *M.O.H. Rept. 1934* (1935), T/MH/1/6

Chapter Seven: Thetford in the past fifty years

1. Thetford Borough Council, *M.O.H. Rept. 1937* (1938) T/MH/1/5
2. ibid., *M.O.H. Rept. 1927* (1928) T/MH/1/5; *M.O.H. Rept. 1938* (1939) T/MH/1/6
3. ibid.
4. *T.B.C.Q.R.* (Report of Public Health and Highways Committee 2 December 1937) T/TC1/18: Thetford Borough Council, *M.O.H. Rept. 1946* (1947) T/MH/1/6
5. Thetford Borough Council, *M.O.H. Rept. 1947* (1948) T/MH/1/6
6. *T.B.C.Q.R.*, 1938-9: T/TC1/18 and T/TC1/19
7. Thetford Borough Council, *M.O.H. Rept. 1946* (1947) T/MH/1/6
8. *The Surveyor*, 5 October 1957, 'Town Expansion at Thetford'
9. *Eastern Daily Press*, 21 September 1955
10. ibid., 20 February 1957
11. Greater London Council, *Expanding Towns: Thetford* (c. 1973)
12. Gretton, J., 'Out of London', *New Society* (15 April 1971)
13. *Eastern Daily Press*, 26 June 1963
14. Greater London Council, *Expanding Towns: Thetford* (c. 1973)
15. Norfolk County Council and Thetford Borough Council, *Thetford Town Map and Written Statement* (1962)
16. *Eastern Evening News*, 24 November 1965
17. *Eastern Daily Press*, 4 November 1966
18. ibid., 26 July 1967 and 17 October 1969
19. Norfolk County Council, *Structure Plan for Norfolk: Written Statement* (1981)
20. Greater London Council, *Expanding Towns: Thetford* (c. 1973)
21. Gretton, J., 'Out of London', *New Society* (15 April 1971)
22. *Eastern Daily Press*, 15 June 1962
23. ibid., 6 February 1963 and 26 July 1967
24. Breckland District Council, *Thetford: Town Centre Plan Review* (1979)
25. ibid.
26. ibid.
27. A valuable summary of the recent expansion of Thetford is to be found in Norfolk County Library, *Thetford Development: Norfolk Parish Studies No. 18* (1982)

BIBLIOGRAPHY AND SOURCES

1. Unpublished and manuscript sources

(a) Held by Thetford Town Council:

The records of Thetford Corporation, Borough Council, and several associated bodies, are with a few exceptions held at either the Kings House or the Guildhall in the custody of the Thetford Town Council. Most have been catalogued by the Norfolk Record Office, and the references below refer to the handlist at the N.R.O. The order followed in the handlist is far from straightforward, and so is not adhered to below.

Thetford Corporation, *Assembly Books* (1574-1835 with some gaps), T/C1/1-5 and T/C2/6-11

Thetford Borough Council, *Reports and Minutes of Quarterly Meetings* (1836-1944), T/TC1/1-19. Within this series there are six volumes (1836-71) which contain numerous handbills, election posters and broadsheets, caricatures, poems and official announcements of poll results, collected and bound in by H. W. Bailey. There are also many manuscript memoranda, annotations and comments by Bailey upon contemporary events and personalities in Thetford politics

Thetford Corporation, *Thetford Town Book* (17th century), T/C1/6

Burrell, G. B., *Scrapbook of material from the records of Thetford Corporation* (compiled early 19th century but including items from the dispersed archives of the town, dating back to the late 13th century), T/C1/11

Thetford Corporation, *Laws, statutes and ordinances made ordained constituted decreed and agreed upon for the better government rule and mayntenance of the Borough of Thetford* (1668), T/C1/19

Thetford Burial Board, *Minutes* (1854-78), T/BB/1

Sir Joseph Williamson's Binding Out Charity Trustees, *Minutes and other papers* (1719-1818), T/MC/1

Thetford United School Board, *Minutes and other papers* (1875-1902), T/SB/1-11

Thetford Borough Council, *Papers relating to Thetford Infants School* (1836-69), T/MC6

Thetford Navigation Commissioners/Committee, *Minutes, ledgers and accounts etc.* (1700-1929), T/N1

Thetford Local Board and Urban Sanitary Authority (T.U.S.A.), *Minutes and proceedings* (1866-1914), T/TC3/0-6

T.U.S.A. and T.B.C., *Annual and quarterly reports of the Medical Officer of Health* (1875-1949), T/MH/1/1-6

T.U.S.A., *Messrs. Gotto & Beesley's Report on the Drainage & Water Supply of Thetford* (1870)

T.U.S.A., *Papers relating to the proposed sewerage and drainage scheme* (1870-6), T/S1/2

T.B.C., *Report of Mr. E Bailey Denton into the proposed sewage scheme for the Borough of Thetford* (1909), T/SS1/1

T.B.C., *Reports of the Sanitary Committee for July and October 1909 into the sewerage scheme of E. Bailey Denton* (1909), T/SS1/1

T.B.C., *Medical Officer's Report on the House to House inspection of the Borough* (1908)

T.B.C., *Statement of health and mortality statistics 1887-1905* (1905), T/TC5/51

Burrell's copy of Martin's *History of the Town of Thetford* (1779, amended in early 19th century), T/C1/17. This volume contains many annotations and insertions concerning topics of antiquarian, historical or contemporary interest. There is also a bundle of 49 loose items formerly inserted in the book but now housed separately. These (T/C1/17/1-49) include notes by Burrell, Leonard Shelford Bidwell and H. F. Killick on matters relating to the history or appearance of the town, as well as transcripts of other documents and miscellaneous observations.

Miscellaneous documents including material relating to:
    Thetford town workhouse, T/MSC/2, 7
    The removal of the Assizes to Norwich, 1830-2, T/MSC/10
    Licensing of entertainments, T/MSC/4
    The rebuilding of the Town Bridge, 1829, T/MSC/11
    Negotiations with the Thetford Gas Company over lighting, 1840s, T/MSC/12
    *Court case over liability of Thetford Corporation to pay the salary of the Borough Recorder,
       late 1890s*, T/TC5/2
    Erection of the first council houses, 1911-4, T/TC5/7
    Amalgamation of the Police Force with Norfolk Constabulary, 1856, T/TC5/12
Burrell, G. B., *Rough draft of town plan of Thetford* (c. 1805), T/C1/17/43
Burrell, G. B., *A plan of the ancient town of Thetford* (1807), map 9
Thetford Corporation, *Acts and Charters transcribed by G. B. Burrell* (c. 1800), T/C1/12
Burrell, G. B., *Notebook containing transcripts of documents relating to the history of Thetford*
    (c. 1800), uncatalogued
Burrell, G. B., *Transcripts of items from assembly and court proceedings* (c. 1800), T/C1/8

(b) held by the Norfolk Record Office:

Beeston next Mileham parish records, *first parish register*, PD377/1
Thetford St Cuthbert parish records, *settlement and removal papers*, PD168/43, 44
ibid., *Overseers Accounts Books*, PD168/36-42
Thetford St Mary parish records, *settlement and removal papers*, PD169/93 and 95
ibid., *Overseers Account Books*, PD169/75-80
ibid., *Note concerning medical care, 1823*, PD169/85
Thetford Poor Law Union Board of Guardians, *Minutes* (1835-7), C/GP/17/1
Norfolk Quarter Sessions, *Road Orders* (1805), Box 3, No. 6
Norwich and Thetford Turnpike Trust, *Minutes* (1786-1870), T/3/1-3
Walsingham (Merton) MSS, WLS XVII and LXI: material relating to the Thetford-Watton road
Petre (NCC) MSS, boxes 4 and 17: deeds etc., and items concerning Thetford market
Tyrrell papers, MC114 T. E. Rudling & Co. 6/8/1975: deeds and leases
Carr papers, MC98/1/1, 543 x 2: letter from Earl of Northampton re selection of M.P.
Thetford MSS 1809 (transcriptions compiled by G. B. Burrell), Thomas 4/1/1971 (R154D)
Evidence Book of Sir Richard Fulmerstone's Estates (compiled c. 1616), (mf. NRO reel 113/7)
    includes inventories of the properties held by the Canons of the Holy Sepulchre and other
    Thetford religious houses 14th-early 16th centuries, as well as transcripts of the title of
    Fulmerstone to his extensive estates
College of Arms MSS (catalogue only): three medieval deeds
Le Neve Collection (Frere MSS), Thetford folder: numerous notes concerning the history of Thetford
    (particularly the religious houses and churches) many in the hands of Blomefield and Martin
Thetford Enclosure Commissioners, *Papers relating to the 1804 Thetford Enclosure Act* (1804-10),
    BR90/11
Thetford Enclosure Act 1804 (copy including draft minutes of the Commissioners), MC30
    MS18623/112,365 x 6 (Watson, Digby and Pope)
Clarke, W. G., *Notebooks concerning the history of Thetford* (derived from printed and mss sources),
    (early 1900s), particularly those concerning sanitation; crime, justice and punishment; and
    parliamentary history (all MS125(T131D) L7322(a)), and industry and miscellaneous topics
    (MS121 (T131D) L7318(a))

2. Published sources

Acts of the Privy Council (Edward VI to Charles I), H.M.S.O.
Albert, W., *The Turnpike Road System in England 1663-1840* (1977), Cambridge U.P.
Allen, C. J., *The Great Eastern Railway* (1968), Ian Allen
Anon., 'What's going on in Thetford?', *Municipal and Public Service Journal*, 1/11/1968

Armstrong, P., *The Changing Landscape: the history and ecology of man's impact on the face of East Anglia* (1975), Terence Dalton Ltd

Barringer, J. C. (ed.), *Aspects of East Anglian Prehistory* (1984), Geo Books

Beacon, T., *Reliques of Rome* (1563)

Blake, E. O. (ed.), *Liber Eliensis* (1962), Camden Society, Third Series vol. 152

Blomefield, F., *An Essay Towards a Topographical History of the County of Norfolk* (1739), vol. II

Boyes, J. and Russell, R., *The Canals of Eastern England* (1977), David & Charles

Bradley, R., *The prehistoric settlement of Britain* (1978), Routledge & Kegan Paul

Breckland District Council, *Thetford Town Centre Plan Review* (1979)

Brown, P. (ed.), *Domesday Book: Norfolk* (1984), Phillimore

Browne, J. O., *Map of the Municipal Borough of Thetford in the Counties of Norfolk and Suffolk* (1837)

Bruce-Mitford, R. L. S., 'A late medieval chalk mine at Thetford', *Norfolk Archaeology*, vol. 30 (1952), pp. 220-2

Calendar of State Papers Domestic (Henry VIII to James II), H.M.S.O.

Carson, R. A. G., 'The Mint of Thetford', *Numismatists Chronicle*, 6th series, vol. IX, nos. xxxv-xxxvi (1949), pp. 189-236

Chatwin, C. P., *British Regional Geology: East Anglia and adjoining areas* (1961), H.M.S.O.

Clarke, R. R., 'The Iron Age in Norfolk and Suffolk', *Archaeological Journal*, vol. XCVI (1939)

Clarke, R. R., *Grime's Graves, Norfolk* (1966), H.M.S.O.

Cornford, B. (ed.), *Studies towards a History of the Rising of 1381 in Norfolk* (1984), Norfolk Research Committee

Darby, H. C., *The Medieval Fenland* (1974 reprint), David & Charles

Darby, H. C., *A Historical Geography of England before 1800* (1969), Cambridge U.P.

Davidson, D. 'Town Expansion of Thetford, Norfolk', *Building*, 27/5/1966

Davison, B. K., 'The Late Saxon Town of Thetford: An interim report on the 1964-66 excavations', *Medieval Archaeology*, vol. XI (1967), pp. 189-208

Dodwell, B., 'The foundation of Norwich Cathedral', *Transactions of the Royal Historical Society*, 5th series vol. VII (1957), pp. 1-18

Dunmore, S. and Carr, R., *The Late Saxon Town of Thetford: an archaeological and historical survey* (1976), East Anglian Archaeology Report no. 4: Norfolk Archaeological Unit

Dunning, G. C., 'The Saxon Town of Thetford', *Archaeological Journal*, vol. CVI (1951), pp. 72-3

Dymond, D., *The Norfolk Landscape* (1985), Making of the English Landscape series: Hodder & Stoughton

Firth, C. B., 'Village Gilds of Norfolk in the 15th century', *Norfolk Archaeology*, vol. 18 (1914), pp. 161-203

Frankel, M. S. and Seaman, P. J. (eds.), *Norfolk Hearth Tax Assessment: Michaelmas 1664* (1983), Norfolk Genealogy vol. XV

Greater London Council, *Expanding Towns: Thetford* (c. 1973), G.L.C.

Green, B., 'Thetford Roman Coin Hoard', *Norfolk Archaeology*, vol. 37 Pt. II (1979), pp. 221-3

Green, B. and Clarke, R. R., *Thetford Castle Excavations 1962* (1963), Norfolk Research Committee Bulletin 14

Gregory, A., 'Excavations at Gallows Hill, Thetford', *N.A.R.G. News*, no. 27 (Dec. 1981), pp. 1-4

Gretton, J., 'Out of London', *New Society*, 15/4/1971

Hare, J. N., 'The Priory of the Holy Sepulchre, Thetford', *Norfolk Archaeology*, vol. 37 pt. II (1979), pp. 190-200

Hart, C. R., *The Early Charters of Eastern England* (1966), Leicester U.P.

Harvey, J. H., 'The Last Years of Thetford Cluniac Priory', *Norfolk Archaeology*, vol. 27 (1941), pp. 1-28

Hewitt, H., 'Chalk Mines at Thetford', *Norfolk Archaeology*, vol. 31 (1957), pp. 231-2

Hudson, W., 'The Assessment of the Townships of the County of Norfolk for the King's Tenths and Fifteenths as settled in 1334', *Norfolk Archaeology*, vol. 12 (1895), pp. 243-97

Hurst, J. G., 'Saxo-Norman Pottery in East Anglia: Part II, Thetford Ware', *Proceedings of the Cambridge Antiquarian Society*, vol. 50 (1957), pp. 29-60

Jennett, S., *The Travellers Guides: Norfolk* (1966), Longman

Killick, H. F., 'The Origin and History of Thetford Hill', *Norfolk Antiquarian Miscellany*, 2nd series Part III (1908), pp. 1–28

Knocker, G. M., *Theodford: The Story of Anglo-Saxon Thetford* (*c*. 1952), priv. pub.

Knocker, G. M., 'Excavations at Red Castle, Thetford', *Norfolk Archaeology*, vol. 34 (1967), pp. 119–86

Le Strange, H., *Norfolk Official Lists: from the earliest period to the present day* (1890), priv. pub.

Lipman, V. D., *The Jews of Medieval Norwich* (1967), Jewish Historical Society of England

Maddock, A., *The Ancient House, Thetford* (1977), Norfolk Museums Service

Maddock, A., *Burrells of Thetford* (1979), Norfolk Museums Service

Maddock, A., *Thomas Paine, 1737–1809* (1983 reprint), Norfolk Museums Service

Martin, T., *The History of the Town of Thetford in the Counties of Norfolk and Suffolk from the earliest accounts to the present time* (1779), John Nichols

Municipal Corporations Boundaries Commission, *Report on the proposed municipal boundary of Thetford* (1837), H.M.S.O.

Municipal Corporations Commission, *Report on the Borough of Thetford* (1835), H.M.S.O.

Murphy, P., 'Prehistoric environments and economies', *Aspects of East Anglian Prehistory*, ed. Barringer, J. C. (1984)

Norfolk County Council, *Structure Plan For Norfolk: Written Statement* (1981)

Norfolk County Council and Thetford Borough Council, *Thetford Town Map and Written Statement* (1962)

Norfolk County Library, *Thetford Development: Norfolk Parish Studies no. 18* (compilation of published sources 1982)

Parliamentary Representation Commission, *Report on the Borough of Thetford* (1832), H.M.S.O.

Patten, J., *English Towns: 1500–1700* (1978) Archon: studies in historical geography

Pigot & Co., *London & Provincial New Commercial Directory* (1822)

Pigot & Co., *London & Provincial Commercial Directory: comprising a directory and classification of the merchants, bankers, professional gentlemen* (1830)

Potter, T. and Johns, C., 'The Thetford Treasure', *Illustrated London News* (April 1981), pp. 54–5

Raby, F. J. E. and Baillie Reynolds, P. K., *Thetford Priory* (1979), H.M.S.O.

Reid, A. W., 'The Rising of 1381 in the South West and Central Norfolk', *Studies towards a History of the Rising of 1381 in Norfolk*, ed. Cornford, B. (1984)

Rigold, S. E., 'Thetford Warren Lodge', *Thetford Priory*, ed. Raby, F. J. E. and Baillie Reynolds, P.K. (1979)

Rogerson, A. and Dallas, C., *Excavations in Thetford 1948–59 and 1973–80* (1984), East Anglian Archaeology Report no. 22: Norfolk Archaeological Unit

Shorten, D., 'Paper Making in Norfolk', *Norfolk Archaeology*, vol. 36 part III (1976), pp. 247–8

Spencer Low, J., *Report to the Local Government Board upon the Sanitary Circumstances and Administration of the three Sanitary Districts comprised within the Thetford Registration District* (1907), Reports of the Medical Inspectors of the L.G.B., no. 269, H.M.S.O.

Stevens, J., *Report on the Sanitary Condition of the Borough of Thetford* (1868), Reports of the Medical Department of the Privy Council, H.M.S.O.

Thetford Moulded Products Ltd., *100 Years of Thetford Moulded Products 1879–1979* (1979), priv. pub.

Thompson, E. M. (ed.), *Letters of Humphrey Prideaux, sometime Dean of Norwich, to John Ellis, sometime Under-Secretary of State, 1674–1722* (1875), Camden Society

Universal British Directory (1790)

White, W., *History, gazeteer and directory of Norfolk and the city and county of Norwich* (1845)

Whitelock, D. (ed.), *The Anglo-Saxon Chronicle* (1961), Eyre & Spottiswoode

Williams, J. F., 'A Bailiff's Roll of Thetford, 1403–4', *Norfolk Archaeology*, vol. 24 (1932), pp. 7–12

Wilson, D. M., *The Archaeology of Anglo-Saxon England* (1976), Cambridge U.P.

Young, A., *General View of the Agriculture of the County of Norfolk* (1804)

INDEX

Plates are indicated in **bold type** at the end of entries, thus: **12**